NO FAULT OR FLAW

THE FUTURE OF THE FAMILY LAW ACT 1996

Being: Papers given to the President's Third Inter-disciplinary Conference on Family Law held at Dartington Hall, Totnes between 24 and 26 September 1999, together with a record of the discussions which took place in the plenary sessions of the conference.

Edited by
THE RT HON LORD JUSTICE THORPE
and
ELIZABETH CLARKE
of Gray's Inn, Barrister, Queen Elizabeth Building, Temple

With an analytical conclusion by
THE RT HON LADY JUSTICE HALE

fl **Family Law**

2000

Published by
Family Law, a publishing imprint of
Jordan Publishing Limited
21 St Thomas Street
Bristol BS1 6JS

British Library Cataloguing-in-Publication Data
A catalogue record for this book is available from the British Library.

ISBN 0 85308 617 6

Phototypeset by Mendip Communications Ltd, Frome
Printed in Great Britain by Hobbs The Printers Ltd of Southampton

NO FAULT OR FLAW

THE FUTURE OF THE FAMILY LAW ACT 1996

The Rt Hon Sir Stephen and Lady Brown

CONTRIBUTORS

Janet Walker, Professor of Family Policy, Newcastle University

Pat Fitzsimons, Manager, Relate Centre

William Arnold, Head of Family Policy, Lord Chancellor's Department

Dr Christopher Clulow, Director, Tavistock Marital Studies Institute, London

Mary Corbett, Marriage Counsellor, Marriage Care

Penny Mansfield, Director, One Plus One Marriage & Partnership Research

Elizabeth Walsh, former Chief Executive, UK College of Family Mediators; Editor, *Family Law*

David Hodson, Solicitor–Mediator, Partner, Family Law Consortium; Vice-Chair, UK College of Family Mediators

Thelma Fisher, Chair, UK College of Family Mediators

Gwynn Davis, Professor of Socio-Legal Studies, Department of Law, University of Bristol

Sarah White, Family Mediation Project Manager, Legal Aid Board

Professor Martin Richards, Centre for Family Research, University of Cambridge

Judith Connell, Newcastle Centre for Family Studies, University of Newcastle

Julia Hennessy, Essex Social Services

Christina Lyon, Queen Victoria Professor of Law, University of Liverpool

Peter Harris, Chairman, National Council for Family Proceedings, Bristol, formerly the Official Solicitor

Dr Judith Trowell, Consultant Psychiatrist, Tavistock Clinic, London

Dr Jenny Stevenson, Consultant Clinical Psychologist, London

Dr Brian Jacobs, Consultant Psychiatrist, Maudsley Hospital, London

Dr Judith Freedman, Consultant Psychiatrist in Psychotherapy, Portman Clinic, London

Dr Anne Zachary, Consultant Psychiatrist in Psychotherapy, Portman Clinic, London

Dr Danya Glaser, Department of Psychological Medicine, Great Ormond Street Hospital, London

Dr Claire Sturge, Department of Child and Adolescent Psychiatry, Northwick Park Hospital, Harrow, Middlesex

Maggie Rae, Solicitor, Clintons, London

Iain Hamilton, Solicitor, Jones Maidment Wilson, Manchester

Peggy Ray, Solicitor, Goodman Ray, London

His Honour Judge Donald Hamilton, Birmingham County Court

Gerald Angel, The Senior District Judge

Lord Justice Thorpe, Lord Justice of Appeal

His Honour Judge Mark Hedley, Liverpool County Court

District Judge Martyn Royall, Norwich County Court and District Registry

Lady Justice Hale, Lord Justice of Appeal

EDITOR'S INTRODUCTION

LORD JUSTICE THORPE

I begin by paying tribute to the ingenuity and scholarship of Nicholas and Margaret Wall who have once again found us our title for this book. The quotation is apt on its own but particularly so when we remember that the words fall from the lips of Gilbert's Lord Chancellor.

In my introduction to *Divided Duties*, I anticipated the present publication when I wrote of the Family Law Act 1996 that *'no statutory implementation has ever presented inter-disciplinarity within the family justice system with a greater challenge'*. But I had not then imagined the 1999 setback. Certainly that development cannot be attributed to any want of inter-disciplinary collaboration. The report of the National Inter-disciplinary Forum shows the commitment of all the disciplines involved in piloting the delivery of information services.

However, I am in no doubt that the anxieties resulting from the Lord Chancellor's June announcement served to ferment the conference to a strength that would not otherwise have been achieved. There was a real absence of internal conflict and a palpable determination to deliver a clear signal to the Lord Chancellor from the united ranks of those who work within or research into the family justice system. The participation of David Lock MP, Amanda Finlay and William Arnold encouraged the conviction that the debate from which the final resolution developed had been well directed and persuasive.

But once again the purpose of this book is to widen the consultation so that those who were not at Dartington, and especially those who were not represented there, may evaluate the evidence and draw their own conclusions. Before you do so, I would offer only this one consideration. At the conference there was a view that the Lord Chancellor should be urged to stand by his earlier statements of intent. There was another view that the Lord Chancellor should be urged to amend the 1996 Act to remove the problems perceptibly created by the parliamentary opponents to no-fault divorce. But the counsel which united the conference was that we should not exceed our expertise. We can tell the Lord Chancellor with no small authority what the family justice system needs. How to meet those needs is not for us but for government. So in the end the message is simple: the introduction of no-fault divorce is the highest legislative priority for the family justice system. That message was subsequently reiterated by the President of the Family Division, Dame Elizabeth, at her inaugural press conference.

Now may I relate the 1999 conference to its predecessor? At Dartington, Arran Poyser was able to report that the Department of Health had acted on the resolution of the 1997 conference by issuing in the previous month a circular setting out higher standards for the design and implementation of care plans. This is further proof of the capacity of the President's Inter-disciplinary Committee to focus on weaknesses and, particularly at its residential conferences, to advocate solutions.

The 1999 conference has done just that and on an issue of far greater social significance that we have ever before addressed. My hope is that the work was not in vain.

The frontispiece illustration is very special. The President has been father to the Inter-disciplinary Committee and has both guided and encouraged all its efforts. Lady Brown has not only supported him throughout but has charmed all who have had the good fortune to meet her at family justice gatherings.

One of the President's last decisions, characteristically shrewd, was to invite Brenda Hale in the midst of the final plenary session to distil the resolutions produced by the small groups. The result has much enhanced the value of the book and the editors are profoundly grateful to her not only for sparing them a difficult task but for achieving so much more than she was bidden to do.

Finally, may I make plain that although this book has two editors it is Liz Clarke who has borne the whole burden of work. She made the contemporaneous notes. She has been responsible for obtaining from each contributor the revisions for publication. She has collaborated with Jordans on the development of the book from first beginning to corrected proofs. She has made light work of every task.

CONTENTS

FOURTH SESSION

Mental Health Services

Legal Services

THE JUDICIARY

National Support Structures

CONCLUSIONS

CLOSING REMARKS   *Lord Justice Thorpe*

APPENDIX

THE PRESIDENT'S WELCOME

The President reminded participants that the concept of inter-disciplinarity had sprung up with the introduction of the Children Act 1989 but its ambit had now extended far beyond that. He recalled that the original intention of this conference had been to consider the implementation of Part II of the Family Law Act 1996 in March 2000. However, in the light of the Lord Chancellor's statement in June 1999 the focus had shifted from simply considering implementation: the task for those attending the conference was to consider the present position and how matters might be taken forward constructively in the light of the Lord Chancellor's statement.

SIR STEPHEN BROWN
PRESIDENT OF THE FAMILY DIVISION

OPENING REMARKS

LORD JUSTICE THORPE

Lord Justice Thorpe began by saying how important these biennial conferences had become: they provided an exceptional opportunity to focus on the most important issues facing the family justice system from time to time. Their production depended heavily on the funding and support of the Government (through the Department of Health and the Judicial Studies Board), and the provision of funding was a reflection of the value Government attached to these conferences. The Lord Chancellor's announcement in June made the topic under discussion even more important than if it were safely established en route to implementation next year. Lots of questions arose for consideration and he expressed the hope that by the end of the conference we would have clear and specific resolutions to take forward for debate and discussion in a wider setting. He closed his remarks by noting that the conference was taking place in the last week of the President's 'reign' and said that it was fitting that he should be there as he had been so hugely supportive of the President's Inter-disciplinary Committee over the years, without which support for these conferences may well not have taken place.

FIRST SESSION

Information Provision

WHITHER THE FAMILY LAW ACT, PART II?

Professor Janet Walker[1]

Professor Walker *opened her remarks by saying that few would take issue with the principles behind Part II of the Act but there was perhaps less consensus as to the changes brought in to support those principles. Part II had several novel elements to it, such as information meetings, marriage support and mediation. The result was a rather difficult juxtaposition between social work and the family justice system. The Lord Chancellor's statement in June 1999 had expressed his disappointment at the results of the pilots. In considering the way forward, one needed to analyse the aims of information meetings and the assumption underlying them.*

The phrase 'saving saveable marriages' was a widely publicised objective of Part II. However, it was important to remember that many of those attending information meetings had already gone beyond the stage of saving the marriage: they had already tried to do so or it was far too late (such as in marriages where the parties had been separated for many years) or one partner very much wanted a divorce. Not all those that had gone on to use the marriage support services had the aim of saving their marriage; they had other objectives such as promoting communication or trying to make their divorce more amicable. Professor Walker expressed the view that the information meetings are having some impact but might not be saving many marriages. They might be about encouraging more reflection and coming to terms with the end of the marriage.

Mediation was another area which had caused some confusion. The information meetings were not intended to divert people into mediation. In the research conducted, 57 per cent of people said they would use mediation in the future if problems arose, for example over the children. The principle of mediation was not one with which people had a problem. In practice, what happens? Evidence was emerging that people were still not sure quite what it is/what it costs/where it fits into the scheme of the divorce process. Also, it was often not felt to be necessary. It also had to be remembered that it required both partners to engage in the mediation process.

As to the involvement of solicitors, it appeared that some people who had attended information meetings were then going on to use solicitors more effectively and/or economically. Also, a striking number of those who had attended information meetings had taken time to reflect and had not taken any formal steps down the divorce route some months after the meeting (although it was important to remember that this did not necessarily mean that they were going to stay married).

In Professor Walker's view, the research findings and the Lord Chancellor's statement raised a number of questions which should be addressed:

(1)   What should an information meeting seek to achieve?
(2)   Should it be a personalised service or a uniform technical guide?
(3)   How should the information meeting package be managed?
(4)   How should the roles of lawyers and mediators be reconciled?
(5)   What should be the measures of success of the meetings?
(6)   Should attendance be mandatory for everyone, for some people (eg those with children) or for no one?
(7)   What are the options if Part II is not implemented?

INTRODUCTION

While many politicians, policymakers and practitioners would like to be able to reverse the current trends which have seen the marriage rate falling and the divorce rate rising, few believe that merely changing the law relating to divorce will provide the solution, nor is it likely to eradicate completely the human unhappiness which so often accompanies marriage breakdown. There is, however, a widely

---

1   Janet Walker, Professor of Family Policy at Newcastle University and Director of the research team which is evaluating information meetings and associated provisions under the Family Law Act 1996. This paper draws on the work and deliberations of the team over the past two years.

held belief that the law can and should provide a responsible and responsive framework within which measures may be structured to address current concerns, and that it can encourage a culture which both supports marriage and seeks to reduce conflict during and beyond marriage breakdown. Evidence shows that existing divorce legislation fails to provide an appropriate framework, and may even make matters worse.

The Family Law Act 1996 (FLA), described as one of the most radical and far-reaching reforms in family justice this century, received Royal Assent on 4 July 1996 after a somewhat tortuous passage through Parliament. The objectives in Part I of the FLA place the emphasis on saving marriages, promoting a conciliatory approach to divorce, reinforcing continuity in parenting, and providing protection from domestic violence and child abuse. In order to promote these objectives, the Act removes the concept of fault as evidence of irretrievable breakdown. It acknowledges divorce as a process rather than a discrete event; it introduces a period of time for reflection and consideration; and it requires that all arrangements for the future are made before divorce can be granted.

The Act encompasses several novel elements. There is general agreement that people facing marital breakdown need better information on a variety of matters than is currently available. Hence the previous Government's proposal that anyone who wishes to start the divorce process should be required to receive a range of information. The former Lord Chancellor stated that giving information:

> '... is intended to be one of the ways whereby, before they take steps towards obtaining a divorce, couples will be made aware of the enormous emotional, social and economic upheaval involved in divorce and, very importantly, the services available to help and support couples ... It will communicate the facts that will help people make decisions on a basis of knowledge.'[1]

The Act seeks actively to encourage people to save their marriage by giving them the opportunity to meet with a marriage counsellor. Furthermore, it provides for the Lord Chancellor to make regulations which will enable eligible couples to obtain State-funded marriage counselling during the period for reflection and consideration. The third novel element is the promotion of mediation as a means of resolving disputes which arise in respect of children, finance or property, funded, for those eligible for legal aid, on the same basis as for legal representation. The court may direct parents to attend a meeting with a mediator to receive an explanation of the availability and benefits of mediation.

Part I (Principles), Part III (Legal Aid for Mediation in Family Matters) and Part IV (Family Homes and Domestic Violence) of the FLA have been implemented. Part II (Divorce and Separation), which contains the most extensive and controversial provisions, has not. Although there was much agreement in Parliament about the principles to guide reform, there was disagreement about the measures which should be employed to achieve the desired objectives. So, for example, while there was widespread agreement that people facing marital breakdown need better information, there was less consensus concerning how such information should be provided and the focus it should have. The (then) Lord Chancellor made it clear that a variety of options for information-giving were being considered and that these would need to be tested in pilot studies.

Between June 1997 and September 1998, 14 pilots had been launched, covering 11 areas of England and Wales, and testing six models of information provision. At the end of the pilots in June 1999, 5,983 people had attended an individual meeting, 2,460 people had attended a group presentation, and 1,468 people had been sent information packs in a postal study. In 1998, the offer of a free meeting with a marriage counsellor was introduced in eight pilots: 561 people attended such a meeting.

Three major research reports[2] have been presented to the Lord Chancellor's Department during the evaluation. In June 1999, the Lord Chancellor announced that he did not intend to implement Part II of the Act in 2000 as previously envisaged, describing the preliminary research results in respect of information meetings as 'disappointing, in view of the Government's objectives of saving saveable marriages and encouraging the mediated settlements of disputes'.[3] This has been widely interpreted as

---

1   The Lord Chancellor, Lord Mackay of Clashfern, in J Walker and J P Hornick *Communication in Marriage and Divorce* (BT Forum, 1996), p 59.

2   J Walker et al, *Information Meetings and Associated Provision within the Family Law Act 1996: First Interim Evaluation Report* (Newcastle Centre for Family Studies, January 1998); J Walker (ed) *Second Interim Evaluation Report: The First Five Pilots* (Newcastle Centre for Family Studies, September 1998); J Walker (ed) *Third Interim Evaluation Report* (Newcastle Centre for Family Studies, January 1999).

3   The Lord Chancellor, Lord Irvine of Lairg, in a written answer, 17 June 1999.

signalling the demise of Part II. Whether or not this is the case, the Lord Chancellor's statement and the accompanying Press Notice raise three fundamental issues: first, the statistics quoted relating to the numbers using mediation, and the numbers expressing themselves as more likely to consult a solicitor, need to be seen in context; secondly, the Lord Chancellor's view renders it essential that the concept of information provision must now be revisited within the framework of the Act as a whole and the principles underlying it; and thirdly, if Part II is not to be implemented in its current form, thought needs to be given to alternative policy options. This paper focuses on the second issue, but in so doing addresses the first and provides pointers for the third.

INFORMATION MEETINGS: A CHANGING CONSTRUCTION

Proposals for the provision of information have shifted and these shifts would appear to be highly significant. The original proposal in the Government's Green Paper[1] was for an information *interview*, which would: offer advice about marriage guidance; allow referrals and enable appointments to be made to appropriate services; influence the decision as to whether to mediate, to negotiate at arm's length through solicitors or to litigate; give information about the likely costs of these services and about eligibility for State funding; and provide a preliminary assessment of the most appropriate way forward, although legal advice would not be given.

The notion of a single first port of call was central to the proposal. The subsequent White Paper[2] listed a number of advantages of this approach. It would provide an opportunity to consider whether divorce is the right course of action; it would ensure that everyone obtains the same access to information about the divorce process and related matters; and it would raise awareness of support services, and encourage couples to consider family mediation. It was noted that any information given must be entirely objective. This could be taken to mean that one service (for example, mediation) was not to be promoted over another (for example, legal services).

Having noted concerns raised about the danger of information-giving spilling over into advice-giving, the Government shifted away from a personal information *interview* towards a proposal for a *group session,* which was viewed as 'a device for providing objective information face to face in the most expedient, comfortable and cost-effective manner', and as a 'much more sophisticated approach' regarding how information might be presented (by the use of a video and talks by experts from different professions, for example). In putting forward the proposal that attendance at a group session would be a condition precedent to starting the divorce process, the Government argued:

> '... it will be essential that the information sessions present a fair and unbiased view of all the services available to couples and of the options open to them. Such a system should result in couples having a better understanding of the emotional, social and practical consequences of marriage breakdown and divorce. It should also mean that parents better understand the effects of separation and divorce on children, and especially the harmful effects on them of continuing conflict.'[3]

The focus was on helping couples to understand the consequences of their actions, and the emphasis was on maintaining 'a level playing field' for the various services. This proposal was embodied in the Family Law Bill presented to Parliament in November 1995. It proved to be contentious. Concerns were expressed about privacy, and by the time the Bill left the Commons, the group meeting had become an *individual* meeting which could be attended by one or both partners, following which there must be a waiting period of at least three months before the making of a statement of marital breakdown. The precise nature of the newly constructed individual information meeting was not decided, this being the subject of the pilots.

The apparent simplicity of this new provision is deceptive. Most people know what information is, and most have some idea of what going to a meeting is like. Yet putting these two elements together and transforming the concept of an individual information meeting from a 'good idea' into reality has not been straightforward. Should the information meeting be akin to a Highway Code of Marriage Breakdown and Divorce – a technical guide which is susceptible to precise formulation? Or should it be more practically oriented, a new service delivered through a personal interview which cannot be

---

1   *Looking to the Future: Mediation and the Ground for Divorce*, Cm 2424 (1993).
2   *Looking to the Future: Mediation and the Ground for Divorce: The Government's Proposals*, Cm 2799 (1995).
3   Ibid, para 7.20.

formulated in rigid rules? Conceptions of what an information meeting should be have been many and varied. The Lord Chancellor's recently expressed disappointment with the research findings in respect of the pilots illustrates this problem.

RHETORIC AND REALITY

Since the three-month period that has to elapse between attendance at an information meeting and the start of proceedings was intended to function both as a clear sign that the marriage may be at an end and as an opportunity for reflection on the possibility of saving it, it would be reasonable for the information meeting to be geared towards an emphasis on marriage support rather than on the divorce process. But most people do not take public steps in respect of divorce after the first marital tiff. The information meeting needs also to provide for those who have thought long and hard. In order to steer a course between different interests and views concerning the purpose and the actual delivery of information, and also to pursue the twin objectives of saving marriages and facilitating consensual divorce, information meetings in the pilots were structured, impersonal and routine. Information was delivered in a standard format which did not permit tailoring to the immense range of individual circumstances in which attendees found themselves.

The evaluation of the pilots suggests that sometimes the elements of the information meeting may clash: saving marriages is an objective distinct from securing civilised divorce. At other times, two related values appear to conflict. The best example of this concerns the objective of promoting mediation. The preliminary findings show that knowledge about mediation increased, and that there was a positive response to the idea. However, as attendees and mediators acknowledge, mediation requires commitment from each partner. Yet recognising the rights of an individual and the significance of confidentiality, particularly in relation to personal safety, has produced a system that militates against couple involvement in information meetings and requires only one party to attend. The vast majority of those attending in the pilots have done so as individuals. While mediation, on the one hand, seeks to balance power between the parties, attendance at an information meeting, on the other, can significantly empower one partner by providing them with knowledge which might not be shared with the other, and which may militate against use of mediation services.

Debate needs to focus on what information meetings or some other form of information provision can realistically be expected to achieve, and on clarification of the primary objectives with respect to the raft of new provisions within the Act. Unless these matters are considered, it is difficult to see how the Government can take a final decision about implementation.

THE SEARCH FOR CLARITY AND FOCUS

Cretney and Masson[1] have described the FLA as being 'conceptually unusual', in that it:

> '... seeks to promote a remarkable collaboration between the legal process necessary to terminate the legal status of marriage, and various applied social work measures intended to minimise the damage done to children and adults by marital breakdown and its consequences.'

It is, perhaps, the integration of social welfare provision with an essentially legal process which causes confusion and discomfort: and it is the information meeting which most starkly embodies this fusion of approaches. The Act seeks to bring together all those working with families at risk of breaking up, in a more inter-disciplinary, co-operative environment which allows for the efficient referral to and use of a range of complementary services, all of which will be explained during the information meeting. It has been suggested that this will 'inevitably shake up and cause some reorganisation of at least three professions, namely family lawyers, family mediators and counsellors'.[2] But not everyone has viewed the FLA, nor indeed information meetings, as desirable innovations. The Act has been welcomed by marriage counsellors and mediators, for whom there is everything to gain. For solicitors, on the other hand, it has created inevitable concerns about the loss of their current role as gatekeepers to the divorce process – the first port of call for the majority of the divorcing population. While solicitors continue to

---

1   S M Cretney and J M Masson *Principles of Family Law*, 6th edn (Sweet & Maxwell, 1997).

2   G Bishop, D Hodson, D Raeside, S Robinson and R Smallacombe *Divorce Reform: A Guide for Lawyers and Mediators* (FT Law & Tax, 1996), p xi.

lack enthusiasm for mandatory information meetings, court welfare officers, mediators and counsellors are generally positive. The problem, it seems, relates to just what it is that information meetings are intended to do. In order to promote greater clarity and focus in the debate, we have begun to explore the various competing conceptions referred to earlier.

Information meetings: a technical guide

In the pilots the information meeting had two principal objectives. The first was to direct a party's attention to the issues which should be considered when contemplating taking steps to end the marriage. The second was to provide information concerning the various options for the resolution of difficulties, including the availability of marriage support, mediation and legal services. In most models the presenter has run through all the topics prescribed in the Act. Only in two models has there been a deliberate and almost exclusive focus on marriage saving and marriage support. In all models, the information provided has been general, not specific to the attendee's circumstances, and the delivery has been prescribed, standardised to a script. Yet attendees have arrived at information meetings with a variety of agendas. People were variously looking to know their rights, to avoid solicitors, to save the marriage, to get information about children and/or finances, to check up on the divorce process, and to be helped in knowing the choices and the possible next steps. Some people wanted very specific information on a single issue, and others were looking for reassurance about what they were doing; but the vast majority wanted information in order to take the next steps.

From the research so far, we have delineated three categories of attendee: there are those who go to an information meeting because they do not know what to do about their marriage; those who do not know how to proceed with the divorce process; and those who do not know how to deal with specific issues, for example arrangements for children. This third group was most likely to express some impatience with the 'basic' nature of the information provided. The different agendas, needs and expectations have considerable implications for the timing and content of information provision. Ensuring that appropriate information is available to people at the optimum time constitutes a particular challenge. If any assessment is to be made about 'appropriateness' or 'optimum timing', the information presentation has in some way to be both sensitive and relevant to the individual attendee.

All the evidence about marriage breakdown and divorce indicates that the transition from one state to the other most frequently entails a long process involving mixed emotions, indecision and reflection. The evaluation reveals that going to an information meeting may mark a watershed, from which decisions and actions flow, or it may serve to slow things down, encouraging reflection and giving people 'permission' to take their time, precisely one of the outcomes desired by those who hoped to prevent over-hasty divorces. Information meetings allow people to consider whether they want to use any services at all, and to realise that they can manage the process by themselves. According to these kinds of criteria the pilot information meetings have achieved some important objectives.

The distinction between information as knowledge (the bare facts) and information as a service (the facts personally tailored) probably takes us to the heart of the main tensions and dilemmas surrounding information meetings. While it is clear that some attendees say they want advice rather than generalised information, it is not so much advice, as in 'what should I do?', which is being sought as information which is tailored to the attendee's particular circumstances, and which is therefore apparently more usable. Disappointment about the 'one size fits all' approach is inevitable if information is to be delivered on an individual basis, yet consist of a structured presentation. Presenters and attendees seemed to be looking for a more flexible process, although the vast majority of attendees in the pilots were positive about the information received, and valued the experience. The extent to which information is recognised and absorbed depends to a large degree on each attendee's notion of its relevance to them given the judgements they face, and this in turn depends on their view about where they are in their relationship – be it in trouble, on the verge of breaking down, or well past the stage of no return.

If Part II is to be implemented unchanged, a meeting akin to the information *interview* mooted in the Green Paper might better meet people's needs and expectations. The extent to which the information given then influences behaviour or promotes the use of certain services, however, is another matter, and consideration of this brings us to the current dilemmas posed by the Lord Chancellor's June 1999 announcement.

Changing behaviour

The information meeting pilots were not set up to 'divert' people into marriage support services or into mediation. Accordingly, the research programme did not set out specifically to test whether such diversion is evident. The pilots were set up to test the 'who, what, where, when and how' of providing information meetings rather than, for example, to establish whether marriages would be saved within the existing legislation. Concerns about the 'low take-up' of marriage counselling and mediation, then, require us to consider whether information meetings or information provision in some other form could and should be attempting to divert people along certain pathways, or whether, as in the pilots, it is more appropriate and acceptable to provide objective information which equips people to make better-informed choices. The former approach would shift the provision away from being akin to a 'technical guide' towards it being an unashamedly persuasive 'consumer guide' which assesses the options and indicates the 'best buys'. Group meetings in Australia are run on these lines, but the current 'level playing field' approach in England and Wales would have to be jettisoned. But even if the shift were made, questions remain about just how many marriages might be 'saved', and just how many couples could and would use mediation. In our view there is likely to be a difference between the Lord Chancellor's expectations and the reality.

Saving marriages

On average, 13 per cent of attendees across all pilots took up the offer of a meeting with a marriage counsellor. Of these, some 47 per cent wanted help to save their marriage. As a result of having attended the meeting, some 61 per cent intended to go into counselling. It is too early to say how many of these have attempted to work on their marriage, or just how many are able to maintain the marriage over a longer period. The meeting with a marriage counsellor has proved to be a significant turning point for many people, enabling them either to accept that the marriage is over or to work on the marriage with a view to maintaining it. The majority of attendees have found it helpful (only 4 per cent have said that they did not find it helpful).

One of the key questions, however, is just what criteria should be used to assess the success or effectiveness of the provision for 'saving saveable marriages'. Many attendees had already tried to save their marriage, and most felt that it was simply too late by the time they went to an information meeting (over half had already separated from their spouse). It would appear unlikely that many will be persuaded that the marriage can survive even though they may 'stop and think' before proceeding down the divorce route. It will make a difference for some, however, and these are the ones who are more likely to take up the meeting with a marriage counsellor. MPs talked about creating 'a window of opportunity'[1] for reconciliation, but were modest in their expectations about the number of marriages which might be saved:

> 'At the end of the day, a relatively small proportion of marriages – perhaps one in 20 – might be saved as a result of the intervention of a counsellor. The number might be less than that – we do not know …'[2]

With this in mind, the initial results from the pilots could be interpreted as promising. The counsellors who have conducted the meetings are extremely positive about the impact, noting that the solution-focused approach was used effectively to help some people work on their marriage and, equally, to help others face the fact that their marriage was irredeemable and move on feeling better able to cope with the consequences. The pay-off in the latter case may be a less conflictual divorce and a more constructive future relationship with a new partner.

Promoting conciliatory divorce

Reducing conflict can be expected to have positive outcomes. That the law should encourage people, especially parents, to mediate any disputes is entirely consistent with the principle of promoting conciliatory divorce. The benefits of mediation are spelt out in the leaflets provided in the information pack. Only in the group presentations, however, was a more determined attempt made to encourage its

---

1   Mr Paul Boateng MP (Brent, South) Official Report (HC Standing Committee E) 7 May 1996, col 124.
2   Ibid, col 128.

use via a demonstration of the process using a specifically commissioned video. In some of the individual meetings, mediation was not even mentioned by the presenter.

Explaining what mediation is and is not has always been problematic, and our evaluation points this up yet again. Nevertheless, the knowledge that is gained about mediation via attendance at an information meeting seems considerable. Attendance acts as a spur to considering mediation as an option: some 57 per cent of people attending the early pilots said they would consider using it in the future if it were to be appropriate. Others pointed to perceived disadvantages of using mediation: mediated agreements are not legally binding; mediation might not serve a party's best interests; it 'takes two to tango', and partners may be unwilling to attempt mediation; it might be costly; and there may be limited local availability (our mapping of mediation services supports this view).

Many attendees at information meetings have described themselves as being either too early or too late for mediation. Those in the first category were not in dispute and had no need for mediation. Those in the second category were well through the divorce process, or had already instructed solicitors to act for them. Estimates that, on a worst-case scenario, 40 per cent of attendees might be expected to use mediation (as suggested in the Lord Chancellor's address to the UK Family Law Conference on 25 June 1999) are, in our view, unrealistic: not all couples are in dispute. Of those who are in dispute, for whom mediation could obviously be an option, some cannot persuade their partner to attend, some fear their partner, some prefer to use solicitors to negotiate on their behalf, and some are confused about where mediation fits in the divorce process. For some, a local service may not be available.

The FLA as a whole is aimed at creating an environment in which the grave matter of marital dissolution is considered differently from at present, but to achieve this there would need to be a radical change in how the various professional groups offer their services and co-operate to guide people through the divorce maze, and, indeed, a more general cultural shift. Traditionally, people considering divorce go to see a solicitor as their first public port of call. Section 8 may change that pattern in an implemented system, but it never would have done so during the pilots. There is evidence, however, that some people manage their use of solicitors differently because they have been to an information meeting, either because they are clearer about what solicitors can do for them, or because they feel less intimidated about approaching a solicitor in the first place. Many attendees have been encouraged to see a solicitor, and in some cases the presenters seem to have recommended this course of action explicitly. Some attendees recognised gaps in the information they had been given at the information meetings, gaps which they could fill only by consulting a solicitor. Also, the information which some attendees sought, especially regarding financial and legal matters, was highly specific to each person and presenters saw provision of it as requiring expert legal knowledge. Solicitors offer more than the negotiation of disputes, and information presenters and, indeed, mediators encourage people to seek appropriate legal advice. Using a solicitor does not necessarily equate with an acrimonious divorce: many lawyers take a conciliatory approach.

Not everyone who has attended an information meeting has sought legal advice, however, and 17 per cent of those in the first five pilots indicated that they were *less* likely to consult a solicitor. These people were most probably managing their own divorce, and felt empowered to remain in control of the process. If the purpose of information meetings is to increase knowledge and empower citizens to take informed decisions, then there is evidence that they are succeeding in achieving these objectives. But it needs to be recognised that those facing marriage breakdown experience many constraints on the choices open to them, and even the desire to use specific services may not be fulfillable.

Later in the study, we shall know whether there is more that could be done to promote mediation and, if so, whether this argues for the provision of information in such a way as to actively divert people into one service rather than another. This would, however, be a very different interpretation of s 8 from that which has appertained until now. There are fine and subtle distinctions to be drawn between neutrality, encouragement and gentle pressure on people to seek help and support.

CREATING OPTIONS

The evaluation is not complete. Nevertheless, there are clear pointers as to the issues which require careful thought before decisions about implementation are finally taken. While the information interview was subsequently transformed into a group information session/meeting, and then into an individual meeting, what is emerging from the pilots is that something akin to a personal interview is what many people expect and hope for from an individual one-on-one encounter. If Part II is implemented, this could be achieved by redesigning the nature and content of the meeting. Unless this happens, it is likely that an opportunity to provide *relevant* information will be lost, and at some considerable cost to the Treasury.

Consistent with the philosophy of the Act, which seeks to offer people information about options on which better-informed choices can be based, it could be argued that people should be offered some choice, however limited, about the mode of information provision which might best suit them. One option might be a one-to-one meeting with a presenter; another might be a CD-ROM program. Given the focus on continuity in parenting, something which encourages fathers to seek the information seems desirable: we have noted that there have been variations in the ratio of women and men attending different kinds of meetings, and the postal pack study attracted a higher proportion of men than did the information meetings. Information-provision could include offering access to written material and a video via libraries, GP surgeries and the Internet. A more flexible approach could promote marriage-saving objectives where it is appropriate to do so, deliver approved messages concerning the needs of children and the benefits of reducing conflict and acrimony, and provide a range of information on which choices could be based.

The Government has declared itself to be committed to 'modernising' justice and to supporting families.[1] The emphasis is on ensuring better access to information so that citizens know their rights and responsibilities, and can avoid or resolve legal problems in a cost-effective way. The interests of children are regarded as paramount, and improving the dissemination of information to parents is a central objective. Whether or not Part II is implemented, it is clear from the pilots that people value information, and that the information about children does have an impact on attendees. The overriding question is whether the information provided is, irrespective of its mode of delivery, to be neutral, or whether it is to be overtly persuasive in seeking to direct people along specific pathways. This is a discussion which is likely to accentuate the differing perspectives of the professionals involved in the divorce business, and it may be one in which inter-disciplinary co-operation is at its most vulnerable. The extent to which the State can or should attempt to change behaviour to conform with notions of what is best for families remains a matter for debate.

---

1   *Modernising Justice*, Lord Chancellor's Department (1998); *Supporting Families: A Consultation Document*, Home Office (1998).

MANAGING AN INFORMATION MEETINGS PILOT

Pat Fitzsimons[1]

INTRODUCTION

As manager of a Relate Centre (for more years than I will say), I found myself following the rather rocky passage of the Family Law Bill 1996 with enormous interest and deep concern for its successful transformation into law. I firmly endorse the principles that underpin the legislation: support for the institution of marriage, an opportunity to save 'saveable' marriages, an intention to minimise the bitterness of the conflict that so often bedevils the parties to a divorce and causes untold misery to children, and action to remove the risk of violence. It all seems eminently sensible to me; numerous marriage guidance clients have said: 'I never meant it to get that far' or 'I never really wanted a divorce'. What they need is time to think and an understanding of all the implications of actions they might take. Once on the divorce roundabout, many find themselves unable to jump off it. Hence my welcoming of this legislation. And then, the undreamed of personal involvement that came my way when the Lord Chancellor's Department invited Relate-Leicestershire to bid for the provision of an information meetings pilot in the East Midlands.

ORGANISATION

Our bid accepted and the Relate Centres in Burton-upon-Trent, Derby and Nottingham all ready to support Leicestershire Relate, we concentrated upon setting up the Local Inter-disciplinary Forum, locating suitable venues, compiling local information directories, publicity and preparing for the launch of the pilot. We did not work in a creative fashion; much of what we did was very tightly prescribed by the Lord Chancellor's Department and by the Research Team at Newcastle Centre for Family Studies and, apart from this pilot's motto which was 'go with the flow', we had a sub-text that meant 'toe the line' which we most certainly did.

PERSONNEL

'We', I must explain, consisted of a small group of the Centre's Trustees and its newly appointed manager as a resource and monitoring unit, myself as project manager, a very young and enthusiastically committed full-time administrative assistant and a more experienced part-time senior assistant who was also responsible for the quality assurance aspect of the presenters' work, and a superb part-time book-keeper, an absolutely essential element; no pilot should be without one.

The Department was very prescriptive in relation to the recruitment of presenters and, in accordance with the guidelines, we advertised for specific categories of professional worker, solicitors, court welfare officers and mediators with the option to recruit counsellors, health visitors, CAB advisers, teachers, librarians; we were to recruit equally men and women, make fair provision for each town, and to take account of the needs of ethnic minority communities.

A total of 435 people applied for the post of Individual Presenter (Model A/B) or Group Presenter (Model B)! We recruited 14 people, three men and 11 women (*pace* gender balance) of whom we trained only 12, amongst them was a solicitor, a barrister, a mediator, four family court welfare officers, four counsellors, a nurse, a teacher and a CAB adviser; we had one black woman, one Asian man, two white women in mixed marriages; we almost managed local town equal distribution.

The first pilot (offering Model A and Model B individual and group presentations) ended in March 1998 and the second pilot (offering Model F CD-ROM meetings) was born in July 1998.

---

1   Pat Fitzsimons, Manager, Relate Centre.

In the second pilot, the same prescriptive terms applied with defined categories of people targeted, computer literate with customer service and training experience. Very different indeed from the first round of information presenters.

The initial training was comparable with the curate's egg but it did one thing superbly; mutual frustration acted like superglue bonding the East Midlands team very tightly together and thus, in my view, contributing substantially to the success we enjoyed.

Training for facilitators was also a mixed bag, as were the facilitators themselves; all had IT skills, all had experience in customer service, all had experience of training others, but from very different backgrounds. A counsellor who had experience in military and police establishments, a mature law student who also taught the flute, a market researcher with a very lengthy CV, a sometime pub landlord and referee with ambitions to write a book, a bank official turned pastoral leader, a lady who was very tuned into community work and women's aid and a lady accustomed to working with groups and training people in fire safety measures. From 124 hopefuls, we recruited eight people: four men and four women; one man fell at the first fence and, because of a close bereavement, one lady did not manage to stay the course. We worked, effectively, with six instead of eight facilitators.

SERVICE DELIVERY

We were given the capacity to offer the service as we saw best. This enabled us to be very flexible in the offering of appointments, service users were our raison d'être and our policy was to make the service fit the user, not the user the service. People were asked where and when it would be easiest for them to attend an individual information meeting and we were invariably able to offer an appointment in accordance with their expressed preference; this system prevailed in both the first and second pilots. Group presentations were different and we were not able to be so flexible; it took a long time to get the first group presentations off the ground as there was a depressingly low demand and even when set up and sourced, a more depressingly low attendance. The courage, fortitude, dignity and the unquestionable skills of group presenters shone like a beacon on these occasions and I realised then why professionals of this calibre had been specified. This is not to denigrate the skills of individual presenters only to highlight the difference in the task. Significantly, individual presenters from Model A were re-trained to do group presentations in Model F and demonstrated the same talent.

We paid close attention to the many and varied venues we used and listened to the views of the presenters who worked in them. This led to underuse of some and perhaps overuse of others; again, our aim was to offer the service users the best possible standards in time, place, the degree of comfort and reassurance and the venue played a very large part in this thinking.

The provision of a professional service was paramount. Good time-keeping by presenters was crucial; no one was to be kept waiting and, whilst presenters needed to enable users to feel at ease during the presentation, the time-limit was not to be exceeded and information only was to be offered. I was filled with admiration for the way in which expert and experienced solicitors, court welfare officers, counsellors all learned to cast off their professional skin and become purveyors of information, resisting the temptation to 'spot the problem', 'feel the vibes of domestic violence' or 'home in on the answers'. It wasn't easy but they all stayed with the script and became expert in the presentation of information.

I was very pleased that from the first telephone call to attendance at a meeting, service users were without exception treated respectfully by all of the pilot personnel with whom they were in contact. I believe this led to people coming to meetings feeling confident and able to participate in the pilot and to their willingness to consent to the research follow up.

In the East Midlands pilot, we had two other tasks:

(1) a special study in domestic violence;
(2) a special study into the needs of the ethnic minority communities.

We had some success in setting up consultations with victims of domestic violence and the people who worked with them, including police liaison officers, women's aid workers, hostel managers and grass root support workers. We also held a number of individual meetings with victims of domestic violence and did some presentations in refuges; it was significant that a comparatively large number of women from ethnic minority communities participated in this special study.

Despite the efforts of a dedicated ethnic minority consultant, we had little success in reaching into the ethnic minority communities in the four towns. We set up consultations to which as many as 80 plus representatives were invited; most attracted a very low level of acceptance and in the event even fewer came. Material describing the proposed changes in the law and invitations to contribute to the debate and to comment on the materials provided was not publicised by the organisations to which it was sent. We discovered that most of it had been consigned to drawers or filing cabinets. 140,000 A4 leaflets printed in five languages and targeted specifically at minority communities were distributed in two tranches via the free newspapers in all four towns, as well as being sent separately to all the agencies concerned with the well-being of ethnic minority communities. There was sadly little response to any of the efforts we made and I think that until the changes in the law are in place, this topic will have little immediacy or acknowledged relevance for members of the ethnic minority communities for many of whom divorce is a taboo subject. It is sad that there was so little feed back and only a minimal opportunity for making the information more relevant to and sensitive of cultural issues.

Towards the latter end of the project we embarked on Information Meetings with Serving Prisoners: here again, we met with limited success, organising several individual meetings with men and women and holding consultations both with members of the prison staff, chaplains and probation service officers, and with serving prisoners. It was not a simple task.

CONCLUSIONS

Managing a pilot project has been a very exciting and satisfying task. I have been conscious throughout that service users have been volunteers who chose to come. It may of course be different when attendance is a statutory requirement and presenters may encounter some reluctance on the part of some attendees. I believe that by offering an immediate, high quality, respectful service, possible resentments could be minimised and attendance at an information meeting could be a very positive experience.

I felt throughout that information meetings should be set up and offered by one agency; a feeling consolidated by the experience of managing the central booking service for the meeting with a marriage counsellor. In this way, an overall high standard of service could be maintained, quality control exercised and there would be total accountability.

Information presenters should be carefully selected, thoroughly well trained, be able to communicate simply and clearly and be well aware of the boundaries within which they need to work; they will also need to be very well supported by management.

These are the thoughts and experience of only one pilot manager and do not reflect anything other than personal experience.

The pleasure of this work stemmed very much from the colleagues who undertook it, liaison with members of the Lord Chancellor's Department and the Newcastle Research Team, all of whom engendered in me a profound respect for their professionalism and dedication to what is still a monumental task and, by no means least, the large number of people who took advantage of the opportunity to 'help shape the future'. I venture to say it has been work well done.

IMPLEMENTATION OF PART II OF THE FAMILY LAW ACT 1996: THE DECISION NOT TO IMPLEMENT IN 2000 AND LESSONS LEARNED FROM THE PILOT MEETINGS

William Arnold[1]

William Arnold introduced his paper by saying that its aim was to try and set the Lord Chancellor's statement made in June 1999 in context. He reminded the conference that the Lord Chancellor remained committed to promoting the Family Law Act 1996 and had suggested some possible modifications in the Supporting Families *document. The question for all those at the conference was what modifications need to be made to that Act to achieve the twin objectives of saving saveable marriages and ensuring less acrimonious conclusions to those marriages which have failed.*

THE DECISION

On 17 June 1999, the Lord Chancellor answered a written Parliamentary Question by Lord Wedderburn of Charlton on whether the Government still intended to implement Part II of the Family Law Act 1996 in 2000. He replied:

> 'No. Before implementing Part II, the Government must be satisfied that the new arrangements for divorce, which it puts in place, will work. The pilot projects, which have been run to test the provision of information meetings under Part II, were concluded at the end of May. The preliminary research results are disappointing, in view of the Government's objectives of saving saveable marriages and encouraging the mediated settlement of disputes. A summary of the research results so far will be published today, and copies will be placed in the libraries of both Houses. The full research results from the pilots will not be ready until early next year, when the Government will consider whether further research is necessary.'

As the Lord Chancellor subsequently explained in his speech to the UK Family Law Conference on 25 June, 'the very least that a responsible Government could do in an area of such importance is to await the final results of its research before deciding how to proceed'. His decision to delay implementation follows automatically from his decision to await the final research results, which are not now expected until late Spring or early Summer 2000. The process of establishing the national provision of information meetings, once a decision to proceed had been taken, would involve a substantial procurement exercise which would take at least 18 months to complete.

However, the Lord Chancellor did not only announce a decision to await the final research results, he also expressed the Government's view that the interim results of the research were disappointing in view of the objectives which the Government hoped information meetings would achieve, in particular, those of saving saveable marriages and encouraging the mediated settlement of disputes. The Government would need to be satisfied that these difficulties would be overcome in an implemented system before it could agree to proceed.

THE INTERPRETATION OF THE RESEARCH

Some commentators have pointed out that the pilot information meetings did not test, and could not test, what an implemented Part II would be like; they merely offered information to volunteers who were either engaged in or considering a divorce under the existing divorce law. The pilot meetings and the research programme were set up in order to test different types of information meeting. They were not set up in order to test whether Part II as such was a good idea or not. Nevertheless, the Government was necessarily interested in the outcomes of the pilot meetings for those who attended them, in terms of their subsequent behaviour, as well as in terms of their reported satisfaction with what had, after all, been free meetings which they had volunteered to attend.

---

1   William Arnold, Head of Family Policy, Lord Chancellor's Department.

The figures which the Lord Chancellor identified as weighing particularly heavily with him – that only 7 per cent of those attending an information meeting have so far gone on to mediation; that 13 per cent have taken up the offer of an initial meeting with a marriage counsellor (about half of these attending with their spouse); and that 39 per cent of those attending reported themselves to be more likely than before to consult a solicitor – are all drawn directly from the interim research reports. There has been no dispute as to their accuracy, but only as to the weight which should be put on them. This, however, is plainly a matter on which Ministers must make and defend a political judgement.

ATTITUDES TO THE 1996 ACT

Three of the four substantive Parts of the 1996 Act have already been brought into force (although Part III will be replaced when the Access to Justice Act 1999 comes fully into force). As far as Part II of the 1996 Act is concerned, the Lord Chancellor has in the past expressed criticism of the current divorce law contained in the Matrimonial Causes Act 1973. Before replacing that legislation, however, he would need to be certain that he was putting something in its place that was better and would be seen to be so. The 1973 Act may not have many friends, but neither is it the object of any popular (as opposed to academic or professional) concern. The Lord Chancellor made clear in his speech to the UK Family Law Conference on 25 June that family law reform is an area where the Government thinks it important to act cautiously, and not to plough ahead with reforms on a doctrinaire basis if research or other evidence calls them into question. The Lord Chancellor emphasised in his speech that family policy is 'too important, too central to people's lives, for us to risk rushing headlong into change for change's sake, legislating in haste and repenting at leisure'.

The Government is also aware of the criticisms that the 1996 Act represents an unduly 'nannying' approach to the way in which adults run their lives and relationships, especially where there are no children concerned. In general, the Government takes the view, expressed in the *Supporting Families* consultation paper, that 'families do not want to be lectured or hectored, least of all by politicians' and that 'we in Government need to approach family policy with a strong dose of humility'.

THE REQUIREMENT TO ATTEND AN INFORMATION MEETING

The requirement to attend an information meeting under s 8 of the Family Law Act 1996 is only one aspect of the reforms under Part II of the Act. Arguably, more important and more significant are the other reforms which abolish fault-based divorce and introduce minimum periods for reflection and consideration before a divorce can be granted. Why then, does the Government not implement Part II with the exception of s 8? The answer to this is that it is not possible because of the way Part II is constructed. The requirement to have attended an information meeting three months before making a statement of marital breakdown is not an optional add-on; it is integral to the new system of divorce and is effectively part of the ground for divorce under s 3. A divorce cannot be granted if this requirement has not been satisfied.

Given the requirements of the 1996 Act, it would require primary legislation to remove the obligation to attend an information meeting before starting the divorce process, or to replace this obligation with a general power for the Lord Chancellor to provide information to divorcing couples. Any proposal for such legislation would have to take its place among the many competing claims for scarce legislative time. Since there is no immediate prospect of such legislation, the Lord Chancellor has taken his decision about implementation on the basis that implementation would mean implementation of Part II as a whole, including the requirement to attend information meetings in their current form.

THE CHANGES SUGGESTED IN *SUPPORTING FAMILIES*

The Family Law Act 1996 was passed after considerable difficulties in Parliament, and represents in its final form a compromise between different views and interests. It does not wholly reflect the original intentions of the then Conservative Government or of the Bill's supporters inside or outside Parliament; it was always clear, for example, that to require divorcing couples to attend information meetings as individuals or as a couple, rather than in a group, would be likely to prove expensive. It is also clear that it is difficult for the same individual meeting to be effective both in trying to save the marriage concerned, and in providing information about mediation, the divorce process and the options available to couples whose marriages are over. The Government therefore suggested in its consultation paper, *Supporting Families*, that it might be better to split the meeting into two, with an individual meeting concentrating on saving saveable marriages, followed by a group meeting providing general information about children, finance and property issues. The group meeting could also be accessible to unmarried parents who applied for court orders over residence or contact.

Out of 127 responses to *Supporting Families* which dealt with the proposed group meetings, 110 supported the Government's proposal, although few gave any detailed views on its implementation. These changes would, however, require primary legislation to amend the Family Law Act 1996 before they could be implemented. A decision not to implement Part II before amending it could therefore entail an indefinite postponement of its implementation. The Government would also wish to consider carefully before implementing a system which would potentially require large numbers of people to go to *two* compulsory meetings before obtaining a divorce; such a procedure might well be open to the accusation that it represented an unduly 'nannying' approach to the private lives of adult citizens.

THE PRELIMINARY RESULTS OF THE PILOT INFORMATION MEETINGS

Although the results of the pilot information meetings were found disappointing in terms of outcomes, the research does enable some preliminary conclusions to be drawn about how information meetings might be run, in the event that they were implemented in something like their current statutory form. These conclusions are explored in the rest of this paper. The most important constraint is the wording of s 8 of the 1996 Act, which stipulates that information meetings must be for individuals or couples, and lays down the categories of information to be provided. Some of the models of information meeting which have been tested (including in particular those involving group meetings or two-stage meetings, such as those suggested in the consultation paper *Supporting Families*) lie outside the scope of the statutory provision and could not be implemented without amending legislation.

THE STATUTORY BACKGROUND

Section 8 sets out the requirement that, under the reformed divorce law, a person initiating the divorce or separation process by making a statement of marital breakdown must (except in prescribed circumstances) have attended an information meeting not less than three months before making the statement. If the other party wishes to make any application to the court regarding children, property or finance, he or she must also (except in prescribed circumstances) attend an information meeting. It is possible for couples to attend the same meeting if they wish, but the Act requires that different meetings must be arranged with respect to different marriages, so it is not possible to implement group meetings. The Lord Chancellor has wide powers to make regulations governing information meetings, but is also constrained by s 8(9) of the Act, which lists nine categories of information, which must be provided. The Government's view is that, in order to conform with the Act, it would be necessary for the meeting to include some element of a face-to-face meeting with a presenter; it would not be enough simply to provide information through the post or over the Internet. On the other hand, it is not legally necessary for all nine categories of information to be covered orally in the meeting; the meeting can concentrate on the information which is most important or most likely to be relevant to the person concerned and it is sufficient for other information to be contained in leaflets handed over at the meeting.

IMPACT OF PILOT INFORMATION MEETINGS

Those attending information meetings had very high rates of satisfaction (over 90 per cent) with the meetings and the information provided. These rates were higher for individual meetings than for group meetings and higher for meetings involving a presenter than for those where the information was given by CD-ROM. The pilots involved volunteers rather than people attending under compulsion before obtaining a divorce, but the University of Newcastle has been working on the problem of how far the results from the pilots can be extrapolated to the general population of those seeking divorce. Studies in other jurisdictions where attendance at information meetings is compulsory have produced very similar satisfaction rates to those found in the pilots.

Information meetings do not only have the objective, however, of satisfying those who attend them. They should also influence the behaviour of those who attend them, by helping them to save their marriages where possible and by encouraging the mediated settlement of disputes where marriages cannot be saved. Information meetings should also give parents a greater insight into the effects of divorce on their children, and should offer information to victims of domestic violence about where to obtain help. It is of course impossible to measure whether any marriages have been saved by the pilot information meetings, but 13 per cent of attendees have taken up the offer of a meeting with a marriage counsellor. 86 per cent of attendees said that they had learned more about mediation, and 56 per cent had considered going to mediation, although in the event only 7 per cent have so far been recorded as having done so. Because information meetings give only general information, and not specific advice, they are likely to prompt some attendees to seek advice which is more tailored to their own cases. 39 per cent of attendees said that the pilot information meeting had made them more likely to go to a solicitor than they were before; this is more than double the percentage of people who said that the meeting had made them less likely to go to a solicitor. 69 per cent of attendees thought that they understood more about how their children feel as a result of the meeting. 14 per cent of attendees said that information provided about domestic violence was relevant to their circumstances.

LESSONS FROM THE PILOT MEETINGS – LENGTH AND FORMAT

The evidence of the pilot meetings suggests that the best length of meeting, from the point of view of providing absorbable information, is about 40 to 45 minutes. Such a meeting is more effective if it concentrates on a few subjects rather than attempting to cover the whole range of subjects listed in s 8(9). The precise contents of the meetings can be varied somewhat according to the circumstances of the individual concerned – there is no point in dealing at length with the welfare of children if the person concerned is childless, for example – but this degree of flexibility is subject to the overall constraint that what is being provided is general information, not individual counselling or advice. All the statutory subjects, including those not dealt with at the meeting, were included in a standard information pack which was given to all those attending.

The pilot schemes experimented with different types of meeting, including group and individual meetings, and meetings where some or most of the information has been provided by video or CD-ROM. Group meetings would, however, not be permitted under the Family Law Act 1996 as it stands. Attendees at the pilots, who often had a poor grasp of the difference between mediation and marriage counselling, found a video on the subject of mediation particularly helpful. The pilots involving CD-ROMs were somewhat disappointing. They encountered some technical problems, and some attendees had difficulty using the technology. Others, who understood it better, were disappointed that what purported to be an interactive CD-ROM was unable to give information tailored to individual circumstances. The use of interactive CD-ROMs also made the length of the meeting difficult to control, as some people revisited sections of information.

LESSONS FROM THE PILOT MEETINGS – CONTENT

One area, which would have to be included orally (even if briefly) in all meetings, is the question of whether the marriage can be saved and the option of an appointment with a marriage counsellor; this is a statutory requirement. In addition, the most important areas to cover, given the Government's overall objectives, would be the availability of mediation as a means of handling the divorce process, and the welfare of children. This approach conforms to the general principles set out in s 1 of the Act, which include: supporting the institution of marriage; enabling marriages which have irretrievably broken down to be ended with the minimum distress to the parties and to the children concerned; enabling questions to be dealt with in a way which promotes as good a continuing relationship between the parties and any children as possible; and limiting the costs incurred in ending the marriage.

Reducing any risk of domestic violence is also one of the principles of the Act, and it would be possible to provide that all information meetings must cover this, in addition to dealing with the subject in leaflets. However, given that only 14 per cent of those attending the pilot meetings said that this information was relevant to them, it might be pointless and counter-productive to force people to listen to material which assumes that they are or may be the (female) victims of domestic violence. Given that the meeting is not in any case intended to provide counselling or individual help other than in the most general terms, it would seem more appropriate on balance that this subject should generally be covered in leaflets, except where the attendee requests further information.

PROVISION OF MEETINGS – PRESENTERS AND PROVIDERS

The Lord Chancellor has the power under s 8 to provide that only persons approved by him can give information. He could, for example, stipulate detailed training requirements for presenters. The pilot schemes, which have been set up, have involved different consortia, including Relate and other voluntary bodies, the Probation Service and firms of solicitors. The presenters have come from a wide variety of professional backgrounds including trained counsellors and mediators, solicitors, court welfare officers, nurses, teachers, psychologists and probation officers.

It had been assumed that the best presenters would prove to be those trained in marriage counselling or mediation, but this was not the case. The best presenters tended to be those who were skilled at dealing with the public and presenting information, but who were not experts in the field of family law or counselling. It was, perhaps, easier for such presenters to avoid being tempted to give individual advice. This could have implications for the types of body that might run information meetings. Meetings might be better delivered by organisations such as banks and building societies, for example, than by voluntary bodies in the family field.

One question which arises is whether it is right to assume, as has generally been done so far, that information meetings should be provided by voluntary or private sector bodies under contract, rather than directly by the State. Since an implemented system of information meetings would require a national network of providers where none currently exists, there is also a question as to whether we should not make use of the existing network provided by the courts.

Other public sector possibilities might be the fledgling Community Legal Service, or the proposed Children and Family Court Advisory Service. Neither of these services yet exists in a form which would enable it to undertake this task, but these options might become more attractive if a decision were taken to implement information meetings in, say, 2002 or later.

LIKELY NUMBER OF INFORMATION MEETINGS

There are currently about 150,000 divorces a year in England and Wales. If Part II were implemented, there would potentially be at least that number of information meetings. It is possible that both parties to every divorce could decide that they want a separate information meeting, which would double the number to 300,000. This seems unlikely, but at least all those who wished to contest any aspect of a divorce would have to attend a meeting, subject again to decisions about exemptions. In addition, once the availability of meetings becomes known, there would be individuals or couples who attended a meeting, but did not go on to seek a divorce and would not have done so in any event. This is an unquantifiable figure, since such people would not be captured in any current statistics. Subject to any decisions by the Lord Chancellor about exemptions, the safest estimate is that there would be about 300,000 information meetings a year if Part II were to be implemented in its current form.

EXEMPTIONS

Section 8 of the Family Law Act 1996 provides that people seeking a divorce, or wishing to contest some aspects of a divorce, must attend an information meeting 'except in prescribed circumstances'. The Lord Chancellor has the power to make regulations prescribing the circumstances in which attendance is not required. One effect of removing the requirement to attend an information meeting would also be to remove the three-month wait between attending such a meeting and making a statement of marital breakdown. When the Act was passed, it was envisaged that exemptions might encompass, for example, the physically or mentally disabled, prisoners and victims of domestic violence. However, one possibility in an implemented system of information meetings would be for Ministers to decide, subject to any questions about *vires*, to take a wide approach to exempting people from the requirement to attend. A wide exclusion of this kind might temper the potential criticism that compulsory information meetings are an unacceptable manifestation of the 'Nanny State' interfering in adults' private lives; the compulsion could be limited to those cases where the State has an undoubted interest in, for example, protecting the welfare of children.

If the Lord Chancellor were to decide to exempt all those without children under the age of 16, 40 per cent of divorce cases would be excluded from the requirement for one or both parties to attend a meeting. The effect of excluding all those without children aged under 16 would also be to speed up their divorces by three months.

There are two rather different areas where exemptions might also be needed.

The first is that of cases in which there is an international element. In some of these, attendance at an information meeting might not be practicable, while there might also be cases where an enforced three-month delay in bringing proceedings could cause hardship, by enabling one spouse to seek divorce in a foreign jurisdiction on more (or less) favourable terms than would be obtainable in the courts of England and Wales.

The second category is in those cases where one spouse suspects the other of disposing of financial assets in order to defeat a claim for financial relief. Such a spouse would seek a court order under s 37 of the Matrimonial Causes Act 1973, restraining the other party from disposing of assets, or setting aside any dispositions already made. An order may only be sought under s 37, however, where proceedings for financial relief have been brought. In these circumstances, it would be undesirable to insist on attendance at an information meeting followed by a three-month delay before proceedings could be initiated by the filing of a statement of marital breakdown.

In both these cases, there might need to be provision for ex parte applications to be allowed to make a statement of marital breakdown, thereby initiating matrimonial proceedings, without attendance or at least prior attendance three months earlier, at an information meeting.

CONCLUSION

The second part of this paper has looked at some of the tentative conclusions which might be drawn from the preliminary research results about the likely shape of information meetings if they were to be implemented under Part II of the Family Law Act 1996 as it currently stands. The larger question, of whether Part II should be implemented in its current form at all, remains to be answered. The Lord Chancellor has expressed the Government's disappointment with the results of research so far. Before implementing Part II, the Government would need to be satisfied that its objectives would be achieved, and that the difficulties which some foresee in operating Part II in the courts would be overcome.

Marriage Support

SUPPORTING MARRIAGE IN THE THEATRE OF DIVORCE

Dr Christopher Clulow[1]

Christopher Clulow *introduced his paper by saying that he had tried to address interdisciplinary perspectives for everyone involved in the 'theatre' of divorce. Part II of the Act had four areas relating to marriage support:*

*(1)   **Reflection:** The thrust of the Act is to prevent marital breakdown. This is perhaps unexceptional but Dr Clulow set out three caveats:*

    (a)   the potential danger of treating reconciliation as the 'gold star' aim of the process;

    (b)   if reconciliation is not possible it may create an unhelpful distinction between a 'good' and 'bad' divorce, encouraging the making of judgements about people's behaviour;

    (c)   a 'good divorce' may be interpreted as an attempt to sanitise the divorce process – it is important to remember that people have 'messy' emotions and a 'neat' divorce is not always possible;

*(2)   **Information:** the information pilots assume a rational model of behaviour which may not adequately encompass the emotional realities of those separating;*

*(3)   **Counselling:** he said he had long argued for the use of the word 'consultation' as an alternative to 'marriage counselling' in this context because it did not imply a desired outcome;*

*(4)   **Funding:** it was suggested that we should consider what kind of training and research we want for the marriage support services and how they are to be funded.*

REWRITING THE SCRIPT

Divorce is a human drama played out on a public stage. Whether the plot is enacted with grand passion or tired resignation, the private experience of loss – and/or fear of loss – will lie at its heart. Like the dramas of classical antiquity, there is a chorus of onlookers providing commentary and response to the unfolding events. The members of the chorus may think they are detached observers of a private drama, but they are, in fact, part of the play and integral to its plot. They will include players in the family justice system whose roles are shaped, in part, by juridical procedures that define the broad structure of what may be the opening, closing or intermediary Acts of the performance. Statute provides a script on which the various actors will base their parts. But there is plenty of room for interpretation, and plenty of scope to be manoeuvred out of role by other players.

When the law changes, so does the script. New parts are written into the drama; established roles are modified or disappear completely. This changes the relationships between the players. A crisis of identity may ensue. When this happens, the members of the chorus are in a similar position to the lead actors; the women, men and children who are, of course, also undergoing a profound process of family change. Family and professional transitions can then become intertwined, and unpredictable consequences may ensue. The psychological processes associated with divorce, and their impact on interpersonal behaviour, cannot in these circumstances be said to apply only to families. Potentially, we are all in it together.

Implementing the Family Law Act 1996 is therefore likely to instil hope and fear in equal measure into the hearts of those who use it and who operate it. In thinking about the interdisciplinary implications of that part of the Act designed to support marriage, I want to adopt a phenomenological rather than a procedural approach; partly because I am less well equipped than others to attend to the procedural niceties, but also because the role of the Tavistock Marital Studies Institute in the family justice system is mainly, as I see it, to create some space for reflecting about experiences of change, and why they are managed in the ways that they are rather than how we would necessarily like them to be.

---

1   Dr Christopher Clulow, Director of the Tavistock Marital Studies Institute.

SUPPORTING MARRIAGE

The fundamental principle underlying Part II of the Family Law Act 1996 is to support the institution of marriage through taking 'all practicable steps' to save those marriages that initially present themselves as candidates for separation or divorce, and to prevent marriage breakdown in the future by ending those marriages that have irretrievably broken down in as constructive a manner as possible. At the heart of the Act lies the 'period for reflection and consideration', a change in process that has introduced new players into the divorce drama – the information provider, the marriage counsellor and the mediator – in an attempt to change the adversarial plot into one that encourages thinking rather than acting out.

There are four provisions that the Act makes specifically to support existing marriages:

(1) a period to reflect on whether the marriage can be saved and to have an opportunity to effect a reconciliation (s 7(1)(a));

(2) information about marriage counselling and other marriage support services (s 8(9)(a)). There is also provision for the Lord Chancellor to make rules requiring a person's legal representative to inform him or her about the availability of marriage support services (s 12(2)(a)(i)) and to provide names and addresses of those qualified to help (s 12(2)(b)(i));

(3) an opportunity of having a meeting with a marriage counsellor and encouragement to attend that meeting (s 8(6)(b)). There are accompanying provisions to ensure the counsellor is qualified and appointed within those terms s 8(11), and to make the meeting free of charge for those qualifying under Part IIIA of the Legal Aid Act 1988, s 8(12). Marriage counselling may also be provided during the period for reflection and consideration, or when that period has been interrupted, subject to terms and conditions that are similar to those relating to the meeting with the marriage counsellor (s 23);

(4) statutory funding for marriage support services, having particular regard to the desirability of these services being available when they are first needed (s 22(1)(a)(3)), and funding for research into the causes of marital breakdown and ways of preventing it (s 22(1)(b)(c)).

Let me comment on each of these four provisions in relation to the implications they may have for interdisciplinary co-operation.

REFLECTING UPON THE AMBIGUITIES OF DIVORCE

The overall thrust of the Act is to prevent marriage breakdown, now and in the future, for all divorce applicants and any children they may have, through encouraging a reconsideration by the parties of the step that at least one of them is proposing to take. When that step is taken, the aim is pursued through attempting to reduce acrimony and encouraging a considered, if not considerate, burial for the broken marriage. Lawyers, information providers, counsellors, mediators, court welfare officers, judges and all the other players who become active in this part of the divorce process are bound by this principle, and by a set of values that discourages fighting over the remnants of marriage and encourages an adult, thoughtful and constructive approach to conflict resolution, one in which the parties are helped to be responsible for managing the consequences of the decision to end a marriage. The period for reflection and consideration is designed to encourage such outcomes.

At one level, there is nothing exceptional about the principle of marriage support and the wish to minimise the destructive potential of conflict. But there are three caveats that I want to add that have implications for everyone working in the family justice system.

The first concerns that part of the human condition that tends to polarise issues, especially when under pressure and in circumstances that are perceived to be threatening. The preferred objective of the Act is that those who present themselves for divorce shall end up being reconciled. This is the gold star outcome of the process given the principles outlined in Part I of the Act. It is not a large step to move from this statement to a position in which reconciliation is counted as the most positive performance indicator for practitioners, at least when it comes to assessing the work of marriage counsellors. If 'marriage' is good, the danger is that 'divorce' will be bad or, at least, a second best outcome in the minds of the chorus of professionals who attend upon families going through this transition. Of course, we have come a long way from the legislation of the past which defined divorce as social deviance, something to be granted only after one of the parties had been 'convicted' of a matrimonial offence. But in the same way that the current Act contains vestiges of the old, there remain questions for those operating the new Act about how they view those who are determined to secure their divorce and who are perhaps impatient of practices and procedures that may feel to them, at best, as irrelevant and, at worst, as infantilising. The attitudes of the professionals will contribute to defining the experience of divorce, and if part of that experience involves reshaping personal identities it will not help to cast those intent on ending what they have been unable to make work into the roles of failures, second best citizens or awkward customers.

On the other hand, practitioners in every discipline need to know about and be able to manage the ambivalence and inconsistencies of those going through a major period of change in their lives. The cast of professionals that has been assembled to assist those going through this family transition is intended to cater for such contradictions. There will be plenty of invitations to us, in our different roles, from those who use the services of the family justice system to relate to colleagues as destructive engineers of marriage breakdown or as useless amateurs in effecting reconciliations. The guilt associated with endings and the feelings of failure that commonly accompany marriage breakdown are often sufficiently unbearable to need to find a temporary home in others. Members of the divorce 'chorus' provide a natural lodging place for such projections.

My second concern is very similar. In the same way that we might be tempted to split our responses to marriage and divorce, so too might we be tempted to distinguish between the 'good' and the 'bad' divorce. The 'good' divorce will be characterised by civilised behaviour, reasonableness, a willingness to 'give and take' in trying to find a solution to persisting differences and an inclination to use the services of mediators in the process. The 'bad' divorce will be conflict-ridden, messy and blaming, with the parties attempting to engage professionals in adversarial approaches to resolving their problems. The invitation to practitioners will be to be drawn into making judgements about behaviour, rather than reflecting upon its meaning in the context of experiences and anxieties that the parties are having to manage. We, as professionals, need the same sort of time for reflection and consideration during the divorce process as our clients if we are not to be drawn into idealising or denigrating ourselves, each other and those who use our services. Being alive to the psychological processes that affect all of us in the work provides some protection against the splitting and dissociation of experience.

My third caveat is related to the preceding two. The drive for reconciliation and the pursuit of the 'good' divorce may attempt to sanitise an experience that depends upon acknowledging and tolerating powerful and messy feelings for there to be a good outcome.[1] Denial, protest and despair are well-recognised features of the road leading from any significant experience of loss. People sometimes do not want to recognise what is happening to them, need to express their rage and hostility to others, and may be unable to mobilise themselves to do the things that they need to do because of the emotional impact upon them of the experience they are going through. If we are intent on recasting angry tigers into docile pussycats (as the strategy has been described by one social scientist) we may encourage a purring within juridical procedures that does nothing to prevent the roaring within families from continuing outside, and its predictable consequences for the children.

PROVIDING INFORMATION IN EMOTIONALLY CHARGED SITUATIONS

The emphasis on providing clear and up-to-date information about marriage support services (and about other options available to the parties prior to registering an application) is one of the very positive features of the Act. Leaflets, information scripts and CD-ROMs have been designed and piloted to test the best ways of informing the public about processes, procedures and options as they go through divorce. A secondary gain from this initiative is that practitioners, too, have access to this information, and so have the opportunity to be better briefed about the range of procedures and services open to families and what they are there to do. The Act has provided additional impetus for those working in the family justice system to learn and become better informed about each other's work. Conferences mounted by the National Council for Family Proceedings and the recent publication[2] explaining the roles and responsibilities of the different players, the systems within which they operate and the

---

1   Sclater, S Day *Divorce: A Psychosocial Study* (Aldershot: Ashgate, 1999).
2   E Walsh *Working in the Family Justice System* (Family Law, 1998).

principles that organise their work, are just two examples of secondary gain that will be crucial to the effective working of Part II of the Act when, and if, it is implemented.

What remains to be seen is how information will be used. Will information encourage couples to use marriage support services and, more importantly, will it help them to use these services in a manner that has beneficial effects? The Lord Chancellor is unconvinced by the results of pilot information meetings conducted so far, although nine in ten of those choosing to attend have said the meetings are useful (especially when information is given personally at an individual meeting), and 13 per cent have gone on to meet a marriage counsellor. Of course, there are likely to be differences between the nature of the experience for those choosing to attend information meetings as compared with those who are compelled to do so (the situation that will prevail once the Act is implemented), so a vital contextual element is necessarily absent from the research and prevents us from knowing what the picture will be like following implementation. I have argued elsewhere[1] that success in conveying information relies on more than cognition. The process of giving and receiving information takes place in an effective context that influences what is heard and how far it can be acted upon. Information depends upon a context of meaning that shapes what is attended to and what is disregarded, a relational context within which it can be processed, assimilated and critically reviewed, and a 'moral' framework that encourages a capacity for concern for others. The view of people as consistently rational beings has its limitations, especially in stressful circumstances. At these times, different personally constructed systems of rationality can come into play, resulting in behaviour that seems quite irrational to the outside observer.

These considerations apply to the professionals as much as they do to those who use their services. We know from earlier legislation how procedural requirements to notify parties of the address of a marriage counselling agency can atrophy into a meaningless formality if the letter of the law is followed at the expense of its spirit. So, too, if the Lord Chancellor creates rules requiring legal advisors to supply the addresses of marriage support agencies this, in itself, will not be sufficient to ensure that they are acted upon, and acted upon appropriately. We know that personal attitudes, professional interests and the dynamics of divorce can combine to propel practitioners into partisan courses of action, depriving the parties concerned of the mental space to review their options.

MARRIAGE COUNSELLING AT A TIME OF DIVORCE

The meeting with a marriage guidance counsellor, and making provision for marriage counselling during the period for reflection and consideration at no cost to those who are unable to pay, are novel features of the Family Law Act 1996. The experience of piloting the meetings is reported on elsewhere, and so I shall restrict myself to a brief comment on timing and resources.

There is something imaginatively self-contradicting in a system that offers marriage counselling to those seeking divorce. While seen as a perverse and obstructive move by some, it has the potential for accommodating the ambivalence and contradictory feelings that so often surround the ending of marriage for one if not both partners. It may also help those who are unsure about what they want. However, most people would accept that the threshold of divorce is likely to be late in the day for mobilising the resources needed to save a marriage. Couples don't activate divorce processes lightly and, when they do, there is usually a history of stuckness with their problems that gives them little hope that things might be different. Even when they are not sure, the term 'marriage counselling' may put them off because it implies a clarity of outcome that the parties are unlikely to share. I think the term 'consultation' is less off-putting than 'marriage counselling' for those going through the transition of divorce. 'Consultation' has widespread acceptance in our culture, does not precipitate the emotional responses that the words 'counselling' and 'psychotherapy' can do, and contains no signposts that might be read as desired outcomes from the perspective of the providers. The words we use to describe the services we offer affect their accessibility in the minds of potential users. More importantly for our purposes, they can affect the behaviour of potential referrers in the family justice system. It is here that some understanding of the nature of the counselling process becomes important.

A key relationship in shaping the nature of marriage counselling services is that between funder and service provider. In the context of the Family Law Act 1996, the funder (government) wishes to save

---

1   Clulow 'Preventing marriage breakdown: towards a new paradigm' (1996) *Sexual and Marital Therapy* vol 11, no 4, pp 343–351.

the saveable marriage and to research, or audit, the outcomes of marriage counselling. I have not been party to the discussions that have shaped the 'meeting with a marriage counsellor', but I can imagine there may have been tensions between funding requirements and professional authority that have had to work themselves out in relation to the nature of the meeting ultimately offered. For example, do people learn what marriage counselling is by having the process described to them, or can they really only learn by experiencing it? Can an agenda-led process such as the meeting with a marriage counsellor properly be described as counselling? If so, who is to determine the model of counselling given the professional differences that exist within the field? The answers to these and similar questions will locate the activity along a continuum of counselling processes that range from information-giving to experiential learning.

There is another dimension to the resource aspect of marriage counselling provision: the fear that one type of service will be funded at the expense of another. It takes little elaboration to indicate how the competition for the same pool of money might affect inter-disciplinary interests and co-operation. Money is a powerful agent of change; it can also create grounds for resistance.

FUNDING MARRIAGE SUPPORT AND RESEARCH

It is, perhaps, the statutory funding of marriage support services and research that, in the context of the Act, is likely to have the most significant impact on preventing and ameliorating future divorce. This part of the Act is already in operation. The Lord Chancellor commissioned an independent review of funding for marriage support that was completed by Sir Graham Hart in March 1999. Part of the evidence reviewed was a discussion paper prepared for the Lord Chancellor's Department by five of the currently core funded marriage support organisations on the nature and value of marriage support,[1] research papers produced by One Plus One on the state of evidence about marriage breakdown and its remedies,[2] and the results of the pilot marriage support projects funded by the Lord Chancellor's Department from the Spring of 1997. The results of this review have yet to enter the public domain, but we already know from his Press Notice of 8 April 1999 that the Lord Chancellor intends to respond positively to the report, a key conclusion of which is that State funding of national support agencies is highly appropriate and worthwhile.

The inter-disciplinary implications of this review remain to be seen. It is clear that future strategic and project-funding decisions will operate within a policy framework. My hope and expectation is that this framework will be constructed through consultation between government, service providers, trainers and researchers, and that there will be the machinery to facilitate and continue this exchange of views between different disciplines which is likely to be the most effective way of ensuring that public money is spent wisely and imaginatively. The principles of diversity and dialogue, so central to the interdisciplinary endeavour, need to be added to the usually stated needs for economy, efficiency and effectiveness.

Nowhere is this more true than in relation to the nature of research into the causes of and remedies for marriage breakdown. Practitioners and researchers have a poor track record of working together on common problems, resulting in separate pockets of knowledge that frequently fail to be linked up. Practitioners have privileged access to the intimate workings of couple relationships, the unconscious processes that bind partners together in relationships that are consciously described as unsatisfactory, and the intersubjective experiences that can communicate more powerfully than words. Researchers have a battery of methodologies, some crude and some sophisticated, that are designed to ensure that, as far as possible, the conclusions arrived at from their investigations are valid and reliable. Each group has much to learn from the other, and it is my belief that the best exploratory processes initiated by therapists and researchers have more in common than either might care to admit, particularly when it comes to tapping into the fine-grained detail of what sustains and erodes the kinds of intimacy and autonomy that make marriages worthwhile for partners and any children they may have.

---

1   Jeffery Blumenfeld, Sarah Bowler, Christopher Clulow, Mary Corbett and Penny Mansfield *Marriage Support and the Secure Society*: Discussion Paper (Lord Chancellor's Department, 1997).

2   Simons J (ed) *Reviews of Evidence on the Causes of Marital Breakdown and the Effectiveness of Policies and Services Intended to Reduce its Incidence* (Lord Chancellor's Department Research Series No 2/99, 1999) vols I and II.

CONCLUSIONS

It is, perhaps, worth concluding with some mention of the ways in which the marriage support aspects of the Family Law Act 1996 have already affected the interdisciplinary workings of the Tavistock Marital Studies Institute.

I have already referred to the collaboration between the currently funded marriage support organisations. The Family Law Act 1996, both during its passage through Parliament and subsequently, has strengthened and provided a focus for joint work between these five organisations which, while sharing a common area of interest, are also quite different from each other. The network of collaboration has extended to include other individuals and organisations as we have played our small part in contributing to the form and content of different media being used in information meetings and the training of information providers. Our contacts with lawyers and mediators have been developed through inviting referrals of individuals and couples who are contemplating divorce to use our recently extended consultation service, and through the interdisciplinary course we run on psychological processes in divorce. We have also been glad to play our part in supporting the work of the National Council for Family Proceedings.

For the future, we hope to offer 'time for reflection and consideration' for small groups of lawyers, mediators, court welfare officers and counsellors, either within or between disciplines, through work consultation groups. These will focus on the experience of practitioners in understanding and managing complex and time-consuming cases. They are predicated on the assumption that what the Act prescribes for the needs of families in transition may equally apply to professionals working with change.

Two other developments are directly related to the aspirations of the Act. The first of these concerns the development of research activities within the Institute, extending case-study and action research methods to include experimental designs, and involving collaborative links with researchers in this country and abroad. We are currently particularly interested in exploring connections between attachment patterns (the web of relatively unchanging assumptions that individuals unconsciously deploy in their dealings with others) and conflict management styles, and in evaluating the process of brief psychotherapeutic interventions with couples. These projects are directly relevant to increasing our understanding of psychological factors that can contribute to marital breakdown, and to providing a contribution to thinking about what constitutes evidence-based practice.

The other development involves our collaboration with a London university that accredits two of our major courses at Masters and Professional Doctorate levels. The intention here is to combine clinical excellence with research-mindedness among practitioners working in the marriage support field. We hope that the students who graduate from these programmes will not only generate original research in the course of their studies but also be equipped to play a leading role in developing good practice and practice-based research in the marriage support field. We expect that these courses will provide a staff development resource for our colleague organisations in the areas of specialist practice, quality assurance, staff supervision and qualitative research.

Other organisations in the family justice system will have similar stories to tell. The Family Law Act 1996, and the process of implementing its marriage support objectives, has provided an important focus for the development of services and research in a relatively neglected and under-resourced area. We are just beginning to identify the possibilities that the Act contains for service users and providers, and the caution of the Lord Chancellor in interpreting the initial findings from research should not detract us from recognising the valuable principles enshrined in it. Our task is to ensure that a spirit of partnership and co-operation prevails in a field that can so frequently demonise difference and dissent.

MEETING WITH A MARRIAGE COUNSELLOR

Mary Corbett[1]

Ms Corbett said her questions for the conference were similar to those of Professor Walker with specific reference to the issue of 'what next for those who attended counselling as a result of their attendance at an information meeting?' It was her view, having been involved as a 'service provider', that many of those couples who had participated in the experiment had found it helpful. It was always going to be difficult for legislation to combine well the two principles of saving saveable marriages and reducing acrimony on divorce. It was worth remembering that the process of marriage support could at least help people deal with the emotional issues arising from the relationship which might help for future relationships.

The opportunity for those who had attended a relevant pilot information session to go to a 'Meeting with a Marriage Counsellor' ended on 30 June. Less than two weeks before (17 June) the Lord Chancellor, Lord Irvine, had confirmed that the Government did not intend implementing Part II of the Family Law Act 1996 in 2000. While appreciating that the experiment is being comprehensively researched, I have chosen to consider the experience of Marriage Care's participation, and spoken to all members who have been involved. The organisation, then known as 'The Catholic Marriage Advisory Council', welcomed the stated intentions behind the White Paper *Looking to the Future – Mediation and the Grounds for Divorce* when it was published in April 1994. An internal consultation about the document took place. The eventual response to government reflected the insight of an organisation with almost half-a-century's experience of dealing with more than half-a-million marriages in difficulty. There was a specific welcome for the inclusion of a period for 'reflection and consideration'; one-fifth of the counsellor responses recorded the fact that they had encountered people (usually women) who had used a solicitor as a means of registering that the marriage was in difficulty and then moved into the divorce process too quickly. There was overwhelming (82 per cent) support for the ending of the need to supply evidence of fault to justify irretrievable breakdown of the marriage.

Throughout 1994, the organisation Marriage Care was part of a working group on a Consortium for Information on Divorce convened by The Nuffield Foundation. The introduction of the Family Law Bill on 16 November 1995 and its subsequent turbulent passage through Parliament afforded a real opportunity for inter-agency and interdisciplinary co-operation. Having observed the shenanigans of the various interest groups and the amazing temporary alliances of libertarians and rigid moralists, it was easy to appreciate the reluctance with which any government would approach the reform of divorce laws. From the perspective of this marriage support charity, the Act which received Royal Assent on 4 July 1996, although flawed, had much to commend it.

Marriage Care members joined emerging local interdisciplinary fora and consortia but the organisation did not tender to become a lead agency for the information pilots. The task did not appear to be sufficiently congruent with the objects of the charity to justify the redirection of time and energy. Individual Marriage Care members became presenters and served in other ways.

In February 1998, agreement was reached that s 8(6)(b) (giving the party or parties attending the information meeting the opportunity of having a meeting with a marriage counsellor and of encouraging that party or those parties to attend that meeting) of the Family Law Act 1996 should be piloted. The Lord Chancellor's Department issued clear guidelines, among them:

- that the meeting should be able to accommodate people at any stage in the divorce process;
- that it should have two sections, one a standard introduction to marriage counselling, the other specific to the agency offering the meeting with a marriage counsellor;
- that the counsellor delivering the meeting should do so in order to achieve one of the following outcomes:

---

1   Mary Corbett, Marriage Counsellor, Marriage Care.

–   that the client(s) leave(s) the meeting feeling that they have received enough information to work on their marriage;

–   that the client(s) agree(s) to come to marriage counselling with a view to saving their marriage;

–   that the meeting enables the client(s) to confirm a decision to divorce, where initially there was uncertainty about this.

The marriage organisations funded by the Lord Chancellor's Department, the Jewish Marriage Council, One Plus One, Relate, Tavistock Marital Studies Institute and Marriage Care were approached to participate in the development of the service. Professor Douglas Hooper joined the group as a participant observer.

The three counselling agencies, Jewish Marriage Council, Relate and Marriage Care, undertook to deliver the first phase of the project, and Relate was chosen as the lead agency for planning purposes.

There were certain professional difficulties about the project (for Marriage Care at any rate).

(i)   the apprehension that counselling might be defined by its outcomes;

(ii)   the importance of the role of supervision in counselling work.

These were not inter-agency problems but were a real reminder that inter-disciplinary work requires patience and understanding so that the integrity and hinterland of each discipline is respected.

Clinical specialists from Marriage Care and Relate devised the training package for the participant counsellors and trainers from both Marriage Care and Relate delivered it. (The section on legal aid eligibility was provided by the Legal Aid Board.) Thirty-five counsellors from six marriage agencies were trained to deliver the service: Relate (14); Marriage Care (13); Jewish Marriage Council (2); London Marriage Guidance (2); African-Caribbean Family Mediation Service (2); and The Asian Family Counselling Service (2).

Part of the 'meeting' was scripted:

–   the opening;
–   the explanation of the meeting;
–   the role of the counsellor in this context;
–   the issue of confidentiality;
–   a statement about domestic violence;

and, towards the end:

–   information about marriage counselling.

The non-scripted part of the meeting was contained within a structured framework to explore the client's current position and to focus on a way forward. It was to concentrate on health rather than pathology.

The Meeting With a Marriage Counsellor was operational within five months of the approach from the Lord Chancellor's Department to the funded agencies. It was offered without charge and entry to the system was made easy by giving the information session attendee one point of contact – a freephone number.

The quality benchmark for the participating agencies was that they offered an appointment within one working day of contact and held the meeting within seven days – unless the attendee wished to delay the meeting.

The Lord Chancellor's Department prepared detailed documentation to brief local agency managers regarding the varied responsibilities incurred and the financial arrangements involved in providing the meeting. As Marriage Care had centrally selected its participant counsellors, it also chose to monitor its contribution to the pilot by accepting requests for meetings centrally.

The organisation is quite small; its counsellors, professionally trained, are volunteers. Many are in full-time work. Although every effort was made to accommodate client wishes, it was not possible in each area to offer daytime appointments. I know from a letter from a current client (who has given me permission to quote him) that he nearly didn't take up the opportunity to attend the Meeting with a

Marriage Counsellor when 'Catholic' Marriage Care was offered as an alternative to Relate. His perception of 'Catholic' included expectations of 'judgement and closed mindedness'. The fact that after four sessions in formal counselling, he has been joined in the process by his estranged wife may show that his original expectations were confounded.

> 'I had previously spoken about my "marriage" to my sister and she confirmed me in my own view that my wife was irrational in her behaviour. Now I am painfully conscious that being "reasonable" does not resolve every situation and whether or not there is a possibility of reconciliation for us, I understand that life is not neat and that order isn't everything.'

From the research information already in the public arena, it seems that most attendees appreciated the Meeting with a Marriage Counsellor. A good proportion indicated their willingness to go on to counselling. Marriage Care found that where counselling could be offered at a convenient location for the attendee, they were likely to begin the process. Ease of access was important.

Twelve of the thirteen counsellors who offered the meeting considered it most worthwhile. The reservation of the one dissident centred on the fact that it took place so late in the process of the disintegration of the marriage. That concern was shared by the others but all felt that the opportunity to 'take stock' to 'take time out' would affect positively existing or future relationships. Their experience as counsellors led them to appreciate the possibility for change and learning which can accompany a time of pain. Some of the attendees were at a crisis point in their second marriage and appeared not to have reflected on the experience of the first break-up.

The counsellors were challenged by the hybrid nature of the meeting but most were satisfied that the approach was appropriate for the task. Many attendees used the meeting to disclose the messiness of their particular situation. None of the models of information meetings had afforded them that opportunity.

All those involved in the project within Marriage Care hope that the delay in implementation of Part II is just that; postponement until the full research reports are available. Marriage Care is concerned to 'save the saveable marriage' and believes that the experiment could work for a few. Even if 5 per cent of couples contemplating divorce could rediscover a meaningful marriage, wouldn't it be cost effective as well as healing?

The whole project has given an unprecedented opportunity for interdisciplinary work. This has involved greater understanding of the roles and respect for other professionals involved in the divorce process. It has allowed for the sharing of information which has the potential to offer better services for people and, for a charity as small as Marriage Care, this is greatly welcomed. Where the inter-disciplinary forum has worked well locally there has been a sense of positive purpose, and a spirit both of challenge and co-operation. Marriage Care is committed to ongoing inter-disciplinary working.

FROM DIVORCE PREVENTION TO MARRIAGE SUPPORT

Penny Mansfield[1]

Ms Mansfield raised the question of how far divorce law can go to support marriage. The concept of saving saveable marriages had to be looked at in the context of the fragile institution which is modern marriage. One should be realistic about the prospects of saving marriages at the point where the parties had reached the stage of wanting a divorce. Evidence suggests that the most effective time to try and save a marriage is much earlier: the focus should be on preventive intervention rather than crisis intervention. It was suggested that varying levels of support could be offered at times such as the birth of a child which typically is a difficult time for a relationship. The aim of marriage support should be to promote stability in marriage, not to try and prevent divorce.

INTRODUCTION

Commenting on his announcement that implementation of Part II of the Family Law Act 1996 would be delayed, the Lord Chancellor told the UK Family Law Conference in June 1999 that the Government remains firmly committed to the principles set out in Part I of the Act; supporting marriage, saving the saveable marriage and, where marriages have broken down, bringing them to an end with minimum distress.[2]

Bringing together these three objectives within the Family Law Act 1996 denotes an inter-disciplinary view of the process of marital breakdown. Family researchers and practitioners working with couples and children experiencing family breakdown have argued that divorce should not be regarded as a discrete event and that the process of marital breakdown begins long before one or both parties consider separation and continues after the decree absolute has been granted.

Section 22 of the Family Law Act 1996 is particularly significant in this respect. It goes beyond the notion of saving marriages and considers the causes of marital breakdown and its prevention. It stresses the importance of research in establishing the reasons for marital instability and effective remedies. In particular, it emphasises the desirability of marriage support services being available when they are first needed. This section of the Family Law Act 1996 is a turning point for family policy because it recognises that saving the saveable marriage is not just a matter of effecting reconciliation for those already involved in the divorce system. Instead, it promotes a comprehensive marriage support service which could prevent marital breakdown rather than the more limited prevention of divorce.

DIVORCE LAW AND MARRIAGE

Whenever divorce law reform is considered, there is unease about its effect on marriage, on the stability of marriage and on perceptions of marriage.

Divorce and marital stability

Has divorce law reform led to an increase in the divorce rate over recent decades? Concern has been greatest in the USA where the greater ease with which a divorce can be obtained under no-fault law has generated a vast body of research into whether this accounts for the rise in the divorce rate.

There is no consensus in the literature on the influence of divorce reform on marital stability; it may be some time before there is any agreement between scholars working in this field.[3] To date, the evidence suggests that there may be some effect, depending on the type of legislation in place, but the effect is

---

1   Penny Mansfield is Director of One Plus One Marriage & Partnership Research.

2   Speech given by Lord Irvine of Lairg, the Lord Chancellor, to the UK Family Law Conference, Inner Temple, 25 June 1999.

3   Mansfield, P and Reynolds, J *What Policy Development would be most likely to Secure an Improvement in Marital Stability?* (Lord Chancellor's Department, Research Secretariat, 1999).

likely to be small and part of a wider process of change. As Glendon[1] notes, developments in family law over the last 25 years: '... have often turned out to be less remarkable than pre-existing and ongoing shifts in ideas about family life or patterns of family behaviour'.

Divorce and perceptions of marriage

Some commentators argue that divorce law reform has led to a change in the perceptions of the nature and permanence of marriage.[2,3,4,5] It is argued that the marriage contract is no longer seen as trustworthy because the no-fault provision permits one partner to divorce the other without their agreement, and because bargaining power has shifted to the spouse who seeks the divorce. The settlement procedure is also criticised on the grounds that it does not usually take account of a woman's financial contribution to the household through domestic labour and child care, or her loss of human capital (foregone earnings and earning potential).

Some theorists predict that the failure of divorce law to protect and compensate vulnerable partners may have contributed to a 'cognitive restructuring' of the idea of marriage which has influenced how people feel about personal commitments.[6] Weitzman[7] writes of the USA:

> 'In a society where one half of all first marriages are expected to end in divorce, a radical change in all the rules for ending marriage inevitably affects the rules for marriage itself and the intentions and expectations of those who enter it.'

Consultees to the White Paper, *Looking to the Future*[8] considered that the law and procedures of divorce should reflect the seriousness and permanence of the commitment involved in marriage. A nearly unanimous criticism of current divorce procedures was that they do nothing to 'save the saveable marriage'. Indeed, many consultees argued that the current system is inimical to the saving of marriages.

How far can divorce law go to support marriage?

Lewis[9] notes that the White Paper proposed a collection of measures to make divorce less expensive and more amicable:

> 'Yet as the Family Law Bill proceeded through Parliament, concern about marriage became stronger. In November 1995 the Lord Chancellor commented that the "debate has been as much about marriage as it has been about the finer details of the divorce system".'[10]

During the passage of the Family Law Bill, a remarkable consensus emerged; politicians, the media and the public focused attention on the state of marriage and the need to reduce marital breakdown. Paul Boateng stated that the Bill 'should not be simply a vehicle for the dissolution of marriage, but a means by which marriage might be supported'.[11] Such a consensus was not present in 1969 when divorce law reform was last debated. Those who then supported reform were positive about divorce, arguing that more people should be given a second chance of finding marital happiness. Three decades later, with greater experience of divorce, we have a better understanding of the complex nature of marital breakdown, in particular its impact on the couple and their children. By 1995, the aim of reform was to prevent marital breakdown, discourage hasty divorce and to minimise discord for the children.

---

1   Glendon, M-A *The Transformation of Family Law – State, Law and Family in the US and Western Europe* (University of Chicago Press, 1989).

2   Fine, M A and Fine, D R 'An Examination and Evaluation of Recent Changes in Divorce Law in Five Western Countries: the Critical Role of Values' (1994) *Journal of Marriage and the Family* May, 56 at pp 249–263.

3   Joshi, H 'Marriage, motherhood and old-age security in the UK' in Maclean, M and Kurczewski, J (eds) *Families, Politics and the Law: Perspective for East and West Europe* (Clarendon Press, 1994).

4   Brinig, S L and Buckley, F 'No-fault laws and at-fault people' (1998) *International Review of Law and Economics,* 18 at pp 325–340.

5   Rowthorn, R *Marriage and Trust: Some Lessons from Economics* (1998).

6   Glendon, M-A *The Transformation of Family Law – State, Law and Family in the US and Western Europe* (University of Chicago Press, 1989).

7   Weitzman, L 'The divorce revolution and the transformation of legal marriage' in Davis, K and Gosbard-Schectman, A (eds) *Contemporary Marriage: Comparative Perspectives on a Changing Institution* (Russell Sage Foundation, 1985).

8   Cm 2799 (1995).

9   Lewis, J 'Marriage saving revisited' [1996] Fam Law 423.

10 HL Deb, 30 November 1995, col 700.

11 HC, Official Report Standing Committee E, Family Law Bill, 25 April 1996, col 4.

The saving of saveable marriages

When the phrase 'the saving of saveable marriages' was used in the Green Paper *Looking to the Future*,[1] it referred to those marriages caught up in the divorce system which 'can be saved but are nevertheless in danger of breaking down irretrievably'. It was a phrase which caught popular imagination because it promised a more effective intervention than trying to reconcile the irreconcilable and implied that modern marriages are fragile and require support. In a letter to *The Times*,[2] the heads of the Government-funded marriage organisations stressed the need to be realistic about how many marriages could be saved on the brink of divorce. Their letter urged Parliament to 'look again at the scope of this Bill, to review what realistically may be done to support marriage in the context of introducing new divorce procedures and to consider the wider legislative framework that supports, or fails to support marriage'.

Incorporating into the divorce system a means of identifying those marriages which may be saved and providing appropriate support to effect reconciliation is a limited form of marriage support. Evidence, and common sense, suggests this is the least effective moment to support marriage; the most saveable marriages are those which are picked up when troubles first arise. The requirement in s 22 of the Family Law Act 1996 for the Lord Chancellor to have regard for marriage support services to be available when they are first needed acknowledges this reality. The challenge for marriage support services is to establish what is a saveable marriage and what is the most effective means of saving such marriages.

DEVELOPING MARRIAGE SUPPORT

Providing marriage support services when they are first needed

The traditional approach to marriage support goes back to 1947 when the Report of a Committee of Inquiry on Procedure in Matrimonial Causes under the chairmanship of Lord Denning favoured the establishment of a 'marriage welfare service':

> 'it should be recognised as a function of State to give every encouragement and where appropriate, financial assistance to marriage guidance as a form of Social Service.'

The service was to be sponsored by the State but not a State institution.[3] In the following half century, marriage guidance has gradually evolved into marriage counselling with an increasing emphasis upon education for personal relationships and marriage preparation. Nevertheless, most of the government funding of marriage support – around £3 million annually – is currently devoted to crisis intervention rather than prevention.[4]

The model of preventive intervention used widely in community, physical and mental health care distinguishes three levels of activity. Primary prevention involves promoting healthy relationships; through education, skills training and information provision. The aim is to enable people to establish and sustain harmonious and cohesive relationships. Secondary prevention is aimed at limiting the intensity and duration of problems, for example early intervention at known stress points in married life, such as the birth of the first child. Tertiary prevention focuses on the treatment of existing problems with the aim of containing distress and limiting their effects. Most counselling and psychotherapy services fall within this area.

From crisis intervention to prevention – new ways of working

A number of researchers and practitioners have concluded that a shift from crisis intervention to prevention is required if a comprehensive and effective marriage support service is to be established. Marriage counselling is not sought by most couples experiencing marital distress and those who do

---

1   Cm 2424 (1993).
2   (1996) *The Times*, 30 April.
3   Cmd 7024 (1947).
4   *Marriage Support and the Secure Society*. Discussion paper prepared by The Jewish Marriage Council, Relate, Tavistock Marital Studies Institute, Marriage Care, and One Plus One Marriage & Partnership Research (1997).

seek help often leave it too late for help to be effective.[1] How can couples whose marriages are in trouble be encouraged to seek help earlier? Clearly, some people find it difficult to use existing services. Making marriage counselling services more accessible and available would help. However, survey evidence suggests that although the majority of people know that relationship therapy is available, a minority regard it as their first choice of help; only one in five of the divorced had actually used it.[2] To encourage couples whose marriages are in trouble to seek help early requires an entirely new approach to marriage support, one which involves a wide range of professionals and new ways of working.

For example, research indicates that the post-natal period can be a stressful time for marriages. Health visitors routinely see mothers in the period following a birth; many are already trained to help mothers with postnatal depression, a condition that can exacerbate and be exacerbated by marital difficulties. A recent study (a randomised controlled trial) carried out by One Plus One Marriage and Partnership Research with funding from the Lord Chancellor's Department, evaluated the feasibility of enhancing the capacity of health visitors to identify and respond to relationship problems experienced by mothers and their partners in the postnatal period. Using a short screening questionnaire, administered to mothers when they attended clinics for the baby's routine '6–8 week check', health visitors were able to identify relationship problems and to respond supportively if problems were identified. The health visitors had received a special four-day training for this role. The results[3] showed that the innovation was strikingly successful in revealing relationship problems and in putting the health visitor in a position to help. Of the 504 mothers in the intervention group, one in four revealed problems in need of attention. In approximately one in sixteen cases, the screening revealed serious problems; frequent rows and evidence of the partners becoming isolated from each other. In most cases, the specially trained health visitors responded supportively; approximately one in five of the mothers received some kind of help with a relationship problem, whereas in the comparison clinics help was given in fewer than one in thirty cases, and by a health visitor without special training for this work.

The period following a birth is not the only time when relationship problems arise or become apparent. Marriages can be under stress when, for example, children leave home and when there is illness, unemployment, and the need to care for a dependent relative. A life-cycle approach to the provision of support is required. Training in the identification of relationship problems and in referral to marriage counselling could be provided for midwives, social workers, general practitioners, the clergy and others. Apart from this gatekeeping role, these professionals may also, with appropriate training, be able to provide marriage support. In addition to seeing clients themselves, marriage counsellors may need to develop ways in which their expertise can be used as a resource for other professionals who provide marital support as part of their routine primary care for families.

A marriage support service which is effective in preventing marital breakdown will need to invest in inter-disciplinary working. Existing knowledge needs to be used more widely; by those involved in marriage support, by those who offer direct help to couples and who refer couples for help, by those who fund the provision of help, and by couples themselves. Research into the causes and prevention of marital breakdown has been identified as a funding priority in s 22 of the Family Law Act 1996; it is clear that research has a vital role to play not only in understanding how marriages break down but also in the identification of effective strategies to support marriage. Understanding marital development is best achieved using data collected in longitudinal research; research that follows couples over time. Such research needs to be guided by theory, and developments in this might benefit from the synthesis of different theoretical perspectives and more inter-disciplinary co-operation.

CONCLUSION

Implementation of the Family Law Act 1996 provides a unique opportunity for inter-disciplinary work among a wide range of professionals who work with families. Marital instability is a feature of modern life. It will not be possible to reverse this trend but it may be possible to build on concern about it. A shift from crisis intervention to prevention in the provision of marriage support is encouraged by the

---

1   Mansfield, P and Reynolds, J *What Policy Development would be most likely to Secure an Improvement in Marital Stability?* (Lord Chancellor's Department, Research Secretariat, 1999).

2   Simons, J *How Useful is Relationship Therapy?* (Lord Chancellor's Department, Research Secretariat, 1999).

3   Simons, J and Reynolds, J *The Use of Health Visitors to Screen for Relationship Problems in the Period Following a Birth: Interim Findings of a Randomized Controlled Trial in an Outer London Borough* (One Plus One Marriage & Partnership Research, 1998).

Act. Further encouragement for this approach has been recommended by Sir Graham Hart in his recently published review of the funding of marriage support, commissioned by the Lord Chancellor. Hart's recommendations, which include a new strategic approach to marriage support services with an emphasis on research and development, and increased funding, have been accepted by the Lord Chancellor.[1] Marriage support services which aim to encourage stability rather than prevent divorce are more likely to be successful, although success is likely to be modest. A cohesive and harmonious marriage brings benefits to the individual and society, benefits that need to be better understood and more widely known.

---

1   Sir Graham Hart *The Funding of Marriage Support* (Lord Chancellor's Department, 1999). The Lord Chancellor announced his acceptance of the recommendations made in the review in a letter to Sir Graham Hart on 24 November 1999.

First Plenary Discussion

INFORMATION PROVISION AND MARRIAGE SUPPORT

It was suggested that the information pilots demonstrated a demand for the provision of information, although there was some agreement that it was a mistake for legislation to try to prescribe the contents of such information meetings in detail. The view was also expressed that the most significant reforms in divorce law since World War II had been achieved through gradual processes of introduction, for example the development of the Court Welfare Service and the concept of the guardian ad litem. There was agreement that people wanted information at the time when the marriage failed, at separation, rather than at the later stages envisaged by the Act. It was also important to remember that children too wanted information. The suggestion was made that parents might be required to inform their child's school in the event of a separation and information could be provided through the school, since separation and divorce clearly had an important impact on a child's education. Julia Hennessy said that this was similar to the Family Group Conferencing operated in Essex where all the professionals and family members involved in a child's life came together at a meeting to provide information for a child (see page 62).

SECOND SESSION

Mediation

FAMILY MEDIATION – THE NEW PROFESSION

Elizabeth Walsh, David Hodson and Thelma Fisher[1]

Elizabeth Walsh *emphasised that her concern was as to the effective regulation of private mediation: given the funding of the public mediation service through the Legal Aid Board, was it right that the Board should be leading the way on regulation of the mediation movement? She also stressed the importance of the commitment of the professionals involved in the family justice system to the idea of mediation: if they were not committed to it, why should one expect others to be? It was important to remember that mediation was only part of the bigger inter-disciplinary picture and one should have in mind what those using the service actually want from it.*

The focus of **David Hodson's** *comments was on the changes needed to get mediation more accepted. In this regard, he reminded the conference that the culture of family law has changed considerably; citing as evidence of this the SFLA Code of Practice, the FDR process and the conciliation appointment in Children Act 1989 proceedings. He suggested that mediation should grow from the 'bottom up': good publicity was needed in Citizens Advice Bureaux, courts and solicitors' offices as to the availability of mediation. Mr Hodson believed that, even without the implementation of Part II, it was still possible to promote the use of mediation through existing means, for example, giving out leaflets with a divorce and changes to court procedures. It was also important to remember that mediation is potentially needed at every stage of the divorce process, not just at the beginning.*

There was also a need to look again at the whole divorce process in order to encourage those couples in mediation, including its terminology and the possible use of joint petitions (which were often requested by couples attending mediation). There was no single easy solution. But, he asked, how can mediation best make progress to greater acceptance and what is its role in a changing culture of family breakdown, what does society expect of mediation, and what do families need?

Thelma Fisher *noted the enormous pressure on mediation as a profession in the past couple of years. One needed to ask why it was so hard to get it established without a change in the divorce culture? She suggested that part of the problem was the word itself: people cognitively did not know what it meant. One might search for a better word for the process. There were also psychological difficulties in trying to get people at the wrong time to engage in mediation when they were emotionally detaching from a relationship; the timing had to be right to persuade people to sit and talk together. She emphasised that there was a need for professional people to work together in the Family Justice System and for there to be a wider understanding of mediation's benefits and possibilities; for there to be 'joined-up separation'.*

INTRODUCTION TO THE UK COLLEGE OF FAMILY MEDIATORS

The UK College of Family Mediators is the professional body for all family mediators in the UK. It was founded in 1996. It is a membership organisation managed by elected and nominated Governors under the Chairmanship of Dame Margaret Booth DBE and, from January 2000, Thelma Fisher. It now has a membership of more than 1,100 including 600 lawyer–mediators. Since it was founded, the UK College has achieved the following.

---

1 Elizabeth Walsh, former Chief Executive, UK College of Family Mediators, Editor, *Family Law*.
   David Hodson, Solicitor–Mediator, Partner, Family Law Consortium, Vice-Chair, UK College of Family Mediators.
   Thelma Fisher, Chair, UK College of Family Mediators (from January 2000).

(1) Promoted mediation

- published three editions of *The UK College Directory* which have been circulated to all county and magistrates' courts, the Principal Registry and the Family Division of the High Court;
- organised 25 judicial seminars for the education of the judiciary, as well as presenting at other conferences and seminars;
- established a media/communications strategy including publication and distribution of leaflets, education pack and professional journal;
- created a website for use by public, mediators and other professionals.

(2) Set standards

- granted approved body status to seven major mediation providers, National Family Mediation, the Family Mediators Association, Family Mediation Scotland, the Solicitors Family Law Association, LawWise, Professional Training and Development and the Academy of Experts;
- established and published a Family Mediation Code of Practice;
- established a UK College Complaints and Disciplinary procedure;
- established practice guidelines on Memoranda of Understanding, Conflicts of Interest, Domestic Abuse and Recording and is currently undertaking the development of guidelines on the direct consultation of children in mediation;
- established and revised professional practice standards for individual mediators and for Approved Bodies, ie set the criteria for membership of the College and the standards for mediation training and practice;
- taking over the Legal Aid Board competency assessment process;
- launching a system of Continuous Professional Development and encouraging continuous education.

(3) Established a family mediators' register

- established a Members' Register, all of whom abide by a Code of Practice and each of whom has a supervisor/consultant;
- established a database of family mediators which provides telephone access for the public and others to the whereabouts of local qualified practitioners, including those assessed as competent for the purposes of Family Law Act 1996, s 29;
- established a supervisors'/consultants' register.

A unifying force

All seven Approved Bodies meet regularly. Consultation is held with the Legal Aid Board, The Law Society, the Lord Chancellor's Department, the Family Law Bar Association and others. At the initiative of the College, a working group was set up with The Law Society (when it announced its intention to set up its own mediation panel) to work towards harmonisation of and/or mutual recognition of the College Code of Practice and The Law Society's Code of Practice.

A membership organisation

From 1 January 1999, the College became a membership organisation with members of the Governing Board directly elected by its members. The College now communicates directly with its membership, not only to strengthen the College's development, but also to empower and unify the membership and demonstrate the establishment of a distinct family mediation profession.

The College management structure

The College is governed by a Board of 14 Governors including an independent Chair (Dame Margaret Booth) and Vice-Chair (David Hodson), and an Honorary Treasurer (Tim Lawrence). Reporting to the

Board are the Executive Committee, the Professional Standards Committee and the Scottish Committee. The College is staffed by a full-time Chief Executive and Administrative Assistant, and a part-time Communications Manager, Clerical Assistant and Accountant.

Vision

In 1998, the College developed a three-year Strategy Plan. The aim is for family mediation to become a widely available, accessible, affordable and popular alternative to the court-based resolution of family disputes. To achieve this:

- the public must be aware of the availability of mediation, understand how to access it and be confident that family mediators are professionally competent;
- family mediation has to become an integral feature of the divorce/separation/family justice and child welfare culture of the UK.

It will also give guidance on matters of mediation policy to government and be the central repository of the profession's intellectual property.

Mission statement

'The aim of the UK College of Family Mediators is to be the statutory regulatory body for family mediation in the UK in order to achieve the quality assurance demanded of family mediation practice for the protection of the clients of mediation and the benefit of all parties concerned.'

The College must be able to give reassurance to the public, as well as its members, that unregulated mediators will not be able to practise in private as well as publicly funded cases. The College also has a strong commitment to supervision/consultancy as the cornerstone of quality assurance.

The strategy plan includes the following areas:

(1) Regulation: quality assurance in the form of a national standard for all family mediators based on assessment and accreditation.
(2) Membership: different levels of membership to be established to allow for different levels of experience – from trainees to Fellows.
(3) Policy: to assist in the implementation of Part III of the Family Law Act 1996 and its statutory successor.

The UK College is now the unifying family mediation organisation in the UK and the professional body for all family mediators, who should be regulated. The UK College is ideally placed to fulfil this vital role.

THE REGULATION OF FAMILY MEDIATORS

No statutory powers

As far as the law of England and Wales is concerned, nothing stops a person practising as a 'family mediator'.

From its inception, the College has stated that protection of the public from poor quality mediation is a prime purpose. If family mediators are not obliged to join the College, we are left with the task of making College membership imperative on a voluntary basis. We are then in danger of falling into the trap of becoming a trade union as well as a regulator. Of course, the College must provide members with information, guidance, services such as insurance, and all the other hallmarks of a professional body. But it is easy to pay lip-service to the public interest while, in reality, protecting professional interests. There are many and varying interests now competing (including with the UK College) in the mediation world. All are presumed to have the public interest as their prime concern but public interest should be protected by statute (or similar), not by aspiration.

Regulation by consent

The College has developed a six-prong strategy for promoting quality assurance and maintaining standards voluntarily.

(1) The Approved Bodies

All seven Approved Bodies have to meet the rigorous training standards set by the College Professional Standards Committee and a Panel carries out annual audits of the Bodies, ranging from the recruitment, selection and training of mediators to the provision of supervision/consultancy and their own complaints and disciplinary procedure.

(2) Individual Members

To become a full member of the College, a mediator must have trained with an approved body, had 30 hours face-to-face mediation practice and received an amount of supervision/consultation every year. To maintain membership, the number of hours face-to-face practice and hours of supervision must be maintained at a certain level. The College is working towards making membership more than a paper exercise and is building on the principle of competency assessment established by the Legal Aid Board.

(3) Code of Practice

The College Code of Practice is mandatory and all members must subscribe to it. It imposes clear duties and obligations and every clause pertaining to practice, qualifications, training and conduct is mandatory. Members sign up to the Code on joining the College, and every year thereafter.

(4) Complaints and Disciplinary Code

The College has produced a Complaints and Disciplinary Code. The College has brought together the Approved Bodies and others to tackle the difficult issue of regulating and disciplining family mediators who may belong to more than one professional body or mediation organisation. According to the College Complaints Code, the ultimate sanction following a complaint which is upheld is removal of the mediator from the College register. While this would no doubt have serious repercussions for publicly funded and employed mediators and those of professional standing and integrity, at the moment it would not prevent mediators practising in the private sector, and so place the public at risk. The College needs the power to enforce its disciplinary procedures on family mediation work in the UK.

(5) Continuous Professional Development

The College requires seven hours of CPD a year and has its own CPD awarding scheme.

(6) Supervision/Consultation

The UK College now consists of more than 1,100 family mediators who have been fully trained, but that is not enough. Only with face-to-face practice and continuous supervision/consultancy can a mediator be said to make that transition from the profession of counsellor, therapist or lawyer etc to family mediator. Quality of performance cannot be assured by written submissions alone, nor by totting up more hours of conferences and seminars. The College insists that every member, no matter how experienced, continues to have a level of individual supervision/consultancy and that each supervisor/consultant is accountable for the practice of those in his/her charge, that he must exercise a management role in respect of the quality of the mediator's practice and continuing training and, not least, give support for a stressful and difficult occupation.

Supervision has an additional role. Family mediators hold a privileged position in the lives of the families that they seek to help. Private ordering, the very essence of mediation, means that agreements are not (always) open to, or at least subjected to, judicial or other outside scrutiny. The competency of mediators must be, and continue to be, assessed rigorously and independently.

The way forward

The UK College has the regulatory framework. What it does not have is the power to enforce it. We have raised standards in mediation and maintained them across the board but this is not enough. The Legal Aid Board has made a welcome contribution to setting standards by its competency assessment programme but the Board has the clout so to do for those at the 'legal aid' level. The choice between completing a portfolio or not doing legally aided family mediation is an easy one. The legal aid sector client is protected but until the external and objective assessment which the College can provide for all mediators becomes obligatory, there is no protection for all. The College continues to call for the statutory or similar regulation of family mediators. High standards must apply to all who practise family mediation and this will be possible only if membership of a professional body with standards of qualification, training and ethical behaviour is made a condition of practice.

MEDIATION AND THE FAMILY LAW ACT: PART II

The loss of some of the features of Part II of the Family Law Act 1996 following the Lord Chancellor's announcement on 17 June 1999 will not be greatly regretted. However, there is much that is good about the Act, individually and as a whole, that cannot be lost. Moreover, there is a danger that the loss could affect the whole infrastructure of the intended complete legislation. Mediation can stand alone and grow in the present law and procedure. However, its preferred foundation and nurturing soil are the various concepts and processes underyling the 1996 Act. The loss of Part II is not fatal to family mediation in England and Wales, but the introduction of certain features of the Act would give family mediation and mediation clients a much better chance of success.

If Part II of the 1996 Act is not to be reintroduced for several years, if at all, a number of its elements should be urgently grafted onto the present law. Mediators, lawyers and the courts have already been working in part in the expectation of the introduction of some of the Act's concepts. The UK College would want to make the most of this anticipated culture and practice change, some of which are as follows.

General principles

Set out in s 1 of the 1996 Act are four fundamental princples. They are recognised by many involved in family cases as crucial to the better conduct of the work and to help families. In part, they are an embodiment of the Codes of Practice of the UK College and the SFLA. They give prominence to helping victims of domestic abuse. But they are applicable only to Part II (and Part III). They should be immediately grafted onto the Matrimonial Causes Act 1973.

Information

The principle of giving parties to a divorce quality, objective and factual information at an early stage is a good one. More thought is needed as to how best to make giving the information more client-friendly. The leaflets with this information are now in a finished state. They should be sent out in their present or shortened form to all petitioners and respondents at the time of issue or service of a petition. The acknowledgement of service and affidavit in support should state that they have been received. This will get good information about mediation (as well as other important subjects) into the hands of the divorcing population, especially those not falling within s 29.

Joint petitions

Some clients want to be able to petition jointly. Many clients have asked for this in the mediation room in order to overcome the public element of blame on one side alone. The Act provided for it. The Booth Committee recommended it 15 years ago. Two-year separation petitions (and perhaps even adultery and behaviour petitions where each have grounds) should be redesigned so they can be issued jointly, with both parties singly or jointly able to apply for decrees nisi and absolute. The experience in mediation is that the issue of one person alone being petitioner can cause real unhappiness and undo much goodwill.

Terminology

Ancillary to the 1996 Act, some terminology would have changed. Where this would produce a more conciliatory and mediatory tone, it should be introduced now. Latin, ecclesiastical and overtly adversarial terms should go including petitions, petitioners, prayers and decrees nisi/absolute and ancillary relief. Why not headings such as 'In the marriage of . . .'? Particularly, we should end the need to claim every conceivable form of financial provision in a petition, which can have a detrimental effect when received by a respondent in person, as seen frequently in mediation when one party comes bearing such petitions. Clients notice such things keenly.

Certificates of reconciliation

These purely paper, often meaningless exercises under the present law are strengthened in the 1996 Act by positive obligations and increased duties to inform clients about mediation and the welfare of children. This should replace the present s 6 of the Matrimonial Causes Act 1973.

Religious divorces

An important, sensitive issue in the 1996 Act was the provision that, where a couple married according to a religious faith/usage, the divorce according to that religious faith should be pronounced before the final divorce decree. It was a particular problem in the Jewish community where some men, who alone can apply for a get, were refusing to give their wives, divorced in law, a proper religious divorce. England was leading the world in the support for wives in such circumstances. This provision in Part II of the 1996 Act should be added to the ability to delay a decree absolute under the present law.

Interim lump sums

This power in the 1996 Act had been keenly awaited, especially after the decision in *Wicks v Wicks*.[1] It is often agreed in mediation but is not possible in law. It cannot be lost.

Adjournments for mediation

Sections 13 and 14 of the 1996 Act give the court specific power to adjourn proceedings at an interlocutory stage to consider the opportunity of the parties to take part in mediation. It is obviously suitable at First Appointments and Financial Dispute Resolution hearings but useful at other times. It 'gets' those who are not subject to s 29, for example because they do not seek legal aid. Some courts are keen to have the power to adjourn. It should be introduced now to help parties and the courts. At the very least, it should be introduced with the Ancillary Relief Procedure Rules for 5 June 2000.

Conclusion

The Family Law Act 1996 had a stormy passage through the Houses of Parliament. Certain elements were much fought over. Some good elements of the reforms came through. Some real hotchpotches resulted from political compromises. Some of the chief practical benefits were in the detail of the legislation which was uncontentious throughout. As family law professionals, whether lawyers, mediators or counsellors, we simply cannot lose these indefinitely. Most can be grafted onto the present law and practice.

Part II of the 1996 Act was carrying more than no fault divorce law reform. It carried the hopes of many as being a symbol for a new future for family law resolution:

  – the increase in co-working of all family law professionals;

---

1   [1998] 1 FLR 470.

- the embodiment of the general principle of the Act, of a conciliatory approach, and a greater awareness of the victims of domestic violence and of the welfare of children;
- a refocusing on saving saveable marriages;
- exploring those cases suitable for mediation;
- the public's understanding of and approach to separation and divorce;
- greater individual responsibility on the parties of the steps taken in the divorce process.

Part II of the 1996 Act may be delayed. However, the momentum of the good and wider aspects of the Act must not be lost. We must identify and then implement within the existing law those relatively minor elements which are good about the Act. Any culture change in the resolution of family disputes may lie as much in a whole series of micro changes as in the macros. Unlike Part II, the culture change must not be delayed.

MEDIATION AND THE FAMILY LAW ACT: PART III

What is continuing in the Act is of the most crucial importance to mediation, ie Part III and specifically s 29. This provides that before a person can be granted a full legal aid certificate for family proceedings, he/she must first meet with a mediator to decide whether mediation is more suitable to the parties, the dispute and all of the circumstances.

However, the Access to Justice Bill repeals Part III of the Act and recreates legal aid funding in a much wider sense with the funding of legal and other ancillary services. It does so in a Funding Code. The Code will incorporate what was Part III but with improvements learnt from the experience of the piloting of s 29. Part III will not be repealed until the Funding Code is finalised and can be brought immediately into effect to replace it.

Eligibility

Limited legal advice to accompany legally aided mediation can be given as before under Claim 10. Clients whose income falls in the gap between Claim 10 and Civil Legal Aid can be given legal advice only by family lawyers approved to give 'linked legal advice' at the ABWOR rate.

Mediators are now routinely assessing clients for their financial eligibility for legally aided mediation at preliminary meetings before they enter mediation.

There is a challenge for researchers in rendering cost comparisons between standard legal aid which is for individuals (about 70 per cent of women and about 11 per cent of men) and the cost of mediation which is for a couple.

Code of practice

Section 27 of the Act contains its own form of Code of Practice for mediators.

Section 7(a) and (b) addresses the issue of domestic abuse screening. Training in this has been developed. The UK College now has a policy on domestic abuse. The preparations for the Act have positively improved mediation practice in this area, which in turn may well inform lawyers' and courts' practice.

Under s 7(c) mediators are required to be aware of the state of the marriage and whether the marriage is saveable. Given the nature of the relationship tensions that lie at the core of mediation, mediators inevitably are well placed to keep this 'under review'. They have skills and capacity to deal with this actively in mediation sessions and by referral.

Section 27(8)(a) and (b) of the Act focuses on the place for the voice of the child in mediation which has become a controversial topic. The UK College is developing a policy on this.

Contracts with the Legal Aid Board

The Legal Aid Board published a draft franchise specification, then a draft mediation contract. There are now quality assurance standards in place and many pilot contracts in operation. These have been developed in four phases with the intention of achieving national coverage by quality assured suppliers by the time of the (as was anticipated) implementation of the Family Law Act 1996.

The benefits of the franchising process have lain in the general sharpening and rationalising of work practices. The not-for-profit sector is particularly vulnerable to delay in the full implementation of Part II. Conversely, for those law practices incorporating mediation work, the delay in implementation of Part II will have very little, if any, impact. The law work will continue alongside a progressive building up of the mediation work of the practice.

Payment of Legal Aid

Payments differ between the not-for-profit and private sector. Not-for-profit services receive set-up grants; the private sector receive loans or self fund in normal small business start-ups. The Family Law Act 1996 puts as an option the statutory charge not being levied in mediation cases. The impact of this is not yet known.

Section 29: meetings with a mediator to assess suitability for mediation

Mediators and others strenuously defended throughout the passage of the Family Law Bill the importance of mediation remaining voluntary. The effort was not prompted by those who wanted it to be compulsory because none did, but by groups, including mediators, who feared that legal aid provisions would in fact make it so for legally aided clients. This anxiety may have contributed to the erroneous belief by the media and some solicitors that mediation itself is compulsory under s 29.

There have been exemptions, concerned primarily with geographical distance, safety for the client from 'significant harm' and the availability of the mediation suppliers to arrange an appointment within 14 days – a limit set to prevent undue delay in accessing full legal representation (early advice is allowed for under Claim 10). Some clients wanting legal aid have seemed to accept this s 29 appointment as a 'given'.

The real problem of entry into mediation, however, lies with the non legally aided client who has been under no obligation to attend such a meeting. However well the meeting is carried out in terms of the opportunity it provides for a significant engagement with the legally aided person, the main limit on its effectiveness is the lack of influence on the non legally aided client.

What is there in it for them? A co-operative approach to problem solving for the sake of their children? An agreed and prudent use of their resources? A potentially cheaper process, including the removal of the statutory charge? However, if they do not become aware of these benefits because they do not attend the appointment offered, then their motivation is not likely to be stimulated. Mediators are learning how to operate this section and are motivated to do so well. It may emerge that the motivation that is most effective is when both are aware that they have something to gain. Perhaps s 29 needs to be revisited in some form later in the court-based process.

To operate s 29, mediators have to be 'recognised' by the Legal Aid Board. At the critical moment when such recognition had to be activated in late 1997, the separate Approved Bodies were not able to agree one way of granting accreditation; each body had developed or was developing its own form of accreditation. The Board therefore undertook to devise its own method using an NVQ occupational standard and testing it by means of a portfolio and an Assessment Board approach in order to establish basic competence. The College is committing itself to it as the 'universal' standard of competence.

The objectives of Part III and the extent to which they are being realised

Some objectives of Part III regarding mediation might be surmised as:

- an increase in the volume of mediation cases. Such an increase would contribute to the achievement of the general principles upon which the Act came to be based;
- savings to the Legal Aid Board and to the public arising from a higher take-up of mediation, on the assumption that it has the potential to be cheaper overall than separate representation. Research findings are awaited;
- control, via franchising, over quality, cost and price of mediation cases to the Board;

- an increase in the availability of mediation suppliers. This is being realised;
- expansion from a lawyer monopoly of all family resolution work. This is not yet fully achieved.

CONCLUSION

Family mediation provides an alternative way of resolving disputes. But for clients to have a choice, they have to have information. The stated aims of the UK College have always been to raise and maintain family mediation standards and to promote good family mediation. It cannot do so alone and it will continue to call upon the government and all professionals in the Family Justice and Welfare Systems to give clients a real choice.

RESEARCHING PUBLICLY FUNDED MEDIATION

Professor Gwynn Davis[1]

INTRODUCTION

I am drafting this paper on 18 June 1999, the day after the Government's announcement that it had no immediate plans to implement Part II of the Family Law Act 1996. I fear that supporters of mediation will have been depressed by this news, but it was, in my view, the right decision, and although I have not been directly involved in monitoring Part II, its probable abandonment ought to be helpful in clarifying the relationship between mediation (which I *am* monitoring) and other divorce processes; a relationship which, also, in my view, has been confused and misrepresented.

Part II of the Act marked an extension rather than a retreat from the presumption that commitment to the marital tie can be reinforced through the law and the practice of courts. It tied the resolution of divorce disputes to the award of the decree; a frail reed indeed upon which to hang inducements to reach agreements on children and property, and one which was obviously open to abuse. It also introduced mandatory information sessions as a means (principally) of encouraging take-up of mediation, the view being that mediation was intrinsically superior to representative negotiation conducted by lawyers and, furthermore, that it offered the prospect of saving money on lawyers' fees.

Most of these ideas can be traced back to the Law Commission's Report *The Ground for Divorce* and to the 1993 White Paper *Looking to the Future: Mediation and the Ground for Divorce* which followed shortly thereafter. Having been in part responsible for the empirical investigation upon which the case for reforming the ground for divorce largely rested,[2] it was indeed depressing to witness the dog's breakfast which our legislators (and in my opinion, at an earlier stage, also the Law Commission) made of the simple, if unsettling, proposal that either party should have the right to a divorce decree following the expiry of a period of notice. As a result, any hope of a rational and humane 'ground' was irretrievably lost, and I shed no tears for the demise of the convoluted procedural gavotte contained within Part II of the Act.

As far as I am aware, there are no experienced practitioners who do not favour no-fault divorce. Unfortunately, this objective is undermined not only by Parliamentarians who have little idea how family law works, and the *Daily Mail*, which doesn't care, but by all those who cling to the notion that divorce law can bolster the institution of marriage. Divorce is, indeed, a process, and it certainly takes time, but it does not follow from this that we should create a divorce law which reaffirms and crystallises those tendencies. That is a complete non-sequitur. Nor, in my 20 years of divorce research, have I heard anyone express the need for an all-purpose information meeting or information pack. Given the reluctance to explain to people in plain terms upon what principles the financial cake falls to be divided (which is the most useful piece of information they could have), one is bound to suspect that the commitment to provide 'information' is, in most aspects, a none too subtle attempt at indoctrination.

I could not in good faith have undertaken to monitor Part II of the Act, but the provision of public funding for mediation appeared to me to raise interesting and important questions to which the answers were far from obvious. We are now over half-way through; I think we've made some progress, and the abandonment of Part II offers the hope that we might get some of the structural relationships right; in other words, that these mechanisms will bear some relationship to the way people actually behave, and the help which they feel they need, rather than being based on some notion of how people *ought* to behave on these circumstances, and the kinds of assistance which they *ought* to find helpful.

---

1   Gwynn Davis, Professor of Socio–Legal Studies, Department of Law, University of Bristol.
2   Davis, G and Murch, M, *Grounds for Divorce* (Clarendon Press, 1988).

MEDIATION AND THE FAMILY LAW ACT 1996

Part III of the 1996 Act provides for legal aid to be made available for mediation in family matters, mainly through the insertion of new provisions into the Legal Aid Act 1998. Whilst mediation is not to be made compulsory, its use is heavily encouraged, with parties who seek legal aid being put in a position where the mediation option must at least be considered.

The 1996 Act provides that anyone seeking legal aid for lawyer representation will first have to attend a meeting with a mediator (although there are a number of important exceptions under which this requirement may be waived). The purpose of this preliminary meeting is to determine whether mediation is suitable given the nature of the dispute and the relationship between the parties. The requirement to consider mediation extends to all disputes concerning money, property, or children where the issue arises from the parties' separation or divorce. The hope is that mediation will become the preferred mode of dispute resolution in these circumstances, although it is envisaged that legal advice will continue to be necessary in addition.

The Legal Aid Board is to have regard to the outcome of a meeting with the mediator when determining whether to grant legal aid for separate representation. The Board is also charged with providing funds for a network of family mediation services.

So, in summary, Part III is intended:

- to transfer business and public funds from lawyers to mediators;
- to reduce (or at least not to increase) Legal Aid Board expenditure overall; and
- to increase (or certainly not to decrease) the parties' satisfaction with both process and outcome.

BACKGROUND TO THE LEGISLATION

Given that the State can afford to support only a fraction of the social needs of its citizens, it is necessary to ask in respect of any service whether the 'need' which it purports to satisfy is one for which the government should accept responsibility. In fact, it is difficult in practice to arrive at any objective measure of the need for dispute resolution services on relationship breakdown and divorce (whether provided by lawyers or mediators).[1] Many people manage to resolve these questions without external assistance, but for the government to pay lawyers and mediators to help tackle the more intractable issues does not seem unreasonable given what is at stake and the fact that the parties may be vulnerable – financially, physically, and through their relationship with their children. (Some would argue that the State should contribute to the resolution of these quarrels because children's future well-being is at stake, but I happen to believe that, for all the rhetoric in which family law is typically encased, divorce disputes are in practice mainly about protecting adult interests and adult rights.)

Hitherto, the dominant mode of dispute resolution in these circumstances has been bi-lateral negotiation conducted by lawyers. This reflects the parties' wish for partisan support, and also for an authoritative statement of the principles upon which these matters fall to be resolved. Legal advice and representation has become part and parcel of our divorce culture, and this is what matrimonial legal aid has traditionally been all about.

Matrimonial lawyers still suffer from a public perception that they exacerbate conflict, but the research evidence does not support this. Rather, lawyers' conduct of divorce disputes has been criticised on the basis that it involves:

- desultory negotiation through correspondence and affidavit;
- in turn permitting a large number of cases to be 'carried' at any one time, often with a very low level of activity on each;
- a final coerced settlement; and
- high cost.[2]

1   Davis, G and Pearce, J 'Privatising the Family?' [1998] Fam Law 614; Pearce, J, Davis, G, and Barron, J 'Love in a Cold Climate – Section 8 Applications under the Children Act 1989' [1999] Fam Law 22.
2   Davis, G, Cretney, S, and Collins, J *Simple Quarrels* (Clarendon Press, 1994).

The pressure to reach a legal settlement can mean that:

- obstinacy is rewarded;
- whichever party experiences less discomfort with the *status quo* enjoys an advantage;
- compromise is sought, irrespective of fairness.

Virtually no case is invulnerable to settlement given these pressures and, indeed, the settlement rate in family proceedings has always been extremely high. Whether despite of, or because of, this, there has continued to be high demand for lawyer services in connection with these disputes. Also, research suggests that client response to lawyer services in the field of matrimonial breakdown is positive on the whole.

The most obvious drawback lies in the expense. Legal aid in the 1980s and 1990s was obviously failing as it catered for the needs of a smaller and smaller proportion of the population at greater and greater cost. Paying private lawyers by the hour out of public funds has proved massively inflationary. The Legal Aid Board had to take steps to control this expenditure, irrespective of the decision to introduce public funding for mediation. The Board has recently begun contracting with a limited number of solicitor firms on the basis that they will deliver a predetermined number of cases at a fixed overall price. This means that legal aid will no longer be a 'demand-led' service. The provision of public money for family mediation is being introduced alongside this other, even more fundamental change.

MEDIATION

Family mediation has risen to its present position on the back of four 'stories':

(1) those who use it like it as a process;
(2) mediation has a high 'success rate' in terms of agreement reached;
(3) the form of negotiation is intrinsically superior, rendering the outcome both more durable and more child-focused; and
(4) mediation has the potential to save public money.

Whilst these advantages are claimed for mediation, public demand over the past 20 years has been less than overwhelming. This picture is not confined to the UK so we have to conclude that the enthusiasm for mediation does not flow in any obvious sense from the divorcing/separating population. However, despite this modest consumer demand, there has been powerful practitioner enthusiasm and, after many years of lobbying, this eventually attracted Government support, or perhaps I should say, the support of the former Lord Chancellor.

The Family Law Act 1996 reflected a view that mediation could be utilised by a much larger section of the separating population. It is argued (and this is a more or less constant refrain) that the lack of any evidence of public enthusiasm for the concept reflects a lack of familiarity or understanding. But divorce law is complex, and people need advice. Also, many of them feel they need support, not just facilitators to help them negotiate. (The Family Law Act 1996 might have been deliberately designed to ensure that all of us, from the Lord Chancellor downwards, could not contemplate divorce without the advice and support of a lawyer.) The Act does not of course deny the need for this advice and support, but it reflects a view that *negotiation* can be as well conducted (indeed, better conducted) with the aid of mediators, face to face, than by delegating this responsibility to legal representatives. The provisions of the Act, and particularly s 29, can be defended on educational grounds, as requiring the parties, before they consume public funds on lawyer services, to get to know what mediation involves.

This question of 'what mediation involves' is not entirely straightforward. There is now a complex relationship between mediation services and the courts, with couples passing back and forth between the two. This is in addition to systems of preliminary appointments on court premises, some of which may also be characterised as forms of 'mediation'. Furthermore, it has become apparent that many family lawyers are themselves attracted to the idea of practising as mediators, either on their own account, or alongside non-lawyer mediators working in the 'not-for-profit' sector.

As a consequence of the way in which mediation is developing in these different directions, it is not safe to assume any particular characteristic of the process simply because the mediation label is applied. Some forms of mediation are quite consciously evaluative and directive. Others claim to be purely facilitative, but may have coercive elements in practice.

Meanwhile, mediation has also influenced lawyers' negotiating practices. It has contributed to a professional consensus which is supportive of the values and principles which mediation is thought to represent.[1]

RESEARCH

These are the questions which my research team is trying to answer.

(1) How do mediation suppliers (and different categories of supplier) compare with one another in terms of: (a) costs; and (b) benefits?

(2) What contracting arrangements should underpin the delivery of publicly funded mediation?

(3) What level of legal advice needs to be made available in addition?

(4) How does mediation (and supporting legal advice) compare with the traditional model of lawyer negotiation and representation in terms of: (a) costs; and (b) benefits?

(5) What proportion of the relevant population is prepared to at least attempt mediation?

(6) Are the mechanisms designed to promote take-up of mediation effective?

It should incidentally be noted that certain kinds of evaluation are not our responsibility. In particular, we are not charged with assessing mediator quality for the purpose of accreditation. The Legal Aid Board has that responsibility, and has made independent arrangements for ensuring that practitioners are of an appropriate standard.

Question (6) is important because the particular *form* of the pilot is bound to have an impact upon the cost-benefit analysis. Under the present arrangements, the parties may choose to avail themselves of mediation at any point but, given the history of modest take-up of mediation, it is inevitable that particular attention is paid to the provisions which positively require consideration of the mediation option. Section 29 requires that mediation be considered at a specific point, but it is clear that mediation may contribute to legal resolution at any stage. We have to consider whether s 29 is an effective means of generating business for mediation services. Might the element of compulsion be applied more effectively when the parties have both come to terms with the decision to end the relationship, and perhaps when they have been exposed to the costs of the litigation process, to the frustrations of bi-partisan negotiation, or to the pains of court attendance?

There are also a number of subsidiary questions concerning the operation of s 29. For example, how will solicitors respond? Might they seek to deflect some clients from a legal aid application altogether, advising them that it is in their interests to pay privately?

Consideration of 'suitability' by the mediation provider is also problematic. Can suitability be equated with willingness, or will the Legal Aid Board feel bound to impose a more rigorous definition if the number of couples who are deemed 'unsuitable' exceeds expectations? How is the determination of suitability to cope with the fact that a person may be willing to mediate and yet at the same time have a pressing need for legal protection, say to prevent assets being dissipated?

The 'savings' issue is perhaps the most difficult of all. Mediation has always claimed to be cheap, but any service provided by a poorly paid or volunteer workforce is likely to be cheap. We now have to grapple with the question of whether mediation is intrinsically cheaper than representative negotiation conducted by lawyers.

In this context, it is important to recognise that there will always be powerful upward pressure on costs. Solicitors argue that their services will continue to be required almost as much as they were prior to the introduction of public funding for mediation. Given that legal aid resources are finite, the Legal Aid Board has to determine which combination of services will deliver reasonable outcomes at a reasonable cost. The question may be posed in terms: what range of services are we prepared to offer, on legal aid, to separating couples? The Legal Aid Board has to control costs, and my team is expected to help the Board determine the best mix of service within those cost limits. That requires judgements on the value of one type of service against another, and of one service deliverer against another. The research focus will be as much on 'benefits' as it is on cost. The fact that expenditure will to an extent be controlled

---

1 Davis, G and Pearce, J 'The Hybrid Practitioner' [1999] Fam Law 547.

through fixed-cost contracts invites us to focus on the value of the services provided; value as perceived by the parties and value measured 'objectively' in delivering good outcomes.

Unfortunately, whilst it is theoretically possible to try and evaluate mediation outcomes and to judge their inherent value, this is hardly a feasible research undertaking. In practice, we have to rely on proxy measures such as: avoiding an application to the court; achieving legal settlement; speed of outcome; and client satisfaction with both process and outcome.

Finally, the research team will advise on the contracts which the Board will enter into with both solicitor firms and mediation providers. Historically, legal aid has been bedevilled by incentives to generate chargeable work. There is now the additional problem of achieving an appropriate mix of services. This means not encouraging a practitioner of one type of service to retain a client whose needs might better be met elsewhere.

I shall now briefly review some preliminary research findings.

THE TAKE-UP OF MEDIATION

The number of referrals to mediation has not changed as rapidly as mediation suppliers (and supporters of mediation generally) would have hoped. The bulk of mediation cases continue to be referred to the 'not-for-profit' sector and involve disputes about arrangements for children (rather than financial issues). Overall, of the 2,270 cases in our database at February 1999, 92.8 per cent were referred to not-for-profit providers of mediation and 6.2 per cent were referred to the 'for profit' sector. Most s 29 referrals also go to the not-for-profit sector, but the weighting is not nearly as extreme. Of s 29 referrals specifically, some 46 per cent have to date been directed to solicitor–mediators. The Legal Aid Board is contracting with an ever-increasing number of mediation providers, and by far the majority of new suppliers entering into contract with the Board in Phase III of the pilot are solicitors. This suggests that if the Government maintains its commitment to support mediation with public funds, the bulk of this work will, in time, be undertaken by lawyers. The position may be compared to the introduction of licensed conveyancing. The anticipated challenge to solicitor' dominance of the conveyancing market has not materialised, and many conveyancers have been taken on by solicitor firms.

MEDIATION STARTS

Prior to the introduction of s 29, the number of mediation starts was modest and relatively unchanging. It might have been anticipated that the provision of Legal Aid Board funding for mediation would itself generate an increase in business, but this has not happened. Section 29, where it has been introduced, has generated a significant increase in the number of intake appointments, but only a modest increase in the number of mediation starts. Of s 29 referrals, just under 20 per cent actually began mediation. The other 80 per cent did not proceed beyond 'intake'.

Prior to the introduction of s 29, the number of mediation starts was around seven cases per month among not-for-profit services and one case per month among for profit services. Following s 29, the mean is of the order of ten cases per month (not-for-profit suppliers) and 2.5 cases per month (for profit suppliers).

If s 29 is retained in its present form, it is likely that couples referred under this provision will come to dominate mediation providers' caseloads, so that the overall 'conversion' rate from intake to mediation will approach 20 per cent and may even fall below that level. The only counter to that will be to increase the scope for exemptions, which is indeed happening. But, of course, each exemption weakens the commitment to require the separating population to explore the mediation option as a means of resolving their disputes.

IMPACT ON COST

The attempt to assess the impact of mediation on a case-by-case basis assumes less significance in the present funding environment because we are confronted with a major imbalance between the Board's expenditure on mediation and the number of cases which are subject to the process. Given current low volumes, it is wholly implausible to suppose that mediation services could pay for themselves through reducing expenditure on lawyer services.

This rather gloomy cost scenario arises because, given the Legal Aid Board's responsibility to develop a network of publicly funded mediation services, it has little option other than to meet the start-up and staffing costs of the not-for-profit sector. Thus, the Board contracts with not-for-profit suppliers of mediation on the basis that it will meet their 'overhead' costs. (This is not true of solicitor providers of mediation, whose overheads are subsumed within their case costs.)

As the number of cases referred to mediation has been lower than expected, the Board has, in effect, been protecting mediation suppliers from the financial consequences of low volumes. As a result, not-for-profit suppliers' actual costs per case have far exceeded their initial estimates agreed with the Board. Cost per case is highly sensitive to changes in volume. There would need to be an increase of about two-thirds in the present number of cases if these suppliers were to bring down their costs to the level initially indicated to the Board. The result is that the Board is paying for mediation at a cost per case which it will not be prepared to support in the long run. The answer, presumably, is that services will have to increase case volume, or cut overheads, or increase income from other sources. None of these is going to be easy.

The Board expects mediation suppliers to charge their private clients the full economic rate, but the volume of cases referred to mediation without any element of compulsion has always been modest, which is why these services had to be run on a shoestring. It has also been the experience of mediation suppliers that potential customers are reluctant to pay for mediation at a level comparable to that which is charged by solicitors. They fear that, if they attempt to charge private clients the full economic rate, this will further undermine their already fragile client base.

If we continue to have only a modest number of cases entering mediation, this suggests that those providers who have but one 'product' (mediation) will find it harder to remain viable than will those who have mediation as but one string to their bow (and a secondary string at that). In other words, lawyer providers of mediation may find it easier to operate in the new funding environment than will the not-for-profit sector who are attempting to stand or fall by the delivery of mediation. This represents a difficulty for the Legal Aid Board which is charged with developing a national network of mediation suppliers, and which furthermore is expected to sustain mediation across both the 'for profit' and 'not-for-profit' sectors. Unless there is a dramatic increase in the number of cases referred to mediation, it is difficult to see how not-for-profit mediation suppliers can become financially viable other than, perhaps, in major population centres.

Any calculation of the impact of an increase in the number of cases referred to mediation must also take into account the potential make-up of this caseload. There is no natural, clearly defined group of cases which require family dispute resolution services. The 'demand' for mediation and lawyer services is not fixed. One possibility is that mediation suppliers will, indeed, increase the number of referrals, but that these additional cases will be ones which would not otherwise have been subject to a legal aid certificate. If this were to happen, mediation suppliers would *appear* more cost effective because they would be dealing with more cases, but the overall cost to the Legal Aid Board would rise as additional cases were 'sucked in' to one form of dispute resolution or another. In order to deal with this problem, the Board will have to impose overall cost limits, presumably on a regional basis.[1]

Meanwhile, solicitors are having to come to terms with the prospect of being relatively modestly paid under the advice and assistance scheme where previously they had enjoyed the blank cheque of a legal aid certificate. The research team will aim to discover whether these restrictions upon the granting of legal aid are effective in limiting the number of certificates awarded, and in cutting solicitor costs overall. We should shortly be able to make a preliminary assessment as to whether the projected saving on the cost of full certificates has in fact been achieved. What is your guess? Mine is that there will be no discernible reduction in the number of legal aid certificates issued. This would be consistent with the evidence of earlier attempts to control legal aid expenditure by indirect means. If I may be permitted to repeat some earlier observations on this theme:

---

1   Bevan, G, Davis, G and Pearce, J 'Piloting a Quasi-Market for Family Mediation amongst clients eligible for Legal Aid', (1999) *Civil Justice Quarterly,* 18, 239–248.

'Whenever steps are taken to reduce this expenditure, for example in simplifying procedure, or in transferring work to a lower court, one observes the legal profession negotiating a higher hourly rate, or increasing the number of applications made in respect of other matters, or simply managing, within each case, to locate more chargeable work. Short of some natural catastrophe which decimates the number of fee-earning matrimonial lawyers, the demands on the Legal Aid Fund will continue to rise. Mediation cannot change this.'[1]

It has been suggested to me that this is a cynical view, or one reflecting a stereotypical image of venal lawyers, but I think it is a matter of the most basic sociological observation. Family lawyers who work on legal aid are amongst the most hard-pressed and poorly paid members of their profession, and they serve a vulnerable population. They are naturally going to resist attempts to cut their income for doing this difficult work. What is more, they need not behave in any way unscrupulously in order to achieve this: the separating population could absorb far more in the way of legal services than the State will ever be able to support. Given the demand, costs can only be controlled directly, by imposing a ceiling on expenditure, never by means of 'diversion' to other services.

FINDING A WAY FORWARD

In contemplating any change to the present arrangements, we have to ask ourselves what kind of dispute resolution services people find helpful when an intimate relationship has broken down. The evidence to date is that most people assume they need legal advice. Lawyers provide partisan support, coupled with an authoritative account of the norms of legal settlement, both of which are valued. At present, it is only a minority of couples who seek a neutral facilitator. The provision of public funding for mediation has not, to date, altered this picture.

Another key observation is that it is a fundamentally different matter to determine legal aid eligibility on an individual basis, for adversarial proceedings, than it is to determine eligibility for mediation. This is because mediation requires a joint commitment to engage in the process. This means, obviously, that the non-legally aided party can undermine participation in a way that he or she cannot undermine participation in contested legal proceedings. This fundamental difference has to date rendered the s 29 requirement comparatively ineffective.

It is also important to ask ourselves whether mediation is rightly conceived as an alternative to litigation. This is the view which is enshrined in the legislation, but it is probably wrong on two counts. First, litigation mainly comprises lawyer correspondence and negotiation, not courtroom battles. Secondly, for most people mediation is probably better conceived as a potentially valuable supplement to (and part replacement of) lawyer negotiation, not as a complete alternative. If that is accepted, it makes little sense to require the parties to explore mediation as soon as an issue is identified.

The experience of the pilot to date is that if mediation is conceived as an *alternative* then it is an alternative that appeals only to a minority. If there is to be more widespread resort to mediation, this will probably have to be on the basis that mediation can make a *contribution* to resolving these disputes, rather than on its being, in effect, the sole mechanism. Also, the requirement to consider mediation is probably imposed too early, when the meaning of this decision may not be clear.

Thus there is a need to develop a mechanism which requires both parties to give serious consideration to the mediation option whilst at the same time allowing greater flexibility as to its timing.

WHERE DOES THIS TAKE US?

It has been apparent for 20 years that, in the absence of coercion, or of a major cultural change, mediation is a minority choice. It need not matter that mediation appeals only to a minority if we accept that it is a distinctive approach calling for certain qualities and skills on the part of the couple themselves. On this view, we might accept that mediation is a minority taste, and allow that it still merits public funding, albeit on a modest scale. Personally, I would regard that as a rational outcome. If, however, we are determined to make mediation part of the mainstream, as is envisaged in the Act, we need to find a means by which it can be more effectively integrated within the early stages of litigation. One experienced mediator whom I interviewed made the point very nicely. She distinguished between

---

1   Davis, G *Partisans and Mediators* (Clarendon Press, 1988) at pp 205–206.

what she called emotional divorce and legal divorce. The ideal starting point for mediation, she thought, was near the beginning of the emotional divorce. However, only a few couples made that choice. The majority would proceed to their 'legal' divorce without having considered the possibility of mediation. Having done that, they needed to understand the processes involved, and to be introduced to the kind of thinking which would be brought to bear in their case. Having been inducted into legal thinking and legal procedure, and the pains of bi-lateral negotiation, the offer of mediation as a means of resolving *legal issues* might come to seem quite attractive, and it is therefore at this (somewhat later) stage that the parties (both of them) should be required at least to consider the mediation option.

The research evidence to date supports this need to review the relationship between the award of legal aid under a full certificate and the offer of publicly funded mediation. One possibility is to allow greater scope for negotiation by lawyers, but to limit the certificate granted for this purpose to the preliminary stages, including obtaining disclosure of the other party's assets. Following this initial exploration and attempted negotiation, consideration of mediation might be made obligatory, subject to whatever exemptions are deemed necessary.

In its dealings with lawyers, the Legal Aid Board is seeking to control expenditure by moving to a system of contracting, requiring the delivery of a fixed number of cases at a predetermined price. It is also entering into block contracts with mediation suppliers based on case throughput. These developments are perfectly compatible with the award of limited certificates covering preliminary exploration and negotiation.

If some such scheme were implemented, reference to mediation might follow the first court appointment, the initial certificate being limited to conduct of the case up to that point (a cash limit would also have to be imposed). It would, of course, remain open to the parties to attempt mediation at any point, including before they consulted a lawyer.

This would be a radical departure from the present scheme, and one which might appear to threaten its cost-saving objectives. But it is probably the only way to embed mediation within the early stages of litigation and thus generate an additional tranche of cases (most of which would have some prospect of being real mediations, not just 'intakes').

As far as the mediation 'industry' is concerned, I have to say that I regard this proposal as two-edged. To what extent do mediators want to become part and parcel of the machinery of litigation and settlement? Were they to agree to go down this road, mediation services would have difficulty in claiming that they provided a distinctive approach to resolving family disputes. They would have become part of the litigation mainstream, putting them under increased pressure to deliver legal settlement. As a result, mediators might well come to experience the ambivalent client reaction that is presently the lot of the family court welfare service.

It may be that mediation providers will seek to have it both ways, perhaps serving the courts and the Legal Aid Board by conducting 'legal' mediations on Tuesdays, but reverting to being purely facilitative as they conduct 'emotional' mediations on Wednesdays. Whatever solutions are attempted, the struggles and dilemmas which have faced family mediation over the past 20 years look set to continue for some time yet.

SECOND SESSION

FRANCHISING FAMILY MEDIATION AND LEGAL SERVICES

Sarah White[1]

BACKGROUND

Following the introduction of the Family Law Act 1996, the Legal Aid Board was given the responsibility by the Lord Chancellor's Department for delivering a network of quality assured mediation services across England and Wales as required by Part III of the Act. The original time-scale for ensuring that the arrangements were in place was April 2000 in order to meet the demand for mediation services which would be created by the implementation of Part II of the Act.

LEGAL AID BOARD'S APPROACH

The Board's approach to delivering a network of mediation suppliers has been:

- by way of a pilot to develop a franchise in family mediation which all suppliers involved in delivering publicly funded mediation services will operate under;
- to identify existing and new suppliers and to assist them in meeting the franchise standards; and
- finally, to conduct an action research programme to identify the most effective supplier arrangements (which is described in the paper written by Professor Gwynn Davis).

INITIAL CONSIDERATIONS

Unlike the legal profession, family mediation can still be described as an emerging profession as there is no regulatory body and, even with the establishment of the UK College of Family Mediators, all of the existing mediation bodies (now members of the College) continue to work to different standards and deliver different training. Developing a franchise category in family mediation has required the Board to take not only a consultative approach, but at times the role of mediator!

The Board also recognises that many practitioners commenced training as mediators following the implementation of Part III of the Family Law Act 1996, and that, as a result, the majority of solicitor–mediators participating in the first three phases of the pilot have little practical experience of delivering mediation services and many of those applying for Phase IV have no experience. The Board has sought to overcome this by establishing participation by the for profit sector through a licensing process. This will operate with new mediators attending training workshops, completing a training portfolio and co-mediating with experienced competence-assessed supervisors/consultants. Following the successful delivery of a specified number of mediation meetings and completed mediations, mediators will then be able to complete the assessment process.

FRANCHISING

Franchising principles

The Board launched its quality assurance scheme in 1994. The Board's objective in franchising remains to work in partnership with the suppliers of legal services to provide an accessible and quality assured service to clients, whilst at the same time delivering improving value for money to the tax payer.

There are four elements to the scheme:

---

1   Sarah White, Family Mediation Project Manager, Legal Aid Board.

(1) the specification of standards of quality assurance that the Board expects suppliers to meet;
(2) audits by the Board designed to ensure that the standards set are being achieved and maintained;
(3) demonstration of continuous improvement in the service that is offered to clients;
(4) control of case costs.

The development of the family mediation franchise category is based on the same principles.

Franchising mediation services

Potential suppliers are invited at intervals (Phases I–IV of the project) to submit an application form expressing interest in participating in the project. On the basis of information supplied, services are short-listed for participation in the project. Only services that meet the requirements relating to practical experience are considered. In addition, all services applying to supply mediation services under the pilot must be affiliated to one of the recognised mediation bodies: Academy of Experts, Balm, Family Mediators' Association, Law Group, LawWise, National Family Mediation, Solicitors' Family Law Association. Mediators must have trained with a recognised training organisation (as listed above) who are members of the UK College of Family Mediators.

As the majority of suppliers applying to participate in the pilot have been new services or have had little experience of the franchising process, it would have been inappropriate to follow the usual franchising process and, instead, the Board has implemented an alternative process for mediation suppliers to obtain contracts. Once services have been granted a contract, they work towards meeting the relevant franchise requirements and obtaining a franchise.

Initially, services are visited by an account manager or project consultant who assesses whether the service can operate satisfactorily on an interim basis whilst working towards meeting the quality assurance standard in full. These requirements include the availability of appropriate premises, that the organisation is capable of meeting the appropriate supervisor standards and are able to develop a set of office procedures that meet the mandatory requirements of the quality assurance standard. On meeting these basic requirements, services are considered for a contract, subject to agreement being reached on service delivery prices. Following Phase III negotiations, there will be 230 mediation suppliers contracted with the Board, two-thirds of suppliers being from the for profit sector.

The Board has undertaken additional development work to ensure that mediation suppliers will be able to meet the franchising standard in the future. Funding has been made available to support supplier development.

After approximately six months of participation in the pilot, preliminary audits are carried out. These focus on the documented procedures of the organisation and ensure that they are working towards meeting the standard required. Suppliers are advised as to what work needs to be completed and are given time scales within which to work.

Thereafter, suppliers receive an interim audit which includes an audit of files against transaction criteria. The transaction criteria were drafted after extensive consultation with all the mediation bodies and The Law Society. The Quality Assurance Standard for Mediation has been revised and services are all currently working toward this standard whilst participating in the project. The final version of the standard will be available by Autumn 1999 following consultation with the mediation bodies, and thereafter all services will need to meet all the requirements.

In the year 2000, suppliers will receive a pre-contract audit and all those services who are able to demonstrate compliance with the franchise standard will be offered a three-year contract.

Post franchise audits will be conducted at intervals of 6–12 months after the contract is let and annually thereafter to ensure that the management system continues to operate effectively and to assess performance against transaction criteria and the file audit requirements.

Mediator assessment

As there are several training bodies for mediation with different practices and standards, the Board also reserves the right in the contract to assess the competence of all mediators in the pilot. The Board devised a competence-based assessment process which all mediators undertaking publicly funded mediation work must complete within the first year of the contract.

All mediators working in an area where s 29 of the Family Law Act 1996 has been implemented must have successfully completed the process before undertaking s 29 meetings with a mediator and s 29 mediations. The UK College of Family Mediators is now adopting the process as a standard for all mediators to achieve.

As mediators with the minimum of experience required initially to participate in the project would struggle to complete the assessment process, the Board has devised a two-tier approach to assessment. This allows those mediators with less experience to be able to participate through a licensing scheme, where they will attend further training in s 29 work, and co-work with an experienced mediator until they have sufficient experience to complete the assessment process.

CONTRACTING

It is the Board's intention to enter into three-year contracts with franchised mediation suppliers in 2000. For the purpose of the pilot, the Board offers services a one-year contract and work schedule which is reviewed annually.

The Board currently negotiates contracts with each service agreeing a volume of work to be conducted by the service over a year and a rate for each category of work to be undertaken by the service.

Monthly contract payments are varied according to the volume of work. It is imperative that the Board maintains a flexible system for payment throughout the pilot as the initial volume estimates are extremely difficult for both parties to establish, particularly when changes such as the introduction of s 29 or the delay in implementation of Part II occur, affecting potential referral rates both positively and adversely.

This has led to difficulties in the not-for-profit sector as most only provide mediation services, have high overheads and are demand-led. In the absence of the expected increase in referrals, it has been difficult for many services to cover overheads. The Board has, to date, assisted those services in the not-for-profit sector, but is strongly advising them to find alternative sources of work and offer other related services in order to be both financially viable and competitive. Where workload falls significantly short of the schedule within the for profit sector, payments are made on a case-by-case basis.

The Board is currently establishing case costs across all categories of mediation and, when the final contracts are offered, these will be done on the basis of an agreed volume of work and an agreed cost for each category. The final form the contract will take has yet to be decided and will be informed by the research.

LEGAL SERVICES

In January 2000, the delivery of all matrimonial and civil advice and assistance to legal aid clients will be through contracts held by quality assured service suppliers. As a result, mediation clients who are in receipt of legal aid will be receiving advice and assistance in support of mediation from a franchised organisation. Whilst this will reduce the number of organisations currently offering the service, client choice will be focused on those who meet the relevant franchise standard. Mediation services will need to be aware of those points of service where clients can access advice and assistance.

Organisations which are contracted to the Board to provide advice and assistance on matrimonial and family matters will receive payment under a contract in much the same way that mediation suppliers are paid now. Whilst organisations will continue to operate in line with guidance, under advice and assistance contracts they will be able to give the relevant advice and assistance in support of a mediation appropriate to the case without automatic reference to the Board.

Exclusive contracting will also resolve the issue of the eligibility gap which affects those who are eligible for legally aided mediation under the pilot but not for the necessary advice and assistance which supports the mediation process.

DEMAND FOR MEDIATION

The introduction of Part III of the Family Law Act 1996 and the anticipation of the effect of Part II, that is referrals from the information sessions and the courts, led many providers of mediation services to expect an increase in mediation referrals which have not and will not in the immediate future be forthcoming. To date, with the implementation of s 29 across pilot sites, albeit initially on a limited basis, the Board reports that currently 40 per cent of applicants for legal aid for those family matters affected by s 29 are required to attend a meeting with a mediator and, of those, approximately between one-quarter and one-third commence mediation. The research outcomes will provide more detailed analysis.

CONCLUSION

Currently, in Phase III, there will be 250 suppliers contracted to provide mediation services, working towards a franchise in mediation. Development work continues with new services ensuring that the network of suppliers in place in 2000 will meet the level of demand for mediation services for the foreseeable future.

The assessment process which has successfully been completed by 450 mediators to date and will be undertaken by another 500 by the Autumn of 1999 has been adopted by the UK College as a standard for all mediators to meet and is being incorporated into the training programmes of key mediation bodies.

Section 29 is being piloted and presently affects approximately 40 per cent of the population and pilot development throughout the year will increase this to 70 per cent.

The research programme is on schedule to inform the pilot development with reports to be delivered in July 1999 and 2000.

The pilot continues to operate to the original timetable to deliver a national network of quality assured suppliers in 2000 in line with requirements of Part III of the Family Law Act 1996.

Second Plenary Discussion

MEDIATION

There was considerable agreement that the fundamental question to be addressed was whether there is a commitment to mediation in the divorce process. If so, the question of how it is to be funded and regulated arises. There was also discussion about the concept of compulsory mediation: should it be, is it necessary?

There was agreement that the constant battle in mediation is funding: unless it is well funded and supported, it was suggested that it may not survive. It was noted that if it is moving from a charitable status to becoming a part of the system, competing within the system, mediation required proper support. The transition was likely to be a hard process.

The question was raised as to what the difference between mediation and the managed negotiations that go on in divorce proceedings through solicitors? Thelma Fisher stressed that the emphasis in mediation was on 'enabling' the parties: assisting them to resolve their difficulties together rather than through solicitors.

The emphasis in discussion was on 'empowering' people to make their own decisions, rather than have solicitors deciding outcomes. It was noted that the new unified Court Welfare Service could offer some aspects of the mediation process, for example the involvement of the Court Welfare Service in direction appointments/conciliation appointments. There was a need to define the roles of the different professionals within that system.

THIRD SESSION

Children's Participation

CHILDREN AND THE FAMILY LAW ACT

Professor Martin Richards and Judith Connell[1]

Professor Martin Richards *drew out three themes from his paper.*

(1) **Research:** *Suggested that for most children their parents' separation was an acute time of distress. For most children, it usually resolved itself over time but there was a small group for whom it does not. For children at separation three things were important: (a) clear information; (b) a need to be able to express what they feel; and (c) that someone is listening to them. The research about listening to children and providing information for them had led to the development of a number of initiatives, such as information leaflets (see (2)).*

(2) **Information leaflets:** *the conference was shown prototypes for these, including a workbook intended to be completed by a young child and an adult, preferably the parent. The aim of these leaflets was to engage children, reaching them directly and enabling them to articulate what they might feel and encouraging them to talk to appropriate adults.*

(3) **Parenting Plans:** *Professor Richards noted that varieties of these had been around for some 15 years, most particularly in North America. They worked as a kind of agenda for separating parents prompting them as to issues which they should perhaps consider. Early research on the use of the Parenting Plan designed for use in conjunction with the Family Law Act 1996 information meetings had elicited the feedback that, although a relatively small group of people had in fact filled them in as a plan, many expressed the view that they had been helpful at some point or other in the process. Irrespective of the implementation of Part II, these things could be developed and used in our present system.*

INTRODUCTION

Over the past couple of decades, there has been a rapidly growing body of research on the possible consequences of parental divorce for children.[2] The work has established that distress at the time of separation is very common for children and that this usually fades with time. However, for a minority of children, there may be continuing adverse consequences.[3] A growing appreciation of the needs of children at divorce has influenced successive legislation.[4] The legislative concern now is not simply the settlement of disputes, the regulation of financial arrangements, and those for children, and protection from domestic violence, but also the provision of information for parents about the needs of children and the encouragement of continuing relationships between them and both their parents after separation.

As recent commentators[5] have put it:

> 'there is [in divorce legislation] a new orthodoxy of child welfare which reflects some, but not all, the principles of the Children Act: namely, that continued contact with both biological parents should be the desired goal; that it is conflict beetween adults which causes most harm to children, and that the best way to ensure that the child's welfare is protected is to endeavour to bring about agreement between parents rather than for courts to adjudicate and attempt to resolve disputed issues through the making of orders.'[6]

---

1   Martin Richards, Centre for Family Research, University of Cambridge.
    Judith Connell, Newcastle Centre for Family Studies, University of Newcastle.
2   Richards, 'Children and Divorce' in Kurczewski and Maclean (eds) *Family Law and Family Policy in the New Europe* (Dartmouth, Aldershot, 1997).
3   Rodgers and Pryor *Divorce and Separation. The Outcome for Children* (Joseph Rowntree Foundation, York, 1998).
4   Maclean and Richards 'Parents and Divorce: Changing Patterns of Public Intervention' in Bainham, Day, Sclater and Richards (eds) *What is a Parent* (Hart, Oxford, 1999).
5   James and James 'Pump up the Volume. Listening to Children in Separation and Divorce' (1999) *Childhood* 189, at 206.
6   Ibid, p 198.

But what is not changing is the lack of opportunity for children to express their own interests in the procedures. At best, it remains the case that their interests will be articulated by adults.

It is a principle of the Family Law Act 1996 that when:

> '... a marriage which has irretrievably broken down and is being brought to an end should be brought to an end –
>
> (i)   with minimum distress to the parties and to the children affected;
>
> (ii)   with questions dealt with in a manner designed to promote as good a continuing relationship between the parties and any children affected as is possible in the circumstances.'[1]

A procedure following these principles is the information meeting which, except in rare circumstances, the initiator(s) of divorce are required to attend before divorce proceedings can begin. The Act lays down nine areas of information which must be covered[2] which include: 'the importance to be attached to the welfare, wishes and feelings of children' and 'how the parties may acquire a better understanding of the ways in which children can be helped to cope with the breakdown of a marriage'.

In this paper, we will discuss some of the ways in which information about children's needs and information for children was being piloted in readiness for implementation of the Act. Following the Lord Chancellor's announcement suspending plans for implementation of Part II of the Act, work on the leaflets for children and parents has continued. The use of material such as these leaflets is not restricted to the context of the Family Law Act 1996 and there is no reason why they should not be provided for parents and their children who are divorcing under the present legislation. We will also consider the Parenting Plans in the paper. While these are not specified in the Family Law Act 1996, these are another technique which was being piloted in the context of the information meeting to encourage parents to focus on the needs of their children and plan for their future in practical everyday ways. Like the leaflets, the use of the Parenting Plan is not dependent on the implementation of Part II of the Act. However, before we consider these aspects of the pilot work for Part II of the Act, it may be helpful to discuss the research on children in a little more detail.

CHILDREN AND DIVORCE: THE RESEARCH EVIDENCE

Recently, Rodgers and Pryor[3] have provided an excellent review of research on children and divorce which draws on over 200 research reports. As these authors state, interviews with children around the time of separation show that most wish their parents had not chosen to separate and that they would get back together again. At separation, children are likely, in the short term, to experience distress, low self-esteem, problems with friendships and loss of contact with a significant part of their extended family. Good continuing communication and contact between children and both parents appears to be especially important in helping children to adapt. But, sadly, research indicates that many parents avoid talking to their children about what is happening and many children do not get the clear explanation of what is happening which is often helpful to them and avoids unnecessary fears and anxieties.

Often the difficulties around the time of separation will fade as children settle into their new patterns of domestic life. However, for a minority, problems persist. There are a number of areas in which difficulties remain, on average, about twice as common in children of divorced families as compared with others of similar social background whose parents remain together. This is the list that Rodgers and Pryor provide on the basis of the published research:

- being in poverty and poor housing;
- behaviour problems;
- performing less well in school;
- needing medical treatment;
- leaving school and home at earlier ages;
- becoming sexually active, pregnant, or a parent at an early age;
- depressive symptoms, high levels of smoking and drinking, and drug use during adolescence and adulthood.
- having lower incomes in adulthood.

---

1   Family Law Act 1996, s 1(c).
2   Ibid, s 8(9).
3   Rodgers and Pryor *Divorce and Separation. The Outcome for Children* (Joseph Rowntree Foundation, York, 1998).

Clearly, in order to intervene successfully to reduce the likelihood of these long-term problems, it is important to understand the process that may link the parental separation with these adverse outcomes.[1, 2] Among the most important processes involved are:

(1) a good relationship with the resident parent and continuing contact with the non-resident parent assists children's adjustment and well-being, except in those rare cases where a parent may be abusive. Not surprisingly, perhaps, what seems to matter is not simply the frequency of contact with the non-resident parent but the quality of the contact; parents and children need sufficient time together to have a 'natural' relationship and to experience some of the ups and downs of daily life together;

(2) money matters. Financial hardship, before, as well as after, separation is influential in limiting children's educational achievements. But lack of money seems less important in its relationship with other adverse outcomes;

(3) conflict between parents before, during, and after separation is stressful for children who may respond by becoming anxious, aggressive or withdrawn. Conflict appears to be an important influence, particularly in relation to behaviour problems. After separation, continuing conflict may have the effect of reducing or ending contact with the non-resident parent;

(4) the upheavals and stresses of separation can produce distress and depression for parents. This may limit their capacity to care for their children adequately and provide the extra support children may well need during the separation. Parents' ability to recover from the psychological stress is influenced by factors such as social and economic well-being and the presence or absence of conflict;

(5) a separation may be only the first step in a series of family changes. The formation of new couple partnerships and changes in 'parent figures' can have a detrimental impact for children. The likelihood of multiple changes will inevitably be highest for those children who were youngest when their parents separated.

It is important to note that children vary widely in their resilience in the face of parental divorce and other family changes. Even in the same family, siblings, apparently experiencing similar circumstances, may fare very differently. As yet, research has paid little attention to such individual differences and we have little understanding of what makes for such differences. In addition, we are still very short of research that evaluates interventions designed to improve outcomes for children and their parents.

FAMILY LAW ACT INFORMATION MEETINGS

Leaflets for parents and children

Various patterns for the information meetings have been trialled as part of the preparations for the implementation of the new Act. At all of these, participants have been given a pack of written information. Among other information, this contains three leaflets, one for parents and two for older and younger children. The reactions to these are being evaluated by the Newcastle action research project.[2] The work, thus far, suggests that the leaflet for parents is the most widely read of all those in the pack and is of wide interest for parents. The research indicates that about one-third of parents pass these on to their children and that some parents find them a useful way of opening discussions with their children. Other parents either did not think that the leaflets were appropriate for their children, that the time was not yet right or that their children were too young for them. In the latter case there was a wide range in the age considered too young, for a few parents even teenagers were considered to be too young to be given the leaflets.

As part of the evaluation, the leaflets were also given to focus groups of children. These children were concerned with both the lack and the content of the leaflets. Most of them wanted a brighter design that would catch the attention of children. Many felt that the suggestion of a number of things that a child might feel at parental separation was too prescriptive for them. Older children indicated that they would

1   Richards 'The interests of children at divorce' in Meulders (ed) *Familles et Justice* (Bruylant, Brussels, 1997).

2   Further information is provided in Walker, J (ed). *Information Meetings and Associated Provisions within the Family Law Act 1996* First, Second and Third Interim Evaluation Reports (Centre for Family Studies, University of Newcastle, 1998) Reports for the Lord Chancellor's Department. See also Professor Walker's paper in this book.

THIRD SESSION

prefer an indirect approach which might, for example, use autobiographical accounts from a number of different children which would provide them with instances that they might identify with. Some younger children favoured a more action-oriented approach which would allow a more hands-on engagement for children. The children who took part in these focus groups, all of whom had experienced parental separation or loss, were very forthright in their views. Almost all of them thought it was a good idea to improve information provision for children but many expressed a reluctance to seek out information in more public places such as schools or libraries. Given that children are often users of the Web, this might suggest that any information provided for children in printed form should also be posted on the Web where children may access it easily.

Thus, research with children, although small-scale, has proved extremely valuable in raising issues which are now being taken into account in the redesign of a second generation of leaflets for piloting. Erica De'Ath of the National Council of Voluntary Child Care Organisations has convened a group of academic specialists and professionals from voluntary bodies with extensive experience of working with children to design a new set of leaflets building on the experience of the initial pilots and other research on information provision for children. Four new leaflets have been designed. For the youngest age group, there is a large format work book, *Me and My Family*, designed for a child to complete in words or drawings with a parent or other adult, with sections such as 'me and my family', 'families change', 'draw pictures of the people you like to talk to' and 'what do you wish for?'. This leaflet is based on one that has been in successful use with children and their parents at the Cambridge Family and Divorce Centre for several years.

The leaflet for middle childhood is entitled 'What's Going On? Dealing with Separation and Divorce'. Again, there are sections for the child to fill in about their own feelings and wishes and people they might talk to. A central section has a snakes and ladders-type board game with spaces for 'situations' which illustrate typical circumstances for children after divorce, 'dilemmas' which describes questions children may face and 'puzzles' which are divorce-related questions for children to solve which may help to hold their attention. The teenage leaflet, 'Working It Out' has a smaller diary-style format that contains a series of young people's stories told in direct quotation, as well as spaces where experiences, feelings and arrangements can be recorded. All three leaflets are heavily illustrated in a bold, bright style. The aim of all three leaflets is to encourage children to articulate and express their feelings about their parents' separation and to talk to their parents and other appropriate adults about these. In addition, there is a fourth leaflet dealing with the same general issues but written for parents.

Parenting Plans

Parenting Plans, while not specified in the Family Law Act 1996, is another technique which has been introduced in the context of the information meetings to encourage parents to focus on the needs of their children and to plan for their future in practical everyday ways.

The Plan consists of a small A4 booklet *Planning for Young Children's Future* which is part information about the needs of children and part a pro-forma plan in which parents can fill in the future arrangements they are making for their children, under nine broad headings. The Plan is a tool or device which can be used by separating parents, on their own or together with a friend or professional (mediator, counsellor, or lawyer) to assist them in making plans for the future of their children. The completed document may be signed by both parents (and perhaps older children) to signify agreement but it is not, as such, enforceable by the court, or, indeed, formally part of the legal process of divorce. It is quite separate from the form setting out the future arrangements for children which must be filed at a court as part of the divorce or separation process. The booklet was produced by Erica De'Ath and Martin Richards by building on the experiences of using Parenting Plans in other jurisdictions, particularly the USA and Australia, where they have been in use for a decade or more. At their simplest, a 'plan' is a set of headings which parents can use as an agenda or aide mémoire for discussions with each other, perhaps with the assistance of others, to ensure that they have covered the various issues that need to be decided about the care of their children after separating. However, some may be much more elaborate and detailed than this, trying to include every possible situation that might arise. The document being used in the Family Law Act 1966 pilot project falls between these extremes. It is designed to be a self-contained document which includes notes on its use, a set of points about various issues that parents might wish to consider in relation to their children's future and a series of headings under which the parents may need to make plans. These sections each include a series of questions with spaces for parents' proposals. The headings are, living arrangements, holidays, special days, staying in contact, school and out-of-school activities, health, religious and cultural upbringing, other arrangements and future changes. There is also a money checklist, but the Plan is not designed for detailed financial planning.

Evaluation of the Parent Plan is being carried out by the Newcastle Team in the context of the action research project for the pilot information meetings. Reactions from professionals toward the Plans have been very positive. More than 2,000 Plans have been distributed to those attending information meetings. Many attendees had either completed the Plan or said that they might use it in the future. Among those who did not intend to complete it, one-quarter said that they had found it useful in other ways. This was often as an agenda for discussions with their spouse or simply as a reminder of the range of issues that they would need to consider. Those with younger children were more likely to make use of the Plans than those with older children. Nor surprisingly, those who had already made arrangements for their children were unlikely to change their arrangements after they received the Plan, but a number of those whose arrangements had not changed found the Plan useful to record the arrangements they had made. Approaching one half of those who had not finalised their arrangements for their children said that the Parenting Plan had influenced them in some way. The main reasons given for using the Plan were:

- a practical and constructive exercise;
- a guide for the future;
- a medium of communication with their partner;
- for reassurance;
- to evoke action and reaction.

These results are at present provisional and a full analysis will be completed in the near future.

As well as this work proceeding in England and Wales, the Parenting Plans are being evaluated with divorcing parents in both New Zealand and Alberta, Canada.

CONCLUSION

A novel feature of the Family Law Act 1996 is that it requires at least one of the divorcing spouses to be given information about a number of issues including the needs of children. This paper describes the work that has been done in producing leaflets for parents and children together with the development of the Parenting Plans. Whilst these materials were developed in the context of the 1996 Act, there is no reason why they should not be distributed and used with the current legislation. The evidence collected thus far suggests that many parents and children would find them valuable. This evaluation research is not yet complete. But if, in the final analysis, the verdict remains positive, it is suggested that these materials should be distributed without waiting for decisions about the implementation of the Act.

THIRD SESSION

THE FAMILY GROUP CONFERENCE PROCESS

Julia Hennessy[1]

Julia Hennessy took the conference through the process of Family Group Conferencing, a scheme which had been developed because of a perceived need to offer children involved in care proceedings a better service. It was based on the belief that a family can usually find their own solutions to problems and on the idea that a child should be at the centre of the decision-making process about its life. She felt that the same approach could be adapted for use in the private law setting, for example contract disputes. The question of getting information to children also raised the point that the Internet was a very useful tool for this: most children had access to a computer and were computer literate and clearly appreciated the availability of information in this form.

GENERAL PHILOSOPHY

The Family Group Conference (FGC) process is a new way of working with families. It is not a one-off meeting, but a process. FGCs are straightforward in their approach, and go some way to redress the power imbalances experienced by children/young people and their families.

The development of FGCs has been, in part, a response to the need to provide more effective services to children/young people and their families. It is based on the belief that families can usually find their own solutions to the difficulties they are facing, and that children/young people have the right to have their families fully involved in their future planning.

This involves clear information being shared, respect towards individuals and no assumptions being made. It is important that the philosophy moves beyond service delivery and becomes part of the implementation and planning process, which has been largely professionally led.

THE BACKGROUND TO FGCS

FGCs developed in New Zealand, and had their origins in the culture of the Maori people. In the 1970s, the Maori people made clear their concerns about the way social welfare services in New Zealand functioned. They particularly highlighted:

- the disproportionately high number of Maori children in the care of the State;
- the over-representation of Maori children on social workers' case loads;
- the almost exclusive placement of Maori children with white European families;
- the lack of Maori social workers;
- allegations of ill-treatment of children in State care.

These concerns were encompassed in legislation in New Zealand in their Children, Young Persons and their Families Act 1989:

'Central to the new legislative structure was the concept of a Family Group Conference charged with empowering family groups to protect and care for their own children and young people.'[2]

The object of this Act was to promote the well-being of children, young persons and their families and gamily groups. The FGC is recognised by the New Zealand Act of 1989 as being the key process by which family groups make informed and reasonable decisions, recommendations and plans in regard to their children and young people.

The concept of what constitutes a family group is open to the widest possible interpretation, and the focus of the FGC is firmly on the 'best interests of the child'.

---

1   Julia Hennessy, Essex Social Services.
2   Wilcox et al (1991).

THE FAMILY GROUP CONFERENCE PROCESS

- – Referrals
- – Preparation
- – Information Giving
- – Private Family Time
- – Agreeing the Plan
- – Monitoring and Reviewing

Referrals

In discussion between families and professionals, agreement is reached that an FGC should be pursued. The social worker will complete a referral form, and an independent coordinator is appointed (this is independent to the case management).

Preparation – Stage One

When the family has been referred for a FGC, it is important that the professionals involved are clear about what the focus for the FGC is, for example, to support a Child Protection Plan or to consider a family placement.

Of absolute importance is the issue of clarity. The family needs to understand what the issues are from the perspective of the professionals in order to be able to act upon it. The information needs to be jargon-free and respectful. In Essex, this information is in the form of a brief report from the social worker.

The adults with parental responsibility and the child/young person must see the contents of the social worker's report, and agree to the sharing of the information contained within it, with other family members; otherwise the FGC cannot occur. Once the parent(s) and child/young person have agreed to share the report with those attending the FGC, the coordinator can begin work.

The coordinator in consultation with the child/young person, with support from their immediate carers, identifies the family network. This may include relatives, godparents, or significant family friends. One of the coordinator's tasks is to prepare these people for the significant family event.

The social worker needs to be clear within his report what the local authority plan will be if the family is unable to produce a plan which fully addresses the professional concerns. This can be referred to as the 'bottom line' and is the Directorate's 'non-negotiable' position.

The social worker will also need to provide information to the family group about the type of resources available and likelihood of accessing them.

When inviting family members, the coordinator will agree with the family a date, time, and venue for the meeting, which is convenient to the family. Preparing family members to participate and focus on the issues are the key responsibilities for the coordinator at this stage. It is important that the family group acknowledges that there is a need for a plan about the child/young person's welfare.

The coordinator has the right to exclude individuals if absolutely necessary. The grounds for doing so should be explicitly stated (eg proven likelihood of violence, or too drunk to contribute), and the family member should have the right to appeal and/or contribute in a different manner.

Who attends the FGC is determined by the coordinator in consultation with the family. The starting point is that all family members are invited, and given a copy of the report for the FGC. This is to avoid any possible collusion amongst the adults, and avoids selection by the adults as to who is significant to the child.

The coordinator will assist all those involved in the process to be clear about what the issues are, and the importance of remaining focused on planning for the child/young person as the main purpose of the FGC.

Information Giving – Stage Two

This part of the meeting is chaired by the coordinator. At the start of the meeting, the professionals are invited to share their information with the family group. The social worker will speak about their report highlighting the concerns the Directorate may have, including being clear about what needs to be different, their statutory duties and responsibilities, including what action will be taken should the family plan not address the areas of concern, and the relevant resources available as a guide.

The family can seek any clarification on the information presented and ask any questions they might have.

Private Family Plan – Stage Three

The coordinator and the professionals then withdraw, leaving the family group to plan in private. The family has three basic tasks:

(1) to develop and agree a plan that meets the care and protection needs of the child/young person;
(2) to agree contingency plans;
(3) to agree how to monitor and review their plan.

The family may take as long as they like, take short breaks as and when they please, and/or refer back to the coordinator should they need any clarification or additional information.

Agreeing the Plan – Stage Four

Once the family agrees a plan, the coordinator rejoins the meeting. The plan is given to the coordinator who may advise if any of the issues to be addressed need further clarification. The coordinator will ensure that the family has included contingency plans, reviewing arrangements, and responsibility for monitoring. The family will be aware, before the private planning time, when their plan will be validated. The plan may need to be validated at a further statutory planning meeting, or by the court, dependent on the individual situation.

The family plan should be agreed if it does not place the child/young person at risk of significant harm.

Should the family plan fail to address any area of concern, the family will be told very clearly and specifically by the social worker what is missing. The family will then be given an opportunity to rectify this situation by meeting again to make the further necessary provision available. The family plan cannot be accepted if it is not deemed to keep the child safe and protected.

Monitoring and Reviewing

Review of the family plan is by a Review FGC. The time and place for this is agreed at the initial FGC, and written into the family plan.

The family will also be asked at the initial FGC to identify a family member, or ideally two, who would take responsibility for informing the local authority if the plan is not working and/or needs minor or major adjustment.

It will be the responsibility of the social worker, at the Review FGC, to update the family group of the current situation in relation to the child/young person, or any significant changes that have occurred since the initial FGC.

THE CONTEXT OF FAMILY GROUP CONFERENCES

It is necessary to view the development of Family Group Conferences in the light of the current legislative framework and knowledge from research.

THE CHILDREN ACT 1989

As mentioned previously, in New Zealand, FGCs are enshrined in law. In England and Wales, they are not. The two Acts, both the New Zealand and England and Wales Acts, do have some similar principles, and these should underpin and inform the development of any way of working. It is impossible to outline all the key parts of the Children Act 1989, but I have outlined some key areas that provide support to the notion of FGCs. These key principles are:

- safeguarding children/young people and promoting their welfare;
- partnership;
- contact;
- parental responsibility;
- family support;
- services to children with disabilities;
- reuniting children/young people with their families;
- taking account of race, culture, language and religion.

WHAT HAVE WE LEARNT IN PRACTICE?

True partnership with families keeping the child as the focus is achievable if we harness the support of the extended family, and provide them with the information that we hold as professionals. The family has a true opportunity to provide a safe protection plan, which is child-focused.

We hold a belief in FGCs nationally that the child has the right to have their family as the key-planning forum, and if the family is able to recognise and accept the need for a plan, then true ownership and participation can be achieved. If the family does not want this ownership, or does not recognise the need for a plan, then it is right and proper that the local authority takes responsibility for the most vulnerable of children. By providing FGCs, we provide opportunities to maximise the potential of families to address their own difficulties.

In evaluations, all participants have voiced their overwhelming support for this process. Family members in Essex have formed a Family Members' Group, which feeds into the FGC Steering Group, therefore harnessing not only their commitment to individual family plans but also to development of policy in this area. Again, an opportunity to promote true partnership with service-users.

In Essex, as part of our evaluation, we attempted to get 'beneath the surface' of the FGC process with professionals and family participants, who were asked to reflect on their experiences and identify what features, if any, differentiated FGCs from traditional child care meetings.

The reflections included:

From professionals –

- shifts in power relationships;
- working in partnership with families;
- jargon-free language of social workers' reports and the FGC;
- uniqueness of each conference, and the way it was able to recognise the specific cultural needs of each family;
- planning rather than procedures led;
- sharing information and family secrets;
- energising and creative development of social work skills.

From family members –

- caring attitudes of coordinators and social services;
- being heard and listened to throughout the FGC process;
- power to make their own plans resulting in ownership and commitment to the plans;
- involvement of significant family members.

THIRD SESSION

ISSUES IN LEGAL PROCEEDINGS

Within Essex, through consultation, we have devised a process where FGCs are considered before care proceedings are initiated. We are also commissioned following a directions hearing during care proceedings.

Where issues of confidentiality are a problem and one family member does not wish other family members to know about a key issue, for example alcoholism, the matter can be listed for a contested hearing by the court to decide what information can be shared by whom. There is a need for guidance regarding confidentiality and there is a need for the Family Group Conference process to be enshrined in legislation. It is effective in most cases where it is applied. Children should not be prevented from benefiting from this process when appropriate.

Following FGC in this arena, the family plans can help to formulate the child's care plan that is validated by the Court. If parents are not in agreement to the FGC, therefore denying the children the right to have their family involved in their planning, there is the legal process of applying for a direction for the judiciary to consider whether an FGC is in the best interest of the child.

DILEMMAS FOR PRACTICE AND DEBATE

While the Children Act 1989 implicitly supports the FGC approach, there is no requirement to practise it. Therefore, the families that are being referred are being provided with an opportunity that other families and their children may not be accessing.

FGCs do present professionals with a challenging model for practice. To empower families requires empowered social workers who have a genuine commitment to working in partnership with children and their families.

Within Essex, we have used this process in many areas of child care practice from Section 17 family support to child protection and care proceedings. The debate is:

- whether FGCs should be incorporated in local authorities' guidance so that all families involved with local authorities can have this opportunity; or
- whether by regulating the quality and creativity of this process it would become a more professional-led process.

CHILDREN'S PARTICIPATION IN PRIVATE LAW PROCEEDINGS WITH PARTICULAR EMPHASIS ON THE QUESTION OF MEETINGS BETWEEN THE JUDGE AND THE CHILD IN FAMILY PROCEEDINGS

Professor Christina Lyon[1]

Professor Lyon addressed the question of what effective support systems exist for children on family breakdown. She told the conference that the very clear message from her research was that children want to know far more about the person who is making the decisions about their life (ie the judge). Children felt rather insulted by the idea that judges needed 'training' in order to talk to them. Professor Lyon was clear that we needed to think far more about how to meet our obligations to enable children who wished to see the judge deciding their case. The present system put up many obstacles before a child could get involved in proceedings: there should certainly be more information provided to children and consultation with them, even if they were not necessarily represented in the proceedings. Professor Lyon's view was that the present family justice system did not fulfil our obligations under the Convention for the Protection of Human Rights and Fundamental Freedoms or the United Nations Convention on the Rights of the Child.

INTRODUCTION

The decision by the Government to delay implementation of much of the Family Law Act 1996 following upon the disappointing results of the pilot studies was greeted with a cheer by many academics. They had criticised the procedural hurdles with which no fault divorce had been hedged around in the new Act as well as the obvious failure to place issues associated with children's welfare at the very top of the lists of concerns to which everyone should pay attention. That children feel marginalised by the current legal process, which intimately affects and impinges upon their lives in so many different ways, is apparent from a range of recent research studies which have directly consulted with children on their experiences of divorce.

By way of introduction, I propose to set out some of the comments made by a number of children who participated in the Gulbenkian research extensively referred to in Professor Murch's paper.[2,3] Some of the quotations were reproduced within the Gulbenkian report, but it was impossible to reproduce all the comments which the young people made under the section headed 'Other Comments'.[4] A return has been made for the purposes of producing this chapter to the questionnaires produced by the children as well as by the adults, to try to elicit such views as may have been expressed with regard to the issue of children seeing the judiciary in private law proceedings. It is assumed that readers are familiar with the Gulbenkian report and will be aware of the range of comments made in response to a number of detailed questions by the 120 children and young people aged between 13 and 21, who participated in that research. More recently, the author returned to two of the schools participating to give them specific feedback on the research and, bearing in mind the questions being asked in respect of this paper, to ask further questions about children and young people's views on this difficult subject.

Those familiar with the Gulbenkian report will recall that one of the reasons for embarking on the research was the view, expressed by a number of boys attending seminars held at the Centre for the Study of the Child, the Family and the Law,[5] that:

---

1   Christina Lyon, Queen Victoria Professor of Law, University of Liverpool.
2   Conducted by myself and others entitled *Effective Support Services for Children and Young People when Parental Relationships Break Down – A Child Centred Approach.*
3   Hereafter referred to as the Gulbenkian report.
4   See *Effective Support Services for Children*, ibid, at pp 81–81.
5   Based at the University of Liverpool.

'when our parents got divorced the Judges never saw us, we never saw them. They were making important decisions about our lives and yet they couldn't even be bothered to see us. At least that was how we saw it.'

Then, looking towards a number of judiciary sitting in the front row, one of the boys, aged 16, indicated with considerable support from his peers sitting around him that:

'You should see us you know. You are making decisions which affect our lives in so many ways. You lot made a decision about me and my brother that has ended up with us spending our lives travelling up and down the M62. Yet you don't have to do the travelling. You don't have to suffer the disruption to your lives every weekend yet you make us do it without any regard for the effects it has on us. How do we get back in front of you to say look, hey, this isn't working. It isn't working for us any more because we're older now and we want to do something about it but nobody will listen because our Dad says "well that's what the Judge says" and our Mum's all for a quiet life so she doesn't want to change things either. Whatever is easy, that's what she wants.'

Moving on to other views expressed in the Gulbenkian report,[1] the following quotations are relevant to some of the issues which will be discussed in this chapter.

'Information should be made more readily available. The more children know about legal procedures, the less intimidated they feel and the more open the discussion the better it will end up for everyone.' (child no 17)

'I think that better counselling and information should be automatically offered to all children. If it is left to them to look for it, many won't know how and will give up. I also agree with the idea of better court representation for the child in private proceedings.' (child no 63)

'I think that there should be Advice Bureaux or drop in centres for people to be able to gain this information. The child should always be treated fairly and no fact should hidden from them. It's their life – it should be their choice.' (child no 95)

'A Children's Officer should exist to signpost services for the child – maybe visiting schools once per month.' (child no 6)

'The whole legal system is a virtual mystery to children. Even for those who are able to get information, the information is poor. The legal profession [and by this the children and young people had indicated that they included the judiciary] don't seem to appreciate the importance of children and their views. Children's views are often more truthful and open than adults and are therefore more applicable.' (child no 81)

'The law cannot stay as it is, children are being forced to live lives which they have no say in. This must be changed. Children must have an extra option when their parents get divorced, because the options open to them at the moment are inadequate. Special counsellors should be used who are able to help the child with information, consultation and representation.' (child no 34)

'In attempting to overcome the woeful arrangements for children in this situation, I would suggest appointing an individual who could inform, consult and represent the child from the moment the divorce is requested. If a partnership breaks down, then both parents should be legally obliged to bring this to the government's attention, so that an information pack, or ideally, a qualified individual can be sent to the child. Then he/she can be carefully informed of the situation they are in, and the rights that they have.' (child no 48)

Finally, comment was made by a number of children about how the child could be included in the decision-making process, particularly concerning the vexed issue of contact. In the Gulbenkian report, there was only room to reproduce a few of the very many comments, but the questionnaires have been revisited for further comments from those children, who had actually been involved in their parents' divorce and from those children whose parents' cohabiting relationship had split up.

'A child involved in a divorce, up to a particular age, should have to remain in contact with both parents (except in special cases). Then after a particular age they should be assessed to see if they are mature enough to make a decision on maintaining contact with both parents in the future.' (child no 7)

As far as the maturity of young people is concerned and their abilities to see all sides of the problem and come to a reasonable decision, one can do no better than quote from child no 62 rather more extensively than we were able to in the report:

'I tried to tell both my mum and dad who I wanted to see and when. I tried to work everything out so that it would be fair to everyone including my nannas and granddads from both sides of the family and my aunties and uncles, but no one listened to me and everything afterwards was just such a mess.'

This child went on to state that:

'It would have been better if I had been able to see the person making all the decisions but all I saw was this person who, I know as result of today, was called a Court Welfare Officer but she didn't really feel interested in my plan and I think, as

---

1   See Chapter 4 pp 81–81.

it has turned out, my plan would have worked for the best for everyone. Why can't kids see the person who is making these decisions? I think it's wrong that they can decide what should happen in your life without seeing you.'

Another interesting point, frequently repeated in terms of the desire to see and speak to the judge, or 'the person who is making the decisions about me' was the contrast which the older young people made with what would have been their position had they been in front of a criminal court making decisions about their future lives.

Merseyside may be an area in which children and young people, particularly in the age range with which we were dealing in 1996, had become particularly attuned to the situation of children involved in a criminal trial. This group of 120 had all been either the same age as, or slightly older than, the two boys charged with the murder of James Bulger and were aware of the vast legal and psychiatric teams working and operating in support of both these children on trial for the murder of the toddler. A number of the young people participating in the research had frequently attended seminars run in the Centre for the Study of the Child, the Family and the Law and therefore were particularly aware of the fact that children caught up in care proceedings not only had their own separate legal representative but also had a specially trained social worker, known as the guardian ad litem, charged with the task of representing their best interests to the court. Indeed, it was just such one of these young people, who had some years ago described to me the relationship he had had, as a young person going into case, with his guardian ad litem and his solicitor. He had referred to his guardian ad litem as his guardian angel since, as he put it, 'she is arguing for what is in my best interests but that's not what I want' whereas he had described the solicitor as 'my devil's advocate because he wants what I want and that's not necessarily in my best interests'. This particular young man has now gone on to complete a law degree, but the extent to which children and young people talk amongst themselves and recognise the intrinsic unfairness between the different systems of law operating in respect of children within this country should sound warning bells to all involved with the administration of justice. This is more especially the case in the light of the implementation of the Human Rights Act 1998 on 2 October 2000, which provides for the Convention for the Protection of Human Rights and Fundamental Freedoms to take direct effect in UK domestic law.

THE UNITED NATIONS CONVENTION ON THE RIGHTS OF THE CHILD

Our concerns for children should thus be influenced by a number of important documents, including the United Nations Convention on the Rights of the Child, as well as the Convention for the Protection of Human Rights and Fundamental Freedoms and the Human Rights Act 1998. The Government has now written its second report to the United Nations Monitoring Committee on the Rights of the Child, the body especially charged with overseeing the implementation of the 1989 United Nations Convention on the Rights of the Child in different countries.[1] When it last visited and took evidence from the UK government, the United Nations Monitoring Committee was singularly unimpressed with legal procedures within England and Wales which did not give children a 'voice' in judicial or administrative proceedings affecting them in accordance with Article 12 of the United Nations Convention on the Rights of the Child.

Article 12 provides that:

'1.   States Parties shall assure to the child who is capable of forming his or her own views the right to express those views freely in all matters affecting the child, the views of the child being given due weight in accordance with the age and maturity of the child.
2.   For this purpose, the child shall in particular be provided the opportunity to be heard in *any* judicial and administrative proceedings affecting the child, either directly, or through a representative or an appropriate body, in a manner consistent with the procedural rules of national law.'

As will be readily appreciated, the Government cannot claim compliance with Article 12 of the United Nations Convention on the Rights of the Child since, in divorce proceedings, the child's voice is not heard either directly or indirectly where parents have made an agreement as to arrangements which should operate post-divorce. Nor do children in England, Wales or Northern Ireland[2] have the right to express their views freely within their families in all matters concerning them.

---

1   See Second Report to the UN Committee on the Rights of the Child by the United Kingdom 1999, London, The Stationery Office.
2   As contrasted with those in Scotland, see s 6 of the Children (Scotland) Act 1995.

THE HUMAN RIGHTS ACT 1998

In addition, the Human Rights Act 1998, which provides for the Convention for the Protection of Human Rights and Fundamental Freedoms to take direct effect within UK law, comes into force, it is hoped, on 2 October 2000. It is arguable that the present processes of law which deny children a right to participate in proceedings which so fundamentally affect them could be deemed to be a breach of Article 6(1) of the European Convention which provides that:

> '1.   In the determination of his civil rights and obligations or of any criminal charge against him, everyone is entitled to a fair and public hearing within a reasonable time by an independent and impartial tribunal established by law.'

Since divorce proceedings fundamentally affect a child's civil rights, an argument in relation to a breach of Article 6 could well be made.

It could be argued that the current provisions affecting children do not accord with Article 8, namely the Article concerned with a right to respect for private and family life and in particular Article 8, para 2 which provides that:

> 'There shall be no interference by a public authority with the exercise of this right [ie the right to respect for one's private and family life, one's home and one's correspondence] except such as is in accordance with the law and is necessary in a democratic society in the interests of national security, public safety or the economic well-being of the country, for the prevention of disorder or crime, for the protection of health or morals, or for the protection of the rights and freedoms of others.'

The way in which children are currently treated by the private family proceedings processes might further be argued to be in breach of Article 14 which prohibits discrimination on any ground and age could certainly be included within this. The Government's concerns about potential breaches of the European Convention on the face of UK law are well known and the mines of litigation, which may be opened up by very many different claims, will undoubtedly be a fertile digging ground not only for lawyers but also for a range of voluntary organisations seeking to represent children's interests.

THE FINDINGS OF RESEARCH STUDIES

An attempt has been made thus far to set out relevant principles derived from international Conventions which might guide thinking on the specific question of meetings between judges and children caught up in residence or contact proceedings and the purpose and extent of such meetings. What is crucial to appreciate about this question is that it *cannot* be considered in isolation from the other important issues affecting children and young people caught up in their parents' relationship breakdown. Thus, the Gulbenkian report, and others, have through the words of the children and young people themselves, conclusively demonstrated that they felt that they were denied participation in a process, which so critically affected them. Thus, the work of Carol Smart, Bren Neale and Amanda Wade on *Post Divorce Childhoods: Perspectives from Children*[1] and *New Childhoods? Children and Co-parenting After Divorce*[2] are in total agreement with the views of the children and young people participating in the Gulbenkian research. To quote from a paper prepared by Ann O'Quigley for the Lord Chancellor's Department,[3] referring specifically to the details of Smart et al's research:

> 'Children's experiences of professional support were less than positive. In most cases they had little choice about participating. They did not receive but would have valued: an informed choice about whether, when and how to participate; knowledge of their rights and what support was available; a flexible range of services (legal and non-legal) tailored to their needs, which offered independent access as and when needed; confidentiality; counselling; consultation over how a problem could be managed (not necessarily a legal route); *and, perhaps most crucially, respect from adults who ignored or re-interpreted their definitions of the problem and failed to acknowledge their wishes and feelings.*' (emphasis added)

Similar supporting findings can be drawn from Caroline Sawyer's work published by the Centre for Socio-Legal Studies at the University of Oxford under the title *Rules, Roles and Relationships: The*

---

1   Nuffield Foundation, 1998.

2   ESRC, 1998.

3   See *Listening to Children's Views and Representing their Best Interests – a Review of the Research* presented to a special consultation meeting organised by the Rowntree Foundation for the Lord Chancellor's Department on Monday 5 July 1999, and now published by the Rowntree Foundation, York, 1999.

Structure and Function of Child Representation and Welfare in Family Proceedings. The conclusions emerging from that research indicated:

'Judicial ideology in private law obscured the voice of the child beneath a near irrebuttable assumption that parents would behave appropriately towards children. Dissent, where seen as opposition to the presumption of contact, was characterised as bad or mad; children so dissenting would have their views attributed either to pressure from the caring parent or to mental illness ... in private law, the voice of the child, or the factual situation of the child, was therefore wholly irrelevant to the prevailing judicial culture of family privacy on a specific model, which was so strong that the social work personnel were unable to resist it. In public law, however, the judicial culture was, if anything *opposed to the private family structure*, and the social work personnel were in any event organisationally and culturally more independent, being child- rather than court-based.'[1] (emphasis added)

Findings from the National Stepfamily Association *Children and Young People Project*, funded by the National Lotteries Charities Board[2] further give support to the Gulbenkian report, in that initial findings suggest that:

'Most children and young people feel powerless in situations of family change. They find themselves in situations which they are forced to accept and yet they feel they have had no say in them ... children and young people want to be consulted in the decisions that affect them; they want to be listened to, not to have the ultimate responsibility however for decision-making.'

Again, the work done by Virginia Morrow on the project entitled *Attending to the Child's Voice: Children's Accounts of Family and Kinship* funded by the Joseph Rowntree Foundation, which has resulted in a number of publications both in 1998 and forthcoming, lends additional further support to the points made by the children in so many of these other studies. Thus, in response to questions exploring 'being listened to', children wanted to be able to 'have a say' in what happens to them, rather than to make decisions themselves.

Finally, research done by Brannen et al on *Children's Views and Experiences of Family Life* funded by the Department of Health has also revealed:

'The great majority of children believed that they should have a say in every day personal matters and some input, with their parents, into major family life decisions which affect them, notably divorce, moving house and choosing a secondary school. Children's views vary by ethnicity, age, number of siblings etc but tend to depend on the particular decision ... 70% of the children thought that they should have some input into decisions about divorce. Almost half thought the decision about who to live with after divorce *should be shared between parents and children. 28% thought that children should decide themselves.*' (emphasis added)

All of these pieces of research, including the Gulbenkian report, were seen by O'Quigley to be key. What all of this research is telling us is that, despite what we as adults may think, children and young people themselves wish to have a say, although clearly not all of them wish to 'decide' what should happen to them.

It is the process of giving the children a say, and more particularly, whether this 'say' should involve seeing the judges where the judges are making such critically important decisions about their lives, which will now be addressed.

MEETINGS BETWEEN JUDGES AND CHILDREN

Background

What does the available evidence tell children and young people about the attitudes displayed by the judiciary towards them? Case-law would appear to tell them that judges are deeply suspicious of the desire of children to make applications for residence, contact or any of the other orders available under s 8 of the Children Act 1989. This suspicion manifested itself very early on in the life of the Act when the case which gave rise to the Practice Direction of 22 February 1993 concerning applications by

---

1   See O'Quigley at p 96.
2   See general findings to date – *Children and Young People Project* (National Stepfamily Association, London, 1999).

children for section 8 orders is considered. This Practice Direction was issued following the case of *Re AD (A Minor) (Child's Wishes)*.[1]

It is quite possible that this Practice Direction, which denies children the rights under Articles 6 and 14 of the European Convention to a fair hearing in matters affecting their civil rights without discrimination on any grounds, could be challenged by a child as it prevents a child having equal access to the courts at magistrates' court and county court level to that enjoyed by their parents. If magistrates' courts and county courts can make decisions as to whether anyone else, including, for example, a child cousin is able to apply for leave to make an application, as laid down under s 10(9), then why can they not make such a decision under s 10(8). The process of insisting that a child seeking leave to even make an application for a section 8 order be transferred for consideration by a High Court judge, means that what should have been a relatively straightforward process now becomes one, which Judith Timms has referred to as the child's obstacle race to representation in private law proceedings.[2]

Those familiar with the various cases on children seeking independent representation, such as *Re S (A Minor) (Independent Representation)*[3], *Re T*,[4] *Re C*,[5] *Re SC (A Minor) (Leave to Seek Residence Order)*,[6] *Re C (Residence: Child's Application for Leave)*[7] and *Re H*[8] will also recall the approach of Sir Thomas Bingham MR in *Re S*.[9] It is suggested that this is worthy of emulation by all the judiciary. Thus, he stated that:

> 'First is the principle, to be honoured and respected, that children are human beings in their own right with individual minds and wills, views and emotions, which should command serious attention. A child's wishes are not to be discounted or dismissed simply because he is a child. He should be free to express them *and decision-makers should listen.* Second is the fact that a child is after all a child. The reason why the law is particularly solicitous in protecting the interests of children is that they are laible to be vulnerable and impressionable, lacking the maturity to weigh a longer term against the shorter, lacking the insight to know how they will react and the imagination to know how others will react in certain situations, lacking the experience to match the probable against the possible ... the process of growing up is, as Lord Scarman pointed out in Gillick, a continuous one. The judge has to do his best on the evidence before him, to assess the understanding of the individual child in the context of the proceedings in which he seeks to participate.' (emphasis added)

As has been highlighted earlier by the quotations from a number of children involved in the research studies, children, even at a very young age, as was highlighted by the example of child no 65 in the Gulbenkian research, are quite able to make the various decisions and judgements referred to by Sir Thomas Bingham MR. Arguably, even more realistic and enlightened are the judgments of Booth J in *Re H*[10] and Stuart-White J in *Re C (A Minor) (Leave to Seek Section 8 Orders)*.[11] In the case of *Re H*, various views were put forward by parties and witnesses that H was not possessed of sufficient understanding to take part in the proceedings. Having heard the evidence, Booth J, before whom the case eventually was heard, favoured the approach of H's psychiatrist and held that H had the relevant understanding necessary to instruct his own legal representative. She also ruled that the services of the Official Solicitor, previously instructed by another court to represent the child, would be retained as amicus curiae. Booth's interpretation of the relevant provisions is key in that it suggests the correct approach which should be adopted on European Convention principles in respect of children seeking to make applications before the court. Furthermore, it is one which does not demonstrate the sort of fear and suspicion of children apparent in so many of the other decisions of the courts on this issue. Booth J's view was that the test of whether a child has sufficient understanding to make an application should be considered in the light of all the circumstances of the case, past, present and future. Although H in this case could not, in Booth J's view, recognise the dangers posed by his former foster father, she took the view that he was not so much under the influence of him that his own ability to think independently had been over-borne. The boy was a young man over 15 years of age and his progress at school indicated that he had a number of abilities. Booth J also made it clear that the boy had already been

1   [1993] 1 FCR 573.
2   See J Timms *Children's Representation* (Sweet & Maxwell, 1995).
3   [1993] 3 All ER 36.
4   [1993] 4 All ER 518.
5   [1994] 1 FLR 26.
6   [1994] 1 FLR 96.
7   [1995] 1 FLR 927.
8   [1994] 4 All ER 762.
9   [1993] 3 All ER 36.
10   [1994] 4 All ER 762.
11   [1994] 1 FLR 26.

involved in the proceedings to a far greater extent than was perhaps initially desirable but that, given that this was the case, it would now be extremely artificial to prevent him putting his own case to the court and testing the evidence. She stated clearly, however, that a child's capacity to litigate without the services of a guardian ad litem required much more than the ability to instruct a solicitor regarding his own views on the desired outcome. She made it clear that the child must also have an ability to enter the court arena alongside the adult parties, to give evidence and be cross-examined. Furthermore, the child must be capable of giving instructions on a variety of matters and making decisions as and when the need arises. One might question how many adults might be able to perform to this level in a court environment? It could also be pointed out that children from as young as 10 years of age (witness the James Bulger case) are expected to perform like adults in the criminal courts when they are charged and prosecuted for offences. Why is it, then, that a far higher ability to understand the proceedings is required when dealing with family proceedings, especially when most adults would not be able to satisfy the participation guidelines detailed by Booth J?

It is also strongly suggested that the approach favoured by Booth J in a case in which the child was already involved in the proceedings and knows what is going on should commend itself to those who have to discuss the question of whether judges should ever see children who have been caught up in their parents' divorce.

The Questions

Should judges in private law proceedings see 'the child in question'?

It is the general understanding that the view propounded by the Judicial Studies Board in its training course for new Recorders and Assistant Recorders in family proceedings is that: 'it is never a good idea to see the child in question' which means, therefore, that little, if any, consideration has been given to the question of the purpose and extent of such meetings.

It appears that the philosophical basis for the view that judges should never see children is influenced by a number of factors including the following:

- seeing the child does not give the judge a different perspective on the case;
- seeing the child does not enable the judge to gather any evidence which can then be used to form a judgment;
- seeing the child runs the risk of the judge obtaining information which nobody else has in their possession (namely the parties, ie the parents or other relatives who may be making an application);
- judges are not trained to talk to children.

These are only a few of the range of factors which might dictate an approach which says that judges should never see children. These reasons should be considered in more detail.

'Seeing the child does not give the judge a different perspective on the case'

Given the very serious consideration which a range of research studies have now demonstrated that children give to these issues, how could it seriously be maintained that seeing the child would *not* give a judge a different perspective on the case?

Why is it that judges should have, potentially, only two perspectives on the case, namely the mother's and the father's?

What is it about the child's perspective that could be so damaging?

Is there a particular age of a child at which a judge would be willing to contemplate seeing a child? In various cases, both High Court judges and Court of Appeal judges have indicated that children: '. . . are not packages to be moved around. They are people entitled to be treated with respect'.[1] Are there issues upon which, perhaps, the child's perspective might be important? Clearly, there are: one only has to

---

1   *Re S (Minors) (Access: Religious Upbringing)* [1992] 2 FLR 313.

look at the huge number of reported cases in which judges have been strongly influenced by the children's views. Thus, if contact orders are being made which necessitate children spending their weekends travelling up and down the M62, is this not a matter upon which the child's views might correctly be sought? Indeed, given the demands of Articles 6, 8 and 14 of the European Convention, could ignoring the child's views and not seeing or hearing them be in breach of the Convention?

'Seeing the child does not gather any evidence which you can use to form a judgment'

The responses to this may be the same as for the previous question.

'Seeing the child runs the risk of obtaining information which nobody else (ie the Parties to the proceedings – note children are not Parties to such proceedings) may have'

This is based upon the presumption that the judge may be seeing the child in private. This could certainly be the case but it could be suggested that the tape-recorder should be switched on and that the judge gives a warning to the child, similar to that given by a whole range of child protection professionals, including Childline telephone response workers, when dealing with calls about child abuse. Given that children have uniformly indicated that they *do not wish* to be asked to make decisions, but they *do wish* to be asked their views about the decisions which are to be made, there is no doubt that children in these circumstances would readily understand the warning which could be given. They would know, just as they are supposed to know when talking to court welfare officers, that what they say is not treated confidentially. All of the children participating in the Gulbenkian study were fully aware, particularly those who had been through the court processes, that court welfare officers were supposed to set out children's views in the report made to the court. Their objection was that sometimes this had not occurred or that, several years down the line, the arrangements were no longer appropriate and the children themselves wanted to know how they could redress the problems, which were caused by unrealistic contact orders.

Judges seeing children and obtaining their views run no greater risks than court welfare officers and could surely be trained to issue the same type of warning as are the range of social workers and other personnel dealing with child protection issues. These groups, of course, include doctors who often also make similar points about confidentiality to those which might be made by judges when concerned about how children will feel in such circumstances.

An alternative approach to seeing the child in chambers with the logger present, or a tape switched on, is to see the child in a more relaxed environment but with another person, usually a court usher present. One or two judges have mentioned this as being an approach which they have sometimes adopted, when they have been *forced* by circumstances to see a child involved in the proceedings. This, it has been said, might be the case where a parent has brought a child along to the proceedings and the judge takes the view that since this is the case he/she had better see the child and explain what is going on or, where the child has known what is going on and has turned up at court of their own volition because they want to hear what is to happen to them.

'Judges are not trained to talk to children'

Who is?

There appears still to be a misapprehension which abounds that social workers, police officers, and probation officers, are 'trained to talk to children'. Courses training police officers, social workers and probation officers serving as court welfare officers have not until extremely recently included training on how to talk to children and, even now, may only include an element, termed 'Observation and Assessment of a Child'. The representatives of the Official Solicitor's Office who go out and make the reports on children involved in cases in which the Official Solicitor has been appointed to represent them do not have any special training in talking to children. Indeed, many of them are not even qualified social workers or probation officers but are civil servants who have never been required to do a course on 'talking to children', and are, in fact, very highly thought of by the members of the judiciary.

What does it take to talk to children? Do judges have the same reservations when dealing with children in the dock in criminal courts? Do they refuse to do cases in which children are defendants because they 'do not know how to talk to children?' It is necessary to be provocative here because this is a very serious question and one in respect of which children feel extremely insulted when they are told that someone has not been 'specially trained to talk to them'. Children have successively made the very valid point in a huge range of research studies now that they are people who have the same rights to be informed and to be involved in decisions made about them as any other person. As Butler-Sloss put it so eloquently in the Cleveland Report 'the child is a person and not an object of concern'.[1]

Are judges in family proceedings working to a number of assumptions?

It has been suggested that, by contrast with those judges who hear child defendants in a range of criminal cases, judges hearing family cases work on the basis that being in court is a bad thing for children. Obviously, one can say that the moment a situation goes to court the whole system has failed because the main desire behind any system of law is that it should avoid cases going into court. Yet it could be argued that the treatment of children involved in divorce processes and family relationship breakdowns generates the cases that come to court. If parents are determined to fight over their children's residence or contact situations, then the system allows them to fight without any consultation with someone such as the court welfare officer until *after* the case has got to court. The system is determined, or so it appears to children, to deny them the right to information, consultation, and where relevant, representation.[2] As child no 65 pointed out earlier, if he had had the organisation and planning of his contact arrangements as well as his residence arrangements then everything would have worked out fine. At least it would have done from his point of view and surely this should be the focus: what would actually work best for the child in his or her new family situation. In so many situations, the child would and should have an input into this decision-making process. Yet, it is generally known, including by those who have engaged in family mediation, that there are parents who have never discussed with their children the situation concerning their divorce and the impact it will have on them.

Assumptions about contact

Influenced, no doubt, by Article 9 of the United Nations Convention on the Rights of the Child as well as by a considerable body of research including Wallerstein and Kelly's *Surviving the Break-Up – How Children Cope with Divorce,*[3] it is assumed that contact between a child and his or her absent parent is a good thing.[4] Although as a result of more recent research on the issue of contact and domestic violence, judges are coming to the realisation that perhaps contact may not be good in all cases, nevertheless the general assumption is that wherever possible contact should be promoted.

But is this always what the child wants and is this always in the child's interest? How is it communicated to children that contact arrangements, which might be approved by the court, are not set in stone, as appeared to be assumed by all of the children involved in the Gulbenkian research? What is wrong with seeing a child to indicate to the child the basis upon which the judge is considering making a particular order?

There is an assumption that seeing a child puts the child under unnecessary stress and strain

Who says that this is the case? Predominantly it is adults, mainly judges, and social work professionals working within the court's setting and some lawyers, particularly barristers. The vast majority of solicitors instructed by children indicate that just as children who are charged with criminal offences have their day in court, a number of children actually find the process of seeing the person who is making important decisions about them therapeutic.

The children and young people involved in the Gulbenkian study indicated very strongly on the consultation day that children involved in the divorce or relationship breakdown of their parents have

---

1   *Report of the Inquiry into Child Abuse in Cleveland* 1987, Cm 412 (HMSO, 1988), para 2, p 245.
2   See Gulbenkian, Lyon, Surrey and Timms, *Effective Support Services for Children when Parental Relationships Break Down – A Child Centred Approach* (Chapter 4).
3   Grant McIntyre, 1984.
4   See also s 1 and s 2 of the Children (Scotland) Act 1995.

already undergone major stress and strain. Simply seeing a judge and being asked their views rather than being asked to decide an issue could be a crucial factor in helping them to adjust to their new family situations. All those children and young people in the Gulbenkian study who had actually been through their parent's divorce indicated that they felt marginalised, and even irrelevant in the whole process, with the consequent adverse effects admirably highlighted by Rogers and Prior in their Rowntree Report entitled *Divorce and Separation: The Outcomes for Children.*[1] The adverse effects of the lack of communication by parents and by those professionally involved within the legal system were highlighted as including: poor performance in school; poor outlook for mental health; poor outlook for health generally, and poor communication skills. A number of people also identified problems later on in life in making adult relationships work and these effects were further highlighted in the work by Cockett and Trip in the *Exeter Family Study: Family Breakdown and its Impact on Children.*[2]

Since English law, in contrast to Scots law,[3] denies children a right to a voice in family decision-making, then one can only anticipate that the call by children and young people for a greater say within the legal process will continue, spurred on by the impending implementation of the Human Rights Act 1998. When children and young people are asked whether they should be consulted, the answer comes out with a resounding 'yes'. If they are asked whether they would like to see the person making such important decisions about them the answer is again 'yes' and, indeed, a considerable number of them feel that they should be able to be represented in front of the decision-maker (see the 42 per cent of children in the Gulbenkian study who felt that they should have a right to representation).[4]

What would be the purpose of judges seeing children or young people?

A number of the reasons for judges seeing children and young people in such circumstances have already been highlighted by reference to the relevant research reports.

The purpose would be to give effect to provisions of the United Nations Convention on the Rights of the Child and, indeed, even the European Convention on the Exercise of Children's Rights,[5] and, more importantly, to comply with procedural requirements as well as other natural justice requirements arising out of the implementation of the Convention for the Protection of Human Rights and Fundamental Freedoms identified in the introduction.

Just as some court welfare officers now tell children and young people that, although they are talking to them and ascertaining their wishes and feelings, it is not necessarily the case that their wishes and feelings would be determinative of any issue, exactly the same warning could be given by judges who see children and young people. The biggest question is, having abolished satisfaction hearings in response to earlier research studies, in the Children Act 1989, is there any purpose to be served in judges routinely seeing children involved in disputed residence and contact order cases? The answer from the children and young people, would, on the basis of all the various research projects, clearly be 'yes' but what are the dangers inherent in going down such a road?

The biggest problem which practising lawyers in the field can see with this proposal is that if it became known that judges would *routinely* see children then the prospect would arise of a parent or other person making an application coaching the child to give particular responses to the judge. Yet, just as these practitioners themselves comment that when 'they have seen a child, they always know if that child has been coached' so, too, should judges, who equally have great experience within the judicial system, be able to reach this particular conclusion. Clear information about the role and purpose of judges seeing children in private law proceedings could be a way of ensuring that such coaching does not take place. The children and young people on the Gulbenkian study also indicated that if the judges were to see children and young people on their own, this would give the judge a much clearer idea of

---

1   Joseph Rowntree Foundation, 1998.
2   University of Exeter Press, 1994. See also Douglas, Murch, and Perry 'Supporting Children When Parents Separate – A Neglected Family Justice or Mental Health Issue?' [1996] CFLQ 121 and see the work of Hetherington, Cox and Cox on 'Long-term Effects of Divorce and Remarriage on Children' (1995) *Journal of the American Academy of Psychiatry* 5.8).
3   See s 6 of the Children (Scotland) Act 1995.
4   See *Effective Support Services for Children and Young People when Parental Relationships Break Down – A Child Centred Approach* (Gulbenkian 1998, Chapter 4).
5   Not yet signed let alone ratified by the UK, see Lyon *Representing Children* vol 8, no 2.

whether implacable hostility to contact by the other parent is really borne out of concern for the child, or whether, in reality, it may in some cases be borne out of embittered emotions of the adult parties generated by the whole process of divorce.

The real purpose behind children being enabled to see judges and express their own views is to give them the opportunity, which it is possible that few will take up, of being able, as the young people in the Gulbenkian study put it, to: 'see the person who is making such important decisions affecting their lives'. How many judges involved in making such decisions have actually been the recipient of the same sort of decisions which they are making themselves? How do they know, and why should they purport to know what children feel about such important issues? How can they presume to know 'best' when they themselves have not experienced the effects of the kind of decisions which they are making?

Even if compliance with the demands of international conventions and the law of the UK is not sufficient, then surely compliance with the demands of justice that: 'it should not only be done, but seen to be done' should ensure that the issue of judges seeing children involved in such proceedings is very carefully considered.

How extensive should meetings between judges and children in such circumstances be?

Earlier research[1] had indicated a considerable degree of dissatisfaction with the then 'satisfaction hearings'. It was felt that hearings which lasted anything between 6 and 18 minutes were not long enough for judges realistically to be satisfied as to the future welfare of children whom they were asked to see. The problem with satisfaction hearings is that they were used in all cases where the fate and future of children under 16 in the family was to be determined.

As a general guideline, it might perhaps be suggested that judges should see children and young people involved in a particular case for somewhere between 30 minutes to one hour. Whilst this may seem rather a long time, it could, in the context of disputed proceedings and the amount of evidence which these days is being called from so-called experts, save a considerable amount or court time and valuable government money.

If the various elements identified in the *Effective Support Services* document were introduced for the long-term benefit of society at large then, as was indicated in that report, it might be expected that the number of contested hearings involving children, children's residences and contact would actually reduce. One of the major problems in this country is the lack, generally, of communication between children and parents which is pointed up in so many different aspects of our social systems. If, as a result of implementing the holistic approach referred to in chapter 10 of the Gulbenkian study, the range and quality of communication about issues such as divorce can be extended to children and young people then, hopefully, the numbers of cases in which judges should be seeing children to discuss their decisions about them would be relatively few. Nevertheless, if judges are to make such decisions then it is suggested here that they should see the children in order to give them a proper voice in the proceedings and in order to enable the UK to say that the legal system fully complies with the demands of all the various relevant Conventions. Those professionals, who as a matter of course, come into contact daily through their work as well as their domestic lives with children and young people never cease to be surprised and impressed by their range of responsible and clear-thinking attitudes. This needs to be acknowledged within the system of private family law proceedings which so fundamentally affects so many of our children's lives. Were this approach to be adopted, the UK may well, over time, reduce the possibility of the divorce statistics getting ever larger by producing parents who, as children had things explained to them properly and who, in turn, will be better able to communicate with their own children.

If judges are to shy away from talking to children except when they are involved in criminal offences or when they overcome the current obstacle race to making an application for a section 8 order, then this part of the legal system can be seen to be failing in its duties to produce the responsible citizens and parents of tomorrow.

---

1   See Davies and Murch, *Justice and Welfare in Divorce* (Sweet & Maxwell, 1981).

CONCLUSIONS

It is extremely difficult to draw conclusions in this particular area of the law. The approach outlined above of judges seeing children whenever there are disputed contact or residence order issues is suggested by the results of the Gulbenkian study. This demonstrates that, above all else, children need to see, like everyone else, that justice has been done and it is very difficult for them to appreciate this if they feel as marginalised and as irrelevant as many of them do.

It has been indicated, by reference to the research studies available,[1] that there are a number of very good reasons relating to children's future mental and physical health as well as their becoming good parents and responsible citizens, which highlight the need for judges in disputed cases to see children and young people themselves. It will be noted that a lower age limit for seeing children has not been suggested. Clearly, disputed residence and contact cases arise in relation to children up to the age of 16, for after that date the court will not normally make orders. I have not suggested a lower age because the courts themselves have consistently moved this ever lower particularly in relation to the sorts of cases with which we are now dealing. Thus, in one case,[2] it was stated that children of 9 and 12 were responsible and mature enough to reach a decision communicated to the court that they did not wish to accompany their mother to Israel but wished instead to stay behind in England to continue their education here and to live with their father. Clearly, in this case, the views of a 9-year-old were influential. But, in the Gulbenkian study, there were young people aged from 13 to 21 who had been caught up in their parents' relationship breakdown many years earlier and who felt that, even at the ages of 6, 7 and 8, they had had views which they had wanted to put forward to the court. In the case of child no 65, at the age of 9, he had had a plan which he thought would work in relation to residence and contact issues.

Several of the children participating in the Gulbenkian research made the valid point that children are not aliens from another planet but real people. They are no more to be feared than the average adult, in fact probably less so. They are expected to be able to take a full part in criminal proceedings concerning them from the age of 10. Yet, in family proceedings, where the judiciary make vital decisions concerning them, including where they should live, with whom they should or should not have contact, and where they may or may not go, they *are treated as and feel 'invisible'*. For some of them, they and their feelings may also have been invisible to their parents, who are so concerned with carrying out their own particular warfare that they do not see the needs and interests of their children. Nearly every family judge will have had experience of such situations, on occasion to such an extent that a warning has to be issued to the parents that they run the risk of a section 37 investigation by social services. Alternatively, the arrangements concerning their children may be of particular interest to the parents, not out of any deep-routed concern for the needs of their children but more as a means of sorting out the day-to-day grind of who is caring for the children, taking them to school and otherwise looking after them. One girl, aged 14 at the time of the research, commented that the mediators involved in her parents' case had come up with a particular nightmarish form of a residence order for her and her younger brother. This took the form of 2½ days of the school week with one parent, 2½ days of the week with the other and rotating Saturdays and Sundays in respect of where they would be staying and with whom. This had the effect of her waking up on Saturday mornings and not knowing where her relevant clothes were for wearing at the weekend. The parents had, as she put it, agreed to this very 'happily' because, she felt, that since both of them were professionals this gave them the opportunity to have at least half of the main working week without the responsibility of having to meet her from one school and go to a different school to collect her brother. As she put it, all of these arrangements were reached by the parents for their convenience and with, as she saw it, no regard at all for her welfare or for that of her brother. She and her brother apparently felt totally confused by the whole situation, and lived with what she viewed as this nightmarish solution for three years until eventually, at the age of 13, she persuaded her grandmother to take her to a solicitor and actually lodged an application for leave to make a section 8 application. It was only at that point that her parents were both persuaded to sit down around a table with her and her brother and sort things out with the children playing a full and vital democratic role in the whole process. This sort of experience again bears out the many research studies referred to in the Introduction of this paper and the very distressing stories heard in the course of the Gulbenkian and

---

1   See the admirable survey by Rogers and Prior, cited above.
2   *M v M (Transfer of Custody: Appeal)* [1987] 2 FLR 146.

other research studies. Children *are* people too – they have a right to their own social lives and the right not to be bussed up and down a motorway over the course of every weekend. This denies them the right of access to their friends and to the same enjoyment of social affairs as their peers.

It should be acknowledged, as was found in the Gulbenkian study, that class and socio-economic groupings play a vital part in this area of the law. Thus, working with children and young people from a range of ethnic groups and across the socio-economic groupings, it was discovered that children were more likely to be the subject of disputed applications when they came from the so-called middle classes than if their parents were working-class or unemployed. Similarly, the children who tended to complain and were able to articulate their views most strongly were those who had either been affected by the divorce process themselves or were middle class with friends who had been affected. Nevertheless, as was identified in chapter 1 of *Effective Support Services for Children*, there was universal anger and resentment about what was seen as almost a conspiracy by adults to deny children relevant information, necessary consultation and, if applicable, representation in the legal process governing their parents' relationship breakdown.

The judiciary cannot afford to ignore the messages from research nor the signposts given by international conventions as well as, now, by UK law. As a society, the UK continues to be concerned about such issues as the rising levels of teenage pregnancy, abuse of alcohol and abuse of drugs.[1] Many of these problems are also caused by a lack of communication as well as by a lack of information. It cannot be denied that, in failing to provide children and young people with the relevant information in so many areas of life as is required by Article 17 of the United Nations Convention on the Rights of the Child, the UK is failing both this generation of children and young people and those yet to come.

Although I have used it before in my writing, there is no more appropriate conclusion to the arguments put forward in this paper in favour of judges seeing children in private and public family law cases than the words of the former United Nations Secretary-General Javier Perez de Cuellar who stated during the drafting of the UN Convention on the Rights of the Child:

> 'The way society treats its children reflects not only its qualities of compassion and protective caring, but also its sense of justice, its commitment to the future and its urge to enhance the human condition for coming generations.'

THIRD SESSION

---

1   See Second Report to the UN Monitoring Committee cited above.

CHILDREN'S WELFARE IN DIVORCE – SOME MESSAGES FROM RECENT RESEARCH

Mervyn Murch

In introducing his paper, **Professor Murch** *identified three key issues:*

(1) as a point of principle, when families split up, does the State have a special role or responsibility towards the children of that family and, if so, what is it?;

(2) within the family justice system as it exists, can s 41 of the Matrimonial Causes Act 1973 be made more effective (on the assumption that the idea of repealing it is politically inconceivable)?;

(3) if s 11 of the Family Law Act 1996 replaces s 41 of the Matrimonial Causes Act 1973, there will be a checklist for the court to consider, including the court's duty to consider the wishes and feelings of the child and the conduct of the parents towards the child: in practice, how is this to be done?

He went on to elaborate a little on the preliminary findings of his research, summarising the three messages as being:

(a) children want and need more information at the time of family breakdown;

(b) they need support and comfort at what is a time of crisis;

(c) they often feel isolated as parents find it difficult to talk to children at the time of family breakdown. There is also an obvious mismatch between the time of separation when children most need information and divorce proceedings, when the family justice system becomes involved. How do we direct resources at the time of separation when children want information: should we use s 41 or s 11 or some alternative process?

(The full text of Professor Murch's paper is to be found in *Modern Law Review* vol 63)

PART II OF THE FAMILY LAW ACT 1996 – CHILDREN'S WELFARE AND WISHES – SECTION 11

Peter Harris[1]

Peter Harris considered the effect of s 11 of the Family Law Act 1996: how might it work if Part II were implemented? He expressed the view that s 11 was not a very effective means of replacing s 41 of the Matrimonial Causes Act 1973: the court still needs information on which to act. Section 11 would need to have a very different procedure if it was going to fulfil its intended role and its effectiveness would depend on how the court was to be provided with information. This also raised questions as to what the relationship between the State and the child was intended to be. Do we need the court to have an overview of these things or is it a private matter for the parents involved? Section 11 is probably intended to change parental behaviour in some ways but it is arguable that the court is not really the best way to tackle that issue.

Peter Harris's suggestions for the sort of information the court might need from parents in order properly to fulfil its duty under s 11 included the example of a pre-school child where the parents might have to answer questions as to whether the child's development has been discussed with a health visitor or, with a school-age child, whether there had been discussion with the child's teacher. The court could even go so far as to say that it required confirmation from an appropriate independent adult such as a health visitor or teacher that these matters had been discussed. Such an approach was more likely to help the court establish which cases needed help or intervention. There were, of course, questions as to resources which flowed from such an approach, and of practicability. Nevertheless, without such a fundamental change in the procedure, s 11 was unlikely to be any more effective a procedure than s 41.

The purpose of this paper is to examine the impact of Part II of the 1996 Act on children whose parents are involved in divorce or separation proceedings and, in particular, the effects of ss 10 and 11.

The policy underlying Part II is to give couples an opportunity for reflection before committing themselves to ending their relationship so that divorce or separation is the outcome only when there is no prospect of the relationship being salvaged. There is an immediate tension here between the laudable wish to save marriages whenever possible, and the avoidance of delay in proceedings relating to children. Although 'children proceedings' are not inescapable if the parties can make arrangements so as to satisfy the requirements of s 11 of the 1996 Act, nevertheless a child is intimately affected by the proceedings between his parents, and delay in those proceedings is likely to have an adverse effect upon the child. The effect of delay is increased by the provision of an added period of six months to the 'period for reflection and consideration' by virtue of s 7(11) and (13) where there is a child of the family under the age of 16 when the application is made. A divorce or separation order cannot be made therefore until 15½ months after the section 6 statement has been filed in the court. This, of course, is in addition to the period of 3 months which must pass following the attendance of one, or both, parties at an information meeting. The general rule (which may be modified in 'prescribed circumstances', ie prescribed in regulations made by the Lord Chancellor) is that at least 18½ months must elapse between one parent initiating the divorce/separation process and the final order. This emphasises the need for the couple to settle the arrangements for the matrimonial home and the children as quickly as possible since the dissolution of the formal marriage relationship will take that minimum period of time. That does not preclude such arrangements being made very quickly if the couple can agree them.

The speedy (or otherwise) resolution of these matters frequently turns upon the use or disposal of the matrimonial home, which is all too often a cause of bitter dispute between the parties. The parents may be unable to agree the arrangements for their children whilst questions about the matrimonial home, and other financial matters, remain unresolved. By there being a period of 15½ months plus to deal with these questions, experience indicates that parties and their solicitors will tend to use all this time to mediate, negotiate and argue. Furthermore, the non-initiating, or responding, parent may fall into the trap of not attending an information meeting until he/she comes to make an application with respect to a

1   Peter Harris, formerly the Official Solicitor, Chairman, National Council for Family Proceedings, Bristol.

child, or contests such an application, when s 8(5) will effectively bar him/her until he/she has attended an information meeting. Delay which is inimical to the interests of the children appears to be a statutory requirement.

How this process will work, and how well it will work, is uncertain because no regulations have yet been made under s 8(8) and (9) regarding information meetings, nor rules under s 12, nor for that matter rules of court by way of the Family Proceedings Rules 1991. However, it will be very important that careful attention is paid to the drafting of the relevant regulations and rules since they will fundamentally affect the complicated process which the framework of Part II of the 1996 Act creates. The difficulty for the rule draftsman, even with the guidance of the rule committee (and here I speak with personal experience as Secretary of the three main civil rules committees, and hence chief draftsman), is to understand the practicalities not only of day-to-day business, but also of the complications which the more unusual circumstances bring. It is essential that those who do have that practical, current experience are enabled to provide advice at an early stage so that the rules and regulations can be effectively tuned to the needs of the business.

SECTIONS 10 AND 11

I now turn to the issues raised by ss 10 and 11 of the 1996 Act. Each section is concerned with the court's power to delay the making of a separation or divorce order, although with rather different criteria.

Section 10 provides, amongst other things, that an 'order preventing divorce' may be made if the court is satisfied that the dissolution of the marriage would result in substantial financial or other hardship to the other party *or to a child of the family*; and that it would be wrong, in all the circumstances (including the conduct of the parties and the interests of any child of the family) for the marriage to be dissolved. Dissolution is, in effect, a means of changing the civil status of the parties – they were married, now they are single and free to marry again. Apart from the ability to marry again, and the ancillary matters upon which divorce enables the court to adjudicate, it does not reorder the lives of the parties in that it has no practical effect upon the making of new relationships, or the arrangements for the children or housing, all of which are dealt with separately from the 'main suit'. Section 10 is in much the same terms as s 5 of the Matrimonial Causes Act 1973, save for the inclusion of the reference to a child of the family, and its extension to all divorces instead of a limited class. Section 5 is effectively a dead letter, since it is very difficult, if not virtually impossible, for a respondent to show that *dissolution* will result in substantial financial hardship. It is the fact of separation, and reluctance to maintain or share financial assets, that causes financial hardship. The civil status of the parties is likely to have little, if any, impact upon their financial standing, or that of any child. I am unaware of any case in which other hardship has been proved so as to justify preventing dissolution. It is difficult to see, also, how dissolution would cause substantial other hardship to a child. This may, of course, give rise to attempts to obtain an 'order preventing divorce', but, in my view, rightly, the courts will be reluctant to issue such an order under s 10, if only because the statute is drawn in such imprecise terms that the courts are given no indication of what criteria should be applied in making a decision of this nature. I doubt that changing the criterion to 'substantial' instead of 'grave' financial hardship will bring many cases to the court, since the court has to be satisfied also that it would be wrong in all the circumstances for the marriage to be dissolved.

Section 11 is intended to replace s 41 of the 1973 Act. It requires the court to consider whether it needs to exercise its powers under the Children Act 1989 in respect of any child of the family. If it appears to the court that it does, or is likely to need to do so, and it is not in a position to do so without giving further consideration, *and* there are exceptional circumstances, it may direct that a divorce or separation order shall not be made until it orders otherwise. In doing this, it must treat the welfare of the child as paramount. There is no indication on the face of the statute what the *exceptional circumstances* might be in which the making of a divorce or separation order would be contrary to the welfare of a child.

The essential difficulty in the operation of s 11 as a means of identifying issues in respect of children is that the evidence upon which the court can base its decision is likely to come only from the parents (unless, perhaps, there has been social services involvement with the children). If there are issues between the parents which they want to litigate, there will be Children Act or other similar family proceedings before the court in any event. The purpose of s 11, like that of s 41 of the 1973 Act, is to safeguard the welfare of children where there are no issues before the court other than a divorce or separation order application, coupled perhaps with ancillary relief applications. How, then, is the court to know whether it should exercise any of its powers under the Children Act, other than when there are concurrent Children Act applications before it? The court is required to have particular regard, *on the evidence before it*, to a number of matters, with which I deal below. But there may be very little, or no, evidence before it, save perhaps for an anodyne statement filed by one, or both, of the parties. Again, much here depends on the details of the procedure to be adopted but, even if the court is provided with investigative facilities, how is it to identify the *exercise of powers* sheep from the *non-exercise of powers* goats?

The matters to which the court is required to have particular regard when considering whether the circumstances of the case require it to exercise its Children Act powers include the wishes and feelings of the child considered in the light of his age and understanding, and the circumstances in which those wishes were expressed. Are those wishes likely to be other than that he/she would prefer the parents not to divorce, or at least that they should continue looking after him/her together? The court must also take into account the conduct of the parties in relation to the upbringing of the child. It must have in mind the general principle that contact with those who have parental responsibility for the child and with other family members, and the maintenance of as good a continuing relationship with the parents as possible must also be given due weight. That at least points to the need to be satisfied that contact is taking place, and if the court has evidence that it is not, and in the absence of evidence to show that contact is not conducive to the welfare of the child, the court will be under a duty to make some inquiry. Finally, the court has to have regard to any risk to the child attributable to:

- where the person with whom the child will reside is living or proposes to live;
- any person with whom that person is living or with whom he/she proposes to live; and
- any other arrangements for his care and upbringing.

The essential question of who is to provide such evidence to the court, and how, has no ready answer. Without a welfare report, it is difficult to see how the court is to have evidence of this or, indeed, of any of the other foregoing matters, before it. If the parents are not litigating children issues, the only source of evidence is, possibly, the local authority, but social workers concerned with the family may not be aware that a divorce or separation application has been made.

The essential purposes of s 11 seem to be twofold. First, to require the court to consider in every divorce/separation order application where there are children of the family under the age of 16, or older children in respect of whom the court directs that s 11 shall apply, whether it should exercise its Children Act powers. Secondly, to decide whether to direct that a divorce/separation order shall not be made until it has been able to consider whether to exercise such powers. In effect, if a question about the welfare of a child of the family arises from the information before it in any proceedings for a divorce/separation order, the court will be able to order a report under s 7 of the Children Act 1989 to address, in particular, the matters canvassed in s 11(4) (referred to in the paragraph above). If it does so, it may also postpone the granting of a divorce/separation order. However, the 'alerting' information may not be readily available, and the rules and regulations will have to fill in a great many gaps in the scheme. At the moment, s 11 bristles with questions to which there are no clear answers, including the fundamental question: will s 11 materially advance the welfare of children caught up in divorce?

THIRD SESSION

Third Plenary Discussion

CHILDREN

The group discussion centred around the question of how we are to balance the fact that it is clear from all the research that children want more information as to what is going on and want to have more of an input into the process against what some perceived as a resistance in adults to the idea of disseminating information to children. How are we to resolve this? The point was made that research suggested that many parents would welcome a neutral third party being involved in talking to their children, recognising that children wish to have more information and support at the time of family breakdown. As to the question of children seeing judges, there is often a perception that judges are afraid to see children. Given that judges typically see children in adoption proceedings, the question was posed as to why this was not more prevalent in other family proceedings. A member of the judiciary made the point that the difference between adoption proceedings and other family proceedings was that the judge saw the childrein in adoption at the conclusion of the proceedings when the litigation was over. This was a very different scenario to that of seeing a child who was at the centre of ongoing proceedings. The suggestion was made that with the advent of the unified Court Welfare Service there might be a greater opportunity to provide more of a 'joined-up' approach between public and private law proceedings, for example one might adopt the model of the guardian ad litem for use in private law proceedings. Guardians were accustomed to providing a voice for children and the view was expressed that children in care proceedings were thus granted a much more effective voice than those involved in private law disputes. The conference was reminded by the senior district judge that the conciliation appointment procedure at the Principal Registry provided children with a means of expressing their views at an early stage of proceedings, as any child over the age of 9 was obliged to attend the appointment and would be seen by a court welfare officer. In a more general discussion, the point was made that health visitors are an under-used resource in this context and perhaps their role could be enhanced. However, given the need for health visitors to have a continuing relationship with parents, it might, in practice, be difficult to expect them also to fulfil a reporting role for the courts in the section 11 process.

FOURTH SESSION

Mental Health Services

MARITAL BREAKDOWN, DIVORCE AND ITS EFFECTS ON CHILDREN

Dr Judith Trowell, Dr Jenny Stevenson and Dr Brian Jacobs[1]

*In introducing her paper, **Judith Trowell** said that the implementation of Part II of the Family Law Act 1996 raised a number of questions, including the following:*

    (a)   *how can we improve our skills in communicating with children (emphasising that listening to children included learning how to listen to what they had to say through non-verbal means eg body language and drawings)?;*

    (b)   *how can we assist the recognition of children and their needs on divorce?;*

    (c)   *vulnerable children, those who were encountering difficulties even before family breakdown arose, may need special assistance: how can we ensure that they are 'spotted' in our system?;*

    (d)   *what role will the new merged court welfare service play in this process?*

Separation of their parents does not have the same effect on all children. How it affects them varies with the age of the child, the child's previous experience and the child's innate constitution (personality and genetic inheritance). This paper starts by looking at child development and how children of different ages react and adapt to the break up of their family. Implicit in this is the view that early experiences are very important and formative, but there is also recognition that early disadvantage can be ameliorated by later good experience. Specific clinical issues are then raised and the relevant research considered.

DEVELOPMENTAL ISSUES

Small children

When do we start to think about the child, as a baby? It seems unlikely that emotional life and feelings start at birth; a primitive mind is thought to be present in utero and the baby does not come into the world as a blank sheet. In the early weeks after birth, a baby gradually learns that it is separate from its mother. Hence, early on, the child does not have specific emotional attachments to particular people. The baby, of course, needs empathic sensitive care-giving from an adult who can anticipate the child's needs, understand the child's communications, show consistency in meeting the child's demands and has a capacity to contain the child's rage and fear and provide love. Most parents can fulfil these needs well enough. Winnicott describes primary maternal preoccupation; Bion uses the word reverie. These are metaphors that explain how the mother is consciously and unconsciously in tune with her baby and also explain why the mother, who is therefore a little out of touch with reality, needs the support of the father or another caring adult. If, at this stage, it becomes clear that one or other parent, or both parents, are totally unable to parent, or the relationship is irrevocably breaking down, then rather than struggle on, if it really does seem set to fail, it may be better to remove the child or for the parent to leave at this early time.

Around six months of age, the child moves from a view of the world that consists of a person as wholly good or bad by the instant with an infant's basic, primitive emotions, to seeing whole people and realising he or she can love and hate the same person. The child begins to feel concern, with a wish to make reparation to the carer when he or she has been angry or aggressive using smiles and cuddles. In other words, the child is aware of and attached to the parent. If all is going well, the child then moves

---

1   Dr Judith Trowell, Consultant Psychiatrist, Tavistock Clinic.

     Dr Jenny Stevenson, Consultant Clinical Psychologist, Tavistock Clinic, London.

     Dr Brian Jacobs, Consultant Psychiatrist, Maudsley Hospital, London.

forward from a secure emotional base to grow and explore. From now on, the adults are significant in their own right.

Six months to five years

Physical development involves increasing mobility, language, bowel control and early, intense relationships with parents and friends. Intellectual and emotional development is built on the early foundation of basic trust. The child begins to develop a sense of self, with self-esteem, as separation and individuation proceed. The child acquires autonomy but still lacks impulse control and finds frustration difficult to tolerate, demanding immediate gratification.

Most children use some kind of transitional object such as a special toy or blanket with which they develop a sense of security and with this there opens up a parental space where curiosity and play is possible; if all goes well, then the older child and adult develop the capacity to play and be creative.

The child's thinking is animistic, concrete and omnipotent. This means that children can feel they are the centre of the world, so that as well as expecting the world to rotate around them, there is also the heavy burden of the belief that, whatever happens, it is somehow their responsibility. Children, at this stage, can have magical thinking; thinking a thought can make the event that was thought about happen, which can increase a sense of responsibility. The magical thinking as well means that they may have very vivid fantasies, a fantasy world. Their sense of time is also different from adult time; events are condensed and displaced. Around the age of 3 years, children become receptive, ready to interact with children of their own age, to play with rather than alongside other children. These other children come to provide increasingly important emotional relationships.

Parental separation, at this time, does inevitably disrupt these growing children's lives and they have a very difficult time. They can use their fantasy world, once it is made very clear to them that it is not in some way their fault, to play out their conflicts and confusions. If the divorce is not too acrimonious, and contact arrangements enable good regular contact with the non-residential parent and the residential parent is not shattered by the emotional upheaval or the financial and legal problems, then the young child can recover. The child will need to talk, to ask questions and to be made aware that both parents still love the child (hopefully, this is the case).

As an example, interviews with a 3½-year-old girl are given. She was the subject of a disputed residence case as part of divorce proceedings, and was seen with both parents separately and also on her own.

Interviews

During the interviews with both parents, Sara oscillated. At times, she was a rather sad, vulnerable child, who needed reassurance, at other times, she was quite assertive. When seen with her mother, she told her mother what to do and generally ordered her around, and when seen with her father, she told him to stop talking. Her father and mother, individually, were both anxious to please and satisfy her. Neither parent found it easy to be firm with her so that the child appeared to be in control.

When Sara was separated from her mother, she became very anxious and was close to tears. When at the end of the interview with her father and Sara knew she would be separated from him, she became distressed and wept. On her own, she was an articulate child, mature beyond her years and had a good grasp of her situation. However, she did not have the security and confidence of the usual child of her age. The sense was more of walking on a tightrope, her attempts to keep her balance and keep Mummy and Daddy happy dominated everything she said and did.

Sara was very clear that Mummy and Daddy loved her. She was also equally clear that what she wanted, ie to have both her parents together, was not likely to happen. Her main preoccupation was how difficult it is when her parents argue or disagree. She wanted to live with her mother and her father and was distressed and yet resigned to the pain and despair of her position.

Whilst talking about all this, Sara looked sad and yet surprisingly sensible, like a little adult. At other times, she became quite autocratic, telling me what to do, what she wanted. She assumed I would comply and was rather disconcerted when I did not. She then became very sweet so it was difficult not to do as she wished.

When I questioned Sara, asking her what she would choose if she had three wishes, she appeared non-plussed. She told me there was no such thing as magic and found it impossible to let her imagination run free. She, similarly, had considerable difficulty in freely exploring the room and the toys I provided, preferring to stick with the toys that had been brought from home with her.

Sara, in the second session, on her own, was much more relaxed. She talked about the meeting we had with her mother and then with her father. Initially, she gave me what felt a little like set speeches, telling me she wanted to live with Daddy, then switching and wanting to live with Mummy. She laughed as we thought that half of her should be with each parent; she told me how she wishes she could be in two places at once. Then, she pulled a face and told me how difficult it all was. She talked with enthusiasm about Granddad and things she did with him.

She went on to tell me of various fears and phobias, for example, a fear of spiders, that make life a problem for her. There was a vivid account of how she has to cope and it was clear that her wish to be bigger was an attempt to take charge both of the things that frightened her and also of both her parents to stop them fighting. Sara explained poignantly about various possessions, some bought by her mother, some by her father, and then, sadly, showed me something she had from before, when Mummy and Daddy lived in the same house.

Summary

Sara is an intelligent, perceptive child who has already learnt to use her situation to her own advantage, playing one parent off against the other knowing they both want to be her preferred parent. The obverse of this is the frightened, vulnerable child who is very anxious about what might happen if she relinquished control. Sara seems to be lacking in normal spontaneity, curiosity and sense of fun and excitement. She does laugh and enjoy activities but she is constantly watching, alert to see how the adults are reacting and she immediately intervenes if she feels she is losing control.

Primary years

The move to school is the major step for child and parents; there is excitement and curiosity at the way intellectual and physical development progresses. At the same time, there is the loss of the very close relationships with parents; other adults begin to play an important role in the child's emotional life and, if there are limitations in the immediate family, these other adults, such as teachers, can be very significant.

Intellectual development is characterised by the acquisition of numeracy and literacy, a sense of time and the capacity to grasp relationships, and logical but still concrete thinking develops. The child becomes industrious and impulse control is good; mastering skills brings pleasure; the peer group grows in importance. Emotional development is very intense but is hidden beneath the surface and is more subtle than in younger children. The range of emotions increases, sexual identity is developing, and there should be a sense of pride and confidence in the self.

Under stress, such as breakdown in the family, this age group tends to respond in several ways. Assuming normal intelligence, the younger age group, five to seven years roughly, are more likely to regress. If the parents divorce, these children retreat into thinking and feeling like the pre-school children.

Children of about eight years of age find stress particularly difficult. They appear to be relatively composed, sensible, coping, but this exterior can belie the emotional distress these children are experiencing. They can no longer regress and escape as the younger children do and the adolescent coping mechanisms are not in their grasp. These children are sometimes very depressed and unhappy. They feel lost, unable to put their feelings into words, perhaps confused, but coping primarily, by keeping their feelings inside, unlike their older or younger siblings.

It would, therefore, seem that these children need very sensitive handling and that external appearances should not be accepted. As an example, there is a description of an interview with an 8½-year-old boy,

Robert. He was seen because of learning problems at school which began soon after his mother and father split up. In the family meeting, his mother came with him and the younger child, Tracey.

Robert marched into the room clutching his work folder from school. He sat down and proceeded to show me his sum book but this was very quickly put away when I saw pages of crosses beside his answers. He told me he did not like sums and that he was angry with his mother; she keeps making him do them and then never bothers to look at them and mark them. He then showed me his writing books and his word cards. The writing was very neat and tidy, but he found the simple words hard or impossible to read; he had clearly copied without reading or understanding what he wrote. He pushed these away and wanted to draw. From looking very down and depressed, he now became very controlling; my paper was no good, the crayons were wrong, the pencils needed sharpening, he needed a ruler. He succeeded in making me quite angry, so I finally said, it seemed nothing was right for him and I wondered if that really was a reflection of how he felt about himself and his family rather than what I had provided.

He decided to draw a bus. He tried very hard; every line was done carefully with the ruler and he kept rubbing out and repeating the lines over and over again, but could not get it right. He became quite distressed, saying he could not do it, wanting me to say it was all right, but then saying it was no good again. Finally, he gave up, saying it was no use.

He then furiously scribbled over the drawing, screwed up the paper and jabbed it with the pencil. I said, he seemed very angry and upset, could he tell me about it? He gave me a long outburst about school, how awful it is and how he hates his teacher, and it's awful at home, and it is all no good, and he can't do it. He turned away and tried to play with some of the toys I had, but wasn't able to concentrate. It was a painful, difficult interview.

Summary

Robert was an angry, unhappy boy who couldn't put his feelings into words but who could communicate his pain and despair indirectly. He has few emotional resources free to learn and needs help with his feelings if he is to make progress.

Older children, 9½ to 11-year-olds, who are under stress, such as parental divorce, find themselves pitchforked precipitately into an adolescent mode of function.

Early adolescence

Intellectually and physically, there is a developmental spurt, the younger person becomes capable of abstract thought and can conceptualise and form hypotheses. The physical spurt leads to an increase in height and strength, but also episodes of exhaustion that are disconcerting to the young person. The peer group is extremely important to this age, they have an identity crisis and a crisis of sexual identity. There may be sexual experimentation. Impulse control is poor again. Their emotional development is characterised by storms; they are vulnerable, arrogant, scornful and contemptuous, all at once. Despair and suicidal thoughts and attempts may be quite a frequent feature. They also experience passionate, excitable enthusiasms, escape routes such as alcohol and drugs can have excitement and allure whereas others find escape in their school work or computers.

Under stress, this age group and the older ones of the previous 'latency' group intellectualise and rationalise. Whatever is happening is explained in a contemptuous, denigrating way; stupid, incompetent adults. Their scorn can be acid, but this cynicism and sarcasm does not deal with the pain and distress. Family stability is not there to act as a buffer to these passions.

Divorce, at this time, can therefore be coped with but at a high price. Girls may become promiscuous or run away from home; premature autonomy. The girls can fear betrayal in heterosexual relationship as happened to their mothers and can be reluctant later on to commit themselves to long-term, deep relationships. Boys are more likely to be in trouble at school or outside the home, some of them present serious discipline problems to their single parent mothers and can be violent. However, the boys often have difficulty separating and leaving their single mothers. Frequent, regular contact with the non-residential parent seems to be extremely important in this age group, but often does not happen.

Older adolescence

Normal development, at this age, sees the settling of the emotional storms. They are functioning well intellectually and physically; heterosexual pairing can begin properly. They are compassionate, arrogant, pedantic and concerned, idealistic and yet angry at the state of the world. There is either a commitment to life or a more definite opting out. Divorce, at this stage, if all has gone well, has a less destructive effect than earlier but can tip young people back into the turmoil of early adolescence.

CLINICAL ISSUES

Children need a coherent story

Many children are given little preparation/explanation, if any, of parental separation or divorce. A parent may feel that they have provided an explanation but the explanation may be limited in that it was a one off and/or a one-sided account rather than explanations from both parents, either separately or jointly. Children often need to be able to talk about the eventual split as they will not necessarily equate the prior arguments and tensions with actual parental departure. They will need help with questions like 'why now', 'why couldn't difficulties be resolved', etc.

They will need reassurances, particularly younger children, and preferably from the parents themselves, that they are in no way culpable. Younger children may feel that they are a causative agent and may also experience 'superstitious' thinking in that if the child is capable of making 'reparation' then the parents may reunite, for example, thinking along the lines of 'if I can get better marks in school this term, they might get back together'.

Contact with parents

It is clear from most research studies that children are better able to cope with the effects of parental separation/divorce if they can maintain contact with both their parents. Children also benefit from clarity about where and with what frequency and with whom they will now see the non-residential parent; in a sibling group with a wide age-span, it will be necessary to differentiate the needs of each child.

Listening to individual voices within a sibling group

Children within a family will often have widely differing needs, different feelings about the divorce, possibly differing 'loyalties' and differing attributions. It is misleading to assume that expressed feelings by one or two children are shared by the other children or, for example, that a communal activity at a regular frequency will be a better option than more individualised activity with the non-resident parent but less often, etc.

The assessment of each child's needs, wishes, current vulnerability often proves complex but necessary; there is no clinical 'shortcut'.

Anxieties about separation/loss

Younger children may experience considerable anxiety about the possible loss of their resident custodial parent and become more clingy with an increase in 'checking' behaviour. It is also common for children to demonstrate behaviour commensurate with a much younger chronological age. This type of behaviour is usually short-lived and should be recognised and understood by adults as such.

Practical stressors

While financial changes and limitations quickly become apparent in divorce settlements, there is less awareness of the psychological accommodation which many children have to make, for example, loss of a bedroom with a house move, changes in routine, etc. These are psychological stressors when the

FOURTH SESSION

child is already mourning the loss of a parent. In adult terms, they are the equivalent to the loss of a loved one while simultaneously moving home. They can lead to feelings of isolation and an inability to complain.

Difficulties with transitions

Children often experience difficulties in the transition to being with the other parent, whether that is the leaving of the family home/custodial parent to be with the non-resident parent for contact, or at the end of contact with a non-resident parent moving back into being with the resident parent.

We need to be attuned as clinicians to the difficulties that fairly 'ordinary' children may have in adjusting to various transitions around contact times. Temperamentally 'vulnerable' children may experience more difficulties. We should expect difficulties around transitions. These should not necessarily be seen as indicative of distress/trauma in relation to the actual contact per se.

RELEVANT OUTCOMES FROM RESEARCH

Long-term mental health of children

One of the most striking findings of more recent research conducted in this decade is that the weight of evidence suggests that, on average, children function competently following divorce/separation.[1,2] 'The distress children face at the time is considerable, yet after a period of individual difficulty, it is clear that the outcome of divorce for most children is not risk but resilience'.[3] None the less, the rate of significant mental health difficulties is increased following parental separation.

Parental conflict

The research evidence overwhelmingly confirms the view that moderate/severe conflict between parents is linked with more psychological difficulties amongst children.[4,5] Indeed, research by Amato and Keith[6] looked at the differential effects of divorce on children re:

(1) parental loss;
(2) economic deprivation; and
(3) inter-parental conflict.

The effects of inter-parental conflict on children was considered to be the most damaging.

There is quite a body of work going on now tending to show that parental conflict may be even more strongly related to children's adjustment than is divorce per se. Many of the problems found among children after divorce in terms of psychological troubles, actually begin before divorce separation occurs.[7]

Parental conflict is also related to the controversy of joint physical custody. Recent research evidence suggests that joint physical custody must be both the best arrangement for some children (with co-operative or disengaged parents) as well as the worst arrangement for others (when parents are in conflict) following divorce.

1   Emery, R E and Forehand, R 'Parental divorce and children's well-being: A focus on resilience' in R J Haggerty, L R Sherrod, N Garmezy and M Rutter (eds) *Stress, Risk and Resilience in Children and Adolescents*.

2   Garmezy, N 'Stress-resistant children: The search for protective factors' J E Stevenson (ed) 'Recent research in developmental psychopathology' *Journal of Child Psychology and Psychiatry* (Book Supplement 4). Oxford (Pergamon Press, 1985).

3   Emery, R E and Forehand, R 'Parental divorce and children's well-being: A focus on resilience' in R J Haggerty, L R Sherrod, N Garmezy and M Rutter (eds) *Stress, Risk and Resilience in Children and Adolescents*.

4   Grych, J H and Fincham F D 'Interventions for Children and Divorce: Towards greater integration of research and action' (1992) *Psychological Bulletin* 111, pp 434–454.

5   Long, N and Forehand K 'The effects of parental divorce and parental conflict on children: An overview' (1987) *Developmental and Behavioural Paediatrics*, 8, pp 292–296.

6   Amato, P R and Keith, B 'Parental divorce and the well-being of children: A meta-analysis' (1991) *Psychological Bulletin* 110, pp 26–46.

7   Elliott, B J and Richards, M P M 'Children and divorce: Educational performance and behaviour before and after separation' (1991) *International Journal of Law and the Family* 5, pp 258–276.

Sibling relationships

The presence of siblings may help protect children from the stress of divorce[1,2] possibly through mutual support.

Extra-familial support

The attention and warm close relationship demonstrated by teachers, the degree of social support from outside the family and from childhood friends appear to relate to a good adjustment on the child's part.[3]

Children's age at time of divorce/separation

The evidence is equivocal. Some research suggests that young children adjust less well than older children but other studies fail to support his conclusion.[4] The recent meta-analysis by Amato and Keith[5] found that school age children faired worse than pre-schoolers.

Conclusions are difficult to reach. Perhaps the safest conclusion at this point is that children of different ages do not necessarily cope better or worse with divorce but they use different styles because of individual differences in cognitive abilities, developmental stage and access to extra familial support.

FUTURE DIRECTIONS AND CONSIDERATIONS FOR RESEARCH

Previous research followed a primary focus on establishing the degree to which divorce proved damaging for children and attempting to identify additional variables associated with greater or lesser risk. Researchers are beginning to investigate protective factors that characterize children as well as the risk factors. Future research should embrace both risk and protective factors. It should recognise that the absence of risk is not synonymous with the presence of protection.

Many factors operate in combination. For example, while contact with both parents may be a protective factor for most children, it might be limited to those children where the parental relationship is less severely conflicted by the time of the divorce.

In term of services for families, is it best practice in terms of a treatment goal to find ways to facilitate divorcing parents' co-operation with each other (and to reflect this in policy goals) or, realistically, a more modest goal with the emphasis on the avoidance of fighting and conflict? Is the appropriate treatment/policy goal necessarily a dual one whereby conflict is always to be discouraged, but when conflict is contained, actively encouraging co-operation.

Divorce research, as in other areas, has undergone distinct trends. Just as it is important to recognise that the outcomes of more recent studies promote the resilience of children on average and that most children's adjustment post-divorce is reasonably good, it is also useful to recognise that unless research in this area has a multivariable approach, outcomes are likely to be simplistic, contributing little to the continuing complex debate.

1   Kempton, T et al 'Presence of a sibling as a potential buffer following parent divorce: An examination of young adolescents' (1991) *Journal of Clinical Child Psychology* 20, pp 434–438.

2   Jenkins, J M and Smith, M A 'Factors protecting children living in disharmonious homes' (1990) *Journal of American Academy of Child and Adolescent Psychiatry* 29, pp 60–69.

3   Cowen, E L et al 'Relationship between support and adjustment among Children of Divorce' (1990) *Journal of Child Psychology and Psychiatry* 31, pp 727–735.

4   Hetherington, E M et al 'Marital transitions: A child's perspective' (1989) *American Psychologist* 44, pp 303–312.

5   Amato, P R and Keith, B 'Parental divorce and the well-being of children: A meta-analysis' (1991) *Psychological Bulletin* 110, pp 26–46.

FOURTH SESSION

DISTURBED ADULTS WHO HAPPEN TO BE PARENTS

Dr Judith Freedman and Dr Anne Zachary[1]

Dr Freedman explained to the conference that the focus of her paper was on parents who were themselves mentally disturbed: how are they to be identified and then involved in deciding what is best for their children? She noted that, in private law proceedings, the way in which these families came to the court's attention was more haphazard (there was also the considerable problem of those who are unmarried parents and, thus, never come before the courts on family breakdown unless a specific private law application was made). She referred to the problems highlighted in her paper which might cause one to worry about a parent (eg drug abuse) and reminded the conference that parental assessment through the mental health services is available and might help the courts in understanding the environment in which a particular child is living.

Disturbed parents are a minority, but a distinct and worrying part of the population of separating parents. The Family Law Act 1996 requires a considerable level of involvement from both members of a divorcing couple, particularly if they are parents and need to address issues of residence and contact in respect of their children. In this paper, we consider some problems of divorcing adults who suffer from a serious personality disorder, a major mental illness or a learning disability. First, how are the courts to identify these problematic parents? Secondly, how are the courts to determine if these parents can engage in thinking about what is best for their children?

In whatever form the law is finally enacted, these are pressing concerns, since the incidence of marital discord and divorce is increased when one or both parents suffers from a psychological disturbance.[2] With the emphasis on parents' participation in the divorce proceedings, the new Act requires us to consider the state of these parents as well as their children.

DISTURBANCE AND THE FAMILY

Psychological disturbance in parents impacts profoundly on children. In addition, psychological disturbance destabilises the marriage, increasing the likelihood of marital breakdown.

Identifying ill parents is the first step towards making decisions about the needs of the children, as well as any special needs that one or both parents may have during the divorce process. However, in divorce courts, where parents are not routinely seen, it may not be easy to recognise the presence of disturbance.

Courts encounter the parents at the time of divorce, which is unsettling and disturbing for any adult. It is then important to distinguish between ongoing mental disturbance and transient distress related to the marital breakdown. This distinction is particularly difficult when there is disagreement about the children. A mother who accuses her ex-partner of abusing their child may seem disturbed. The problem for the Courts is to determine if she is troubled by what is happening with her child or if she is herself intrinsically disturbed.

A useful indicator in identifying troubled parents is that one has what we often call 'a bad feeling' about them. Rather than discounting this experience, it helps to recognise its presence and investigate further.

In addition, particular disturbances in behaviour signal the need for further investigation. These include the following: domestic violence; alcohol or drug abuse; past or present history of child abuse; neglect or other indications of inadequate parenting and learning disability. In addition, a parent may suffer from a hitherto undiagnosed serious mental illness, such as depression, schizophrenia or severe personality disorder. Other worrying signs include: a history of criminal behaviour, particularly violent or recurrent criminality; a general presentation of inadequacy; difficulty in engaging in negotiations, leading to a total breakdown in communications; implacable hostility.

---

1   Judith Freedman and Anne Zachary, Consultant Psychiatrists in Psychotherapy, Portman Clinic, London.
2   Quinton and Rutter 'Family pathology and child psychiatric disorder: a four-year prospective study' in A R Nicol (ed) *Longitudinal Studies in Child Psychology and Psychiatry* (Wiley, Chichester, 1985).

These behavioural indicators should stand out as warning signs that the parent may be suffering from a disturbance in mental functioning. Often there is a need to look further. For example, substance abuse or criminality are not in themselves diagnostic of psychological disturbance, even though they often occur together with depression or personality disorder. Likewise, social class does not determine mental disturbance. Personality disorders and depression, in particular, occur across society and are not caused by race, culture or socio-economic status.

When a warning sign is identified in a divorcing couple, the court needs a detailed understanding of the parental disturbance. This will help determine the parent's capacity to participate in complicated decisions about divorce, residence and contact. The investigations should also focus on the impact on the children, in both the present and the future. In other words, decisions about contact and residence must take into account the parental disturbance. It is also important to consider the possibility that the children are already traumatised by the disturbance in the parents and may be in need of specialised mental health interventions.[1]

Whilst it may seem obvious that it is necessary to undertake careful assessment of the child, we suggest that, equally, assessment of the parents is needed.

PARENTAL ASSESSMENT

When the court identifies worrying signs about a parent in a divorcing couple, the judge can ask for a section 7/37 report from the local authority. In addition, a specialist mental health facility can provide a full parental assessment. The parent's problems will dictate which professionals to instruct: for example, forensic, learning disabilities or alcohol and drug abuse.

Whatever the specific concerns, it is crucial that *both* parents participate in the assessment. Even though the parents are deciding to put an end to their marriage, the psychological partnership is not so easily put to rest. In any two-person relationship which endures over time, there develops a mutual sharing of psychological features. Some of these, in gross form, are easily recognised in everyday life: for example, the domineering husband and the submissive wife or the mothering woman and the childish man. Couples unconsciously realign their personality traits so that they complement each other. Thus, the domineering man will enact all of the aggressive behaviours that may be required on behalf of both himself and his wife. At the same time, the submissive woman will undertake all of the vulnerable emotions on behalf of both herself and her husband. In normal couples, this is a fluid process that changes over time to accommodate the individual growth and change of each partner. However, in disturbed couples these processes are more rigid and constraining. In our example, the domineering husband must always be aggressive and never show any vulnerable feelings; the submissive wife must always be passive and weak and never show any strength or aggression.

Sometimes, the marriage breaks down because of the discomfort experienced by one or both members of the couple with the constraints imposed by this process. At other times, one partner may manage, despite the constraints, to change, and this will upset the equilibrium, leading to breakdown of the marriage.

The existence of these processes (which psychoanalysts call 'projective identification'[2]) implies that it can be extremely difficult to get a clear picture of how the parent functioned within the marriage, unless both partners are seen. We need to understand both who each parent is as an individual and who each parent was as a partner in the couple.

At the Portman Clinic, we assess parents when sexual or criminal acting out, including child abuse, is a problem. Our stance is to understand who the parents are, both as individuals with a past history and as members of a couple. Often this leads us to a view of their illness rather than just their badness. This shift in focus, whilst it may not change the outcome for the children, sometimes helps the parents to feel that the court has listened sympathetically to who they are.

We routinely ask that both parents are involved in the assessment. We offer individual assessments to each parent to develop a psychodynamic understanding of them. We do this by focusing on the parent's

---

1   Wallerstein et al 'Children of divorce: a 10-year study' in E M Hetherington and J D Arasteh (eds) *Impact of Divorce, Single Parenting, and Stepparenting on Children* (Erlbaum, USA, 1988).

2   S Ruszczynski and J Fisher (eds) *Intrusiveness and Intimacy in the Couple* (Karnac, 1995).

own experiences in the family of origin during childhood and the course of the parent's development into adulthood, as well as the emotional states and the quality of thinking that are present during the interview. We also listen for what the parents may reveal about their unconscious preoccupations and motivations. We are interested in what each parent has to say about him or herself as well as what they say about the other parent. We use these twin pictures to try to put together a picture of the marriage in which both these parents as well as the children existed. It is like bringing together the two pictures in a viewer to get one, stereoscopic picture.

In addition, we offer the possibility of a joint interview if the parents can tolerate it. Their willingness to engage together in a joint interview usually augers well for their ability to fulfil their roles as parents in thinking about needs of the child, even after the marriage is over. Sometimes, we also ask our child psychotherapy colleagues to interview the children. This gives us further information, from the child's perspective, about what it was like to grow up in the family environment created by this parental couple.

We present some clinical examples of disturbed parents who came to mental health attention in the course of their family law proceedings.

THE MOTHER WHO COULD NOT WORRY ABOUT A RISKY FATHER

A difficult problem faces family courts when, in the setting of a divorce, one parent, usually the mother, accuses the other of sexually abusing the child and stops contact. Often, there is no clear evidence of sexual abuse. The court is faced with the dilemma of determining whether the father is a child sexual abuser or whether the mother has instilled in the child a lie or a fantasy based on her anger and resentment toward the father. We present here a case with a somewhat different twist: this mother could not worry enough about a father who really was a risk.

Mr and Mrs A were married for six years. They had a daughter, Julie. Mrs A knew that Mr A's daughter from his first marriage had accused him of sexual abuse, but she did not believe the allegations. Even though he was convicted and served a prison sentence before he met Mrs A, she did not understand the seriousness of the charge. Mrs A minimised the danger her husband presented, even when the local authority registered Julie as at risk. When no further evidence emerged after a few years, the local authority de-registered the child.

Mrs A became dissatisfied with Mr A's lack of interest in family life, even though she also felt that he was too controlling of her life. When Julie was 5 years old, Mrs A left the marriage, taking her daughter with her. A divorce ensued, with parental agreement about contact. Mrs A did not tell the court about past concerns about Mr A, so they were not taken into consideration when contact arrangements were made.

Relations between Mr and Mrs A were amicable during the divorce proceedings. However, their relations deteriorated when Mrs A became involved with a new boyfriend, a man who was a friend of Mr A. Mr A began intimidating Mrs A, following her in his car and making nuisance phone calls. Around this time, Mr A took Julie for a contact visit and kept her overnight, without her mother's consent. The next day, Mrs A called the duty social worker, who fortunately had worked with Mr A's previous family. The social worker told Mrs A that she should not leave Julie unsupervised with Mr A. On hearing this, Mrs A felt able to retrieve Julie from her father's house. She found her in the care of a young teenage girl, who Julie later told her had shared her father's bed the previous night.

Mrs A suspended contact, and Mr A applied for a contact order. The court welfare officer assigned to the case felt uneasy and unable to determine the level of risk. She felt that Mr A's history was worrying, but she did not understand why Mrs A was only now becoming concerned. It emerged that Julie had begun soiling in the last months of the marriage, but the mother had not connected this to concerns about the father. The court welfare officer recommended a specialist assessment of both parents and a section 37 report from the local authority.

We met with Mr and Mrs A separately. Mrs A felt too intimidated by Mr A to agree to a joint meeting. Although Mr A was working and seemed capable and personable, we found him to be a disturbed man with a serious personality disorder. In the interviews, it emerged that his grasp of the truth and his ability to take responsibility for his actions was poor. Instead of accepting his feelings of guilt, he defended himself as a man who had done nothing wrong. To maintain this self-image, he had to constantly blame others and hold on to confusing and contradictory thoughts. We also found that he seemed emotionally empty and devastated, particularly in relation to the loss of his wife to his friend. His wish for contact with Julie seemed motivated by his longing to have contact with his ex-wife and to take revenge against her.

The puzzle was why Mrs A failed to recognise and act on these worries before. It emerged during our interviews with her that she had engaged in prostitution during the marriage. Mr and Mrs A disagreed about who initiated this activity, each of them blaming the other. Mrs A felt ashamed and thought that she could only stop the prostitution by leaving the marriage. Mrs A never considered what effect her activities had on Julie, believing that she was too young to understand what was happening.

We recommended that Mr A should only have contact with Julie under close supervision by the local authority. In the course of our assessment, we encouraged the local authority to take a more active role in their investigations of the family. We also recommended that Julie should attend her local child and family clinic.

In this assessment, the mother was helped to face the terrible secret that paralysed her and prevented her from taking a properly protective stance for her daughter. The risk presented by the father was clarified to all parties, so that a safe plan for continuing the father's contact with his daughter could go forward. It remains uncertain whether Mr A abused Julie. Hopefully, events came to a head before she suffered the same fate as his first daughter years earlier.

WHEN BOTH PARENTS ARE MENTALLY ILL

Parents with sustained mental illness present difficulties to the courts in how to work with them in a meaningful way. We present here a case that became a public proceeding under the Children Act 1989. Equally well, these same aspects of working with the parents could have occurred in private law proceedings.

Miss B and Mr C met in hospital when they were both suffering schizophrenic breakdowns. Rebecca was born one year later. Unfortunately, Miss B broke down again soon after Rebecca's birth, and she returned to hospital. Mr C successfully applied for parental responsibility, as he was looking after Rebecca. When Miss B left hospital, the local authority offered the family intensive support.

Unfortunately, when Rebecca was 2 years old, both parents returned to hospital. They arranged for the maternal grandmother to look after their daughter. Rebecca remained with her grandmother after both parents left hospital. The parents had separated by this time, but together they had frequent contact with their daughter during the week, and she stayed with them at weekends. When Rebecca turned 3, the grandmother noticed that she seemed distressed and displayed sexualised behaviour. A short time later, Mr C disclosed to his community psychiatric nurse that he touched Rebecca's genitals when he changed her nappy.

At this point, the case moved from voluntary arrangements into the arena of the Children Act 1989. The local authority asked us to see the family to assess the residence and contact arrangements for Rebecca, including the risks posed by the father and the mother's ability to protect the child.

We began with a meeting of the parents and the grandmother. Miss B was back in hospital, and it remained uncertain until the morning of the meeting whether she would attend. On the day, she was deemed able to travel independently, and she arrived on her own, still highly disturbed. It emerged in the meeting that these three adults, who shared the care of Rebecca, had never before spoken all together. It was a tense and difficult meeting, with Miss B deeply angry and refusing to participate. Mr C tried to be helpful, but he was clearly frightened of Miss B and her mother. The grandmother was both pained to see how ill her daughter was and furious at Mr C for abusing Rebecca. Miss B refused to attend again. Mr C, in his individual session, divulged that the couple had decided to end their relationship on the eve of the joint meeting, but neither of them could mention it.

Our assessment continued with the grandmother and Rebecca, looking at what they needed to ensure a safe future together. At the beginning of this process, there was an assumption that Miss B could participate in discussions and planning about residence and contact arrangements for Rebecca. The joint meeting made it clear that she was incapable of conducting her own affairs. Her solicitor asked the Official Solicitor to represent Miss B.

Mr C was more capable, but he still communicated very little about himself. We made guarded recommendations about his contact with Rebecca. Some months later, he admitted to his mental health team that he had persistent paedophilic fantasies about his daughter. Contact was suspended while he engaged in further treatment.

This case required specialist involvement, both from our team and from the local mental health team, to establish the limitations in the mother's capacity to participate as well as to assess the level of risk that the father posed. The process unfolded over several months in a way that could not have become apparent in routine proceedings.

DOMESTIC VIOLENCE AND LEARNING DISABILITY

Our next case involved domestic violence, learning disability, alcoholism, and mental abnormality.

Miss D has learning difficulties and attended a special school. In her early 20s, she met Mr E, 20 years her senior. They had two children, Edward, now age 5, and Deborah, age 4. Unbeknown to any authorities, Mr E was violent to Miss D whenever he became drunk, a frequent occurrence. The beatings were particularly severe during her pregnancies. Miss D felt that she had to put up with the violence, perhaps because she was accustomed to beatings from her parents. She also believed that she had nowhere else to go.

However, when the children were aged 3 and 2 respectively, Mr E came home drunk and inflicted a particularly severe beating on Miss D, including breaking her nose. Edward was present and became distressed. Miss D picked him up as Mr E tried to hit her again, but caught Edward instead with a hard slap. Fortunately, the neighbours heard the commotion and rushed in as Mr E was trying to strangle Miss D. They rescued her and the children and called the police. Subsequently, Mr E was convicted and spent two months in prison. In the aftermath, Miss D determined not to return to Mr E. She and the children moved into a refuge. Two years later, when we saw them, Miss D had obtained accommodation for herself and the children at a secret address.

One year after the separation, Mr E filed applications for contact and for disclosure of the children's whereabouts. The court welfare officer recommended that Mr E have indirect contact with the children until he undertook treatment in a domestic violence programme. However, the programme did not accept Mr E. The court welfare officer then felt unable to make a recommendation about Mr E's application, and so a specialist assessment was requested. There was also concern about the impact of the violence on Edward, and we agreed to provide an assessment of him as well.

We met individually with Mr E and Miss D. Given the history of violence, we did not offer the parents a joint interview. The child psychotherapist on our team met with Miss D and Edward together.

We found that Edward was definitely traumatised by the violence and that the prospect of contact with his father terrified him. The child psychotherapist made suggestions for his special needs in school. She felt that, over time, it would become possible to distinguish the extent to which his deficits were trauma-induced or were the result of other special needs.

We found that Miss D, despite her learning difficulties, was able to engage in interviews. When she related her abusive early history, we wondered whether her deficits might also be at least in part trauma-induced. At the end of the assessment, she accepted a referral for psychotherapy.

Unfortunately, Mr E demonstrated no real concern for the children. He was unable to consider what they went through and the effects of this experience for them. His capacity to take responsibility for his behaviour was severely limited. He claimed no memory of any violence, apart from the episode that led to his conviction. Even this, he blamed on Miss D, saying that she behaved aggressively toward him. He was continuing to drink. Mr E's mental state was of concern, as he seemed to have difficulty in following a logical line as he spoke.

We recommended to the court that there be no contact with the father so that the children could achieve a period of safety and stability. However, we recognised that as the children grew older, they might wish to see their father. In that case, we suggested that contact should be supervised.

Although the court was concerned about Miss D's ability to engage in the legal process, we found that she was capable of understanding quite complex issues. What we uncovered, instead, was a mental abnormality in Mr E that raised concerns about his ability to participate.

A MARRIAGE BASED ON ILLNESS

Human nature being what it is, there are always situations that are difficult to fit into our professional frameworks. Many of the disturbed parenting couples we see are not married. Even so, the issues of appropriate child care may be similar to those in a divorce case.

In this family, the children's mother presented as if she was one of the children, while her partner tried to care for the entire family. Should the mother receive successful treatment, she might 'grow up' and leave her partner. In fact, this couple declined treatment, lost their children into permanent care and then married in a rather paradoxical fashion. The possibility now is of more children and ongoing risk.

Ms F and Mr G's three children were taken into care against their wishes. Social Services were concerned about physical and emotional abuse but the main problem was that the children were not getting enough to eat.

Ms F is a pretty, childlike young woman in her early twenties. Mr G is twice her age and looks old, careworn, ill and slightly suspect. It was hard to believe they could be the parents of three young children. At first, we thought that he was her father.

Ms F's initial interview revealed a complex and colourful family history. She had a dozen mixed-race siblings, most sharing her father but by different mothers. She had little contact with her father, who left early in her childhood. Ms F lived with her mother and her subsequent partners. She idealised her father and spoke about all his children individually by name. She described a continuous round of visiting her extended family, remembering these visits like idyllic summer holidays. She spoke about the death of a male friend of her mother, whom she had known and loved in childhood. She burst into tears about the loss of this man who sounded like Mr G, another father substitute. We wondered about sexual abuse during her childhood. Ms F confirmed a minor incident with a male guest at her mother's party. She stressed that her sexual experience was different from her mother's in that before Mr G she had only one partner.

In the second interview, Ms F could talk about her children by name, and her love for them was evident. She was defensive about the concerns of social services, such as that she preferred cleaning to child care. She was angry that they noted weight loss but ascribed it to the wrong child. This was the nearest she came to acknowledging that the allegations were true. Her first two children were girls, Jenny and Jane, whilst she had longed for a boy. She was afraid girls would grow up to be as promiscuous as her mother. The youngest child, a boy, was failing to thrive. An incident in the reports gave a poignant insight into Ms F's rigid and punishing internal world. The foster-carer reported that Jenny had been cross with Jane. She overheard Jenny saying that she would not speak to Jane again if she forgot about Mummy and Daddy. Ms F, rather than accept this as the children's loyalty, was furious with Jenny. She said that it was all right for them to fall out at home, but when they were away they must stick together.

Mr G arrived for his interview dressed smartly in a suit and carrying a briefcase, whilst incongruously reading a comic. He cast light on how depressed Ms F had been. It was as if he had four small children to look after. He was angry about social services, saying they had made 'a big mistake'. He was the middle child in a large family and was used to helping with his siblings. Prior to meeting Ms F, he had had a long career as a lorry driver. He 'rescued' her, becoming a substitute for her idealised father, and their different vulnerabilities led to them rapidly creating an idealised family of their own.

Meeting together, Ms F was able to admit in her partner's presence how depressed she had been. It was also evident how Mr G used her illness and his sense of being needed to boost his own feelings of inadequacy. They had slipped into chronic poverty, due to Mr G giving up work in order to look after his wife and children. He described how she would lie in bed upstairs so that the children should not see her depression. He saw social services as demanding and 'blackmailing'. He was unwilling or unable to adapt. Whilst refusing a family residential assessment, he explained that their lease was about to run out so that the couple faced homelessness.

The court was extraordinarily sensitive to this family's needs, and social services were unusually generous in their offer of residential assessment. However, the fixed dynamics in the family made it difficult for change to occur. Mr G needed Ms F to be ill to maintain his self-esteem. Ms F remained ill to keep her father substitute engaged. Ms F, cleaning excessively, projected anything 'black' into the children, particularly Jenny, who was scapegoated and punished to help her parents cling desperately to a rosy view of life. All this meant that nothing could be done to preserve the family and a decision was taken to place the children in permanent care. At least for Jenny this was hopeful in that she received therapeutic help to lighten the burden of the projections she carried.

What can be done in these paradoxical situations where the parents are not married and family breakdown is imminent? In this case, the parents lost their children in their efforts to stick together and then went on to marry and no doubt produce more children. We are left feeling disjointedly out of step with their actions and helpless in our endeavours. Within a framework of helping them towards a constructive 'divorce', they marry, after losing their children. It is as if their every move is based on the chronic inter-twined psychopathologies of each needy parent. It suggests that long before the need for divorce intervention, pre-marital and pre-natal input are needed.

CONCLUSION

Our cases demonstrate a variety of difficulties faced by the family courts in applying the Family Law Act 1996. By way of conclusion, we want to stress how our four examples demonstrate poignantly that the problems that disturbed parents bring to the courts have been in the making for a long time. To understand and respond to these parents properly and fairly, we are required to engage with them in exploring and coming to know about their long-term problems. This is a tall order, particularly in a crowded court system where there is pressure to move matters along quickly. We suggest that specialist mental health practitioners, working in concert with the courts, can help to address these difficult problems.

DIVORCE AND SEPARATION: IMPACT OF PARENTAL FACTORS ON CHILDREN: ALERTING PAST AND PRESENT CIRCUMSTANCES

Dr Danya Glaser and Dr Claire Sturge[1]

Dr Sturge emphasised the point made in her paper that children have rights in the situation of family breakdown. Her suggestion was that there were a number of 'alerting circumstances' (as outlined in her paper) and that someone needed to vet the cases which came before the court to ensure that none of those 'alerting circumstances' were present. If any of them were found to be present, the court could use s 7 of the Children Act 1989 or use the new merged Court Welfare Service to obtain information. Occasional cases may require an expert to assist the court.

Dr Glaser made the point that the fact that s 11 is in the Family Law Act 1996 at all is important: the question is who should be ensuring that the checklist is fulfilled? Health visitors and, in some cases, mental health professionals can point up areas of concern but ultimately it is for the legislators to decide as to what can be done and when. One needed to consider the question of whether the s 11 route is an effective way of alerting the court to problems in the private law field in circumstances where the child would not otherwise be before the court.

All children are affected by a breakdown in the relationship between their parents, whether the parents are still together or as a result of their separation. Social class does not confer immunity to any of these issues to be considered here. Poverty increases vulnerability but is not causal. Most poor families function adequately under difficult circumstances.

What will concern judges in addressing applications for residence, contact or other parental issues is whether the arrangements around the parental separation are the best and most appropriate that can be achieved in the interests of the children. This paper is designed to help inform such decisions by highlighting child mental health issues that should alert judges and which need to be considered when making orders.

Consideration of the issues listed here need normally only apply in cases where there is a dispute about residence or contact. However, if a judge has concerns about cases in which both parties appear to have freely agreed to contact or residence arrangements, the judge might refer to the list.

PARENT FACTORS AND COUPLE RELATIONSHIP ISSUES

Whenever concerns initially appear to apply only to the adults, questions need to be asked about whether and how these might be affecting children in the family and whether the effects on children are sufficient to influence decisions about contact or residence. This will be of particular importance if the child may have unsupervised contact with one troubled parent without the protective presence of the other parent.

Parent factors

This section deals with problems in a parent which to varying degrees can affect the welfare of the child. They include the following:

- parental alcohol and drug misuse;
- major mental illness in a parent;
- significant learning difficulties in a parent;
- violent criminality in a parent.

1 Dr Danya Glaser, Department of Psychological Medicine, Great Ormond Street Hospital, London.
Dr Claire Sturge, Department of Child and Adolescent Psychiatry, Northwich Park Hospital, Harrow, Middlesex.

FOURTH SESSION

Adult mental illness and substance abuse can affect children in a number of ways, the magnitude and nature of some amounting to emotional abuse. Some parents thus affected are emotionally unavailable and unresponsive to their children's needs, making the children feel unwanted and neglected. Other children have duties and responsibilities imposed on them which are age-inappropriate, which they cannot fulfil or which interfere with their education and normal peer relationships. These include their own and younger siblings' physical care, and care for the mentally ill parent, including the summoning of help when the parent is in urgent need of help. The children often feel responsible, guilty and sometimes a failure in such circumstances. Exposure to the parent's behaviour while mentally ill or under the influence of drugs or alcohol may be frightening and/or distort the child's understanding of reality.

Parental alcohol and drug misuse

In assessing the impact on the child, the following have to be considered:

- is the parent able at all times safely to parent the child and/or arrange appropriate safeguards, for example an available safe adult to cover times when the parent might be incapable?;
- does the habit produce secondary risks for the child, for example strangers in and out of the house, drinking parties, unsavoury drug dealers, etc?;
- how involved is the child in the alcohol/drug culture? Does he/she witness drunken adults, people 'shooting up', arguments around money or drugs? Has the child become over-aware of the symptoms or habits, for example is able to sense or is involved in a parent's drug craving? Is the child continually on the lookout for the first signs of inebriation in the parent? Is the child involved in procuring?

Comment

There are always risk factors for the child in these situations. Poor supervision is a likely consequence and if the child is also exposed to a variety of people, he/she is likely to be at risk of sexual and other abuse. Overall parenting may be affected and the child may have to mature rapidly in an inappropriate way in order to look after himself or herself.

Drugs producing an urgent and overwhelming drive to procure often present the greatest risk particularly to young children, for example crack cocaine.

Vignette: Alan

When Alan was 5 years of age, after his father had successfully undertaken treatment for his alcoholism and been dry for one year, the mother consented to his living with his father as he had expressed this wish. For several years all went well but, by the time Alan was 8 years of age, the father became awkward about contact for Alan with his mother and at the age of 9 it ceased. The mother issued a contact application. The father did not co-operate with the legal system. Eventually, after Alan was found wandering late at night, social services intervened. The living situation was described as appalling and it became apparent that Alan had been both buying and cooking food himself for months. The father was continually under the influence of alcohol and seemed unconcerned about his son.

Major mental illness in a parent

In assessing the impact on a child, the following need to be considered:

- the disorder: it is illnesses which involve psychosis that present the greatest risks. The main illness in this category is schizophrenia but also severe depression;
- the course of the illness, prognosis and compliance with treatment;
- whether any of the delusions or hallucinations have ever been in relation to the child. This increases the direct risk of physical harm or even death to the child;
- whether there is a 'healthy' adult in the household who can identify problems early and act to protect the child.

Comment

Most mental disorders will have some impact on the child. A less severe mental illness which can have far-reaching effects is obsessive compulsive disorder if the parent's obsessions and compulsions override attending to the child.

Conversely, in most psychotic states, the basic protective instincts survive but can become distorted by the illness. In personality disorders, ie disordered rather than mentally ill adults, the impact on the child will vary according to the type of difficulties the parent is experiencing.

Munchausen's Syndrome By Proxy is in a category of its own as there is sometimes an absence of any obvious psychiatric disorder. It is defined in relation to behaviours towards the child and is, therefore, by definition a risk to the child.

Vignette: John and Peter

John and Peter were aged 9 and 7 respectively when their father applied for residence on the grounds of the mother's mental illness. She had had four episodes of illness and showed a pattern of complying with treatment for up to one year after each admission and then ceasing treatment and gradually becoming ill. Her sister looked after the childen when she needed admission. The mother's general care of the children was considered good and they were devoted to her, hardly knowing their father.

The child psychiatric assessment revealed that, for the previous five months, no electricity had been used. They went to bed at dusk (it was autumn/winter); they had seen no television nor could they use their computer games; their mother cooked on a primus stove and washed their clothes only in cold water.

It emerged that although averring the opposite, the mother had ceased seven months previously to take her medication. She was guarded in what she said, sensing the risk of losing her children if she talked freely. However, it became clear that she believed both her neighbours and a group of unidentified men were trying to brainwash her and her children, and poison them through electric waves. The children were confused, having some recognition that what their mother believed was all wrong but half believing it. With the pressure of the case, she became more obviously very unwell and had to be sectioned.

Significant learning difficulties in a parent

In assessing the impact on children the following need to be considered:

- the general principles of decision-making are no different than those in assesssing a parent of normal IQ. The issues are around the quality of the parenting and its meeting the child's needs;
- there are serious problems if the IQ or overall functioning is so low as to not be able to attend to basic child care needs and the child's needs more generally. Such low functioning is unusual;
- if the learning disabled parent is with a much higher functioning partner, there will be power issues and the question of whether the disabled parent can protect;
- as in any person, emotional factors and failures in their own parenting when they were children is highly relevant and can be more relevant than the learning disability. Deprivation in the parent will result in their functioning more poorly than can be explained by the IQ alone;
- there are interactional factors in relation to the level of functioning of the child. Learning disabled parents are more likely to have learning disabled children. While such children will have special needs which will present a challenge to the parent, a learning disabled parent has something unique to offer that child in terms of his or her own experience and acceptance of limitations. Where the child is higher functioning than the parent and likely to 'outstrip' them, this needs addressing.

FOURTH SESSION

Comment

Such parents need careful assessing. Their limitations in themselves tell us little about their capabilities as a parent unless very marked, for example an IQ under 70. Most parents with mild learning difficulties do a remarkably good job.

Vignette: Isobel

A father of normal intelligence sought residence of his daughter, Isobel, aged 3, on the grounds of neglect. His ex-partner had mild learning difficulties. A parenting assessment was undertaken at a local Family Centre. This showed that the mother was meeting the child's needs in terms of attention, and emotional sensitivity and support. Her house-keeping skills were poor and Isobel often arrived at nursery looking dishevelled. With input from the Family Centre, this improved and weekly support to the mother was organised.

Violent criminality in a parent

This refers to a parent who has a record of violence to people outside of the home. While some of the issues are similar to those in domestic violence (see below), others are not. In particular, there are issues of morality and the standards and role modelling conveyed to the child.

As with drug abusers/pushers, the child may be indirectly or directly drawn into criminal practices or the criminal sub-culture. Concerns are greater in relation to male children.

There may be frequent separations from the criminal parent because of incarcerations which disrupt the child's life and sense of security.

Such a parent may have a temper control problem that spills over into the home.

Vignette: Johnny

A prolonged contact and residence dispute had been going on for years between the estranged parents of Johnny, aged 12. The father had a record which included amongst other things, three convictions for GBH in the course of robberies. He had spent four years in gaol during Johnny's life.

Johnny adored his father and his expressed wish was to leave his mother to live with his father. He had begun running away to be with him. There had been an incident of shop-lifting while with his father and the mother believed he had been set up. Johnny had been involved in several serious fights in the neighbourhood.

The father presented well without any diagnosable personality disorder or mental illness. He had high expectations of his son despite his son's poor attendance and poor academic progress at school. This did not bother him as he 'had lots of connections and could easily set him up in a good job later'.

The couple relationship

There are, by definition, problems in this relationship if the parents have separated. Many parents are able to put their child's interests first and, whatever their own distress, can make appropriate arrangements for the child. Many fathers do, over quite short periods of time, disappear from the child's life for a variety of reasons. In cases reaching court, the father has remained involved, which can be seen as positive in itself. However, there is a dispute bringing it to court. These can be seen as a continuum from breakdowns in communication to violence and even murder and on an emotional continuum from breakdown in communication to implacable hostility and false allegations.

Couple relationship issues impacting on children

- Domestic violence;
- Implacable hostility;
- Disputed allegations;

- Breakdown in communication;
- Other disputed issues.

Domestic violence

In assessing the impact on children, the following need to be considered:
- Children exposed to violence directly or indirectly are at greatly increased risk of:
  - developing anti-social disorders;
  - being violent;
  - developing emotional and other psychiatric disorders;
  - developing post-traumatic symptoms.
- There is evidence that with very young children, ie pre-school, helplessly witnessing marked violence or trauma to his or her main carer produces more serious effects than direct abuse to him or her.
- Women experiencing chronic domestic violence become totally demoralised, feel inadequate in their parenting as well as in other areas of their lives and may be depressed.
- Some women develop marked post-traumatic symptoms and any arrangement that brings the partner into proximity, for example contact, can trigger symptoms.
- Some women exhibit as much violence in the relationship as their male partners.
- Pathological jealousy can be the basis for the violence. Such men often continue to harass their partners after separation.
- Alcohol often plays a part in one or both partners.

Children in such families are always affected even when they have no direct knowledge of the violence itself. The dynamics of the family functioning is distorted and the atmosphere is a violent one. Injuries may be all too apparent. The child usually becomes part of the secrecy around the violence.

These experiences often amount to significant emotional abuse.

The ill-effects in the child may be apparent at the time or not become apparent for months or years, for example in adolescence.

The level of parental functioning, independent of the domestic violence, can often not be judged until some time after the separation.

Even when the non-resident parent poses no direct physical threat to the child, indirect ill effects may be produced, for example, deviant attitudes to women or denigratory feelings towards their main carer; deviant attitudes to violence; confusion to the child if he or she knows the other parent has seriously damaged their main carer.

The killing of one parent by the other is the extreme of domestic violence.

Working out how to best meet the needs of the child, within the battle that often ensues between the two extended families, can be very complex.

Vignette: John and James

John aged 6 and James aged 4 are living with their mother. Their father is awaiting trial on a charge of actual bodily harm brought by his partner. He denies the charge and seeks residence on the grounds of his partner's instability and drinking and, in any case, contact.

John tells the court welfare officer that the father still visits the home, that he and Mum drink lots of cans and he is sent to bed but can hear shouting. He says his mummy (at his nursery) sometimes cannot walk properly. James is worryingly withdrawn. He has mentioned Mummy having a broken nose.

Implacable hostility

In assessing the impact on children, the following need to be considered:

- the child's wishes and views are almost certainly contaminated and that contamination is most likely to come from the parent with whom he or she resides: this amounts to emotional abuse;

FOURTH SESSION

- the differences in the two parents' reports may be so fundamentally at odds that it is very difficult to assess what the child's experience of the family and of life has been;
- allegations usually abound; these are always disputed;
- the parent with whom the child resides, usually his mother, may present as on the brink of breakdown as the result of their partner's previous traumatogenic behaviour, his applications or the court proceedings: differentiating a manipulative mother from one who may become so destabilised as to be unable to care for the child is often nigh impossible; the child is often caught up in this, being put in a position of needing to show dysfunctional symptoms in support of the mother or may be genuinely distressed about the situation and coping poorly;
- there are issues about how long the two parents are likely to keep up hostilities and how this will affect the child over time; against this, some contact orders are followed despite expectations to the contrary and the child does gain the right to access to both parents;
- one or both of the parents' behaviour is often highly traumatic or depriving to the child but, even when it can be established which parent is exhibiting the abnormal behaviour, this may not of itself determine the best options for the child as regards contact and residence.

Comment

If the outcome in such a case is to largely exclude one parent, careful consideration is needed as to how the reasons for this might be communicated to the child at some stage in her or his life. This could be a reason for a judgment so that there is a written record.

Disputed allegations

These often have many of the hallmarks of implacable hostility as described above.

Where the allegation is about the child, the child involved in assessing the allegation and the allegation later deemed to be false, then the accusing parent has effectively caused emotional abuse to the child. Where this has involved sexual allegations there may be secondary or indirect sexual abuse of the child, ie the child becomes inappropriately involved in sexual matters and/or focused on in a sexual way.

Sexual abuse allegations that are real do arise after parents separate. These usually emanate from the child rather than the parent and reflect the safer situation, post-separation, in which the child feels able to speak out.

Vignette: Lauren

Lauren is 5 years old. Her mother, one year after separating from Lauren's father in acrimonious circumstances, alleges that the father is masturbating himself by having Lauren on his lap and has been inserting things into her vagina. She repeatedly tape records discussions between herself and Lauren.

These do not appear suggestive, nor does Lauren say anything negative about her father when first interviewed by the police. When interviewed six months later because her mother's allegations persist, Lauren seems very different, behaving coyly, making bizarre statements that could be seen as sexual but no allegations. The judge found that sexual abuse had not occurred but that Lauren was being emotionally abused by her mother.

Other disputed issues

There are many other disputed issues.

We assess the impact on children of two of these as follows.

Parental responsibility

The issue of parental responsibility usually affects the child only indirectly, ie his or her life will be affected by who has responsibility for the decisions in her or his life.

When children reach an age where they can begin to understand such issues, what is particularly bewildering is when a natural parent does *not* have parental responsibility.

Paternity including surrogacy and artificial insemination

The issues of paternity, including surrogacy and artificial insemination, can have a major impact on children not just through the implications of such issues but directly to the child in terms of what the information means to them, at the time or later.

Finding out that the man you believed was your father is not can be devastating; realising your mother must have had 'sex' with someone other than your 'father' can be very hard to accept; learning no one knows who your father or your genetic mother is can be destabilising; surrogacy challenges the very basic belief of children about coming out of your mother's tummy.

The handling of these matters cannot ignore the meaning for and the impact on the child.

Vignette: Sarah

Sarah was 12 years old. She had moderate learning difficulties. Her 'parents' had split up and her mother, who also had learning difficulties, was with an old boyfriend. The mother now said this was the father of Sarah and that the man, whom Sarah saw as her father, should not have contact. She sought DNA testing and had told Sarah about this.

Sarah told the child psychiatrist involved that she was very worried about people saying her 'father' was not her father and she did not want any blood tests. She could not explain why she did not, but had grasped that it could mean 'losing' the man she new as Daddy.

Breakdown in communication

Breakdown in communication is the sine qua non of cases reaching court with a residence or contact dispute.

Those divorces and separations where the two parents can communicate result in the parents mutually agreeing what arrangements are in their child's best interests.

Children whose parents have separated desperately need both parents to continue in their parenting roles and this is what can ameliorate the ill effects.

If parents cannot communicate over their child's progress and needs, and make flexible child-centred arrangements over contact, then the child will be the subject of emotional pressures, distress and the pain of divided loyalties.

Other types of contact disputes

Siblings

Siblings are very important in children's lives and offer children the opportunity of the longest lasting family relationships in their lives.

Studies of contact sought by adopted children shows that the commonest request is to trace siblings.

Knowing and having contact with siblings is important in many areas of development and particularly in relationship to identity formation and the development of a sense of shared origins and life story.

Grandparents

If there are disputes about grandparental contact, this almost inevitably relates to issues between the parental couple. Emotions and hostility may be less intense about the grandparents, in which case, such contact may afford a means, albeit a compromise, of keeping the child in touch with the family of the non-resident parent.

Parenting issues

A past history of child abuse or neglect and/or inadequate parenting is sometimes encountered in cases of separation and divorce. If children have continued to live with their parents, the assumption can be made that they are considered to be protected and that their needs have been adequately met. However, it may be that protection has been afforded by the presence of both parents.

New risks might, therefore, arise if one parent leaves and there is now proposed contact or residence with one of the parents alone. This particularly applies to child sexual abuse, or severe mental illness, where the other parent has been the protecting person. Physical abuse and neglect may have arisen during times of stress within the family. Permanent separation and divorce, particularly if this leaves one parent to care for the child(ren) on his or her own, may reintroduce the risk of neglect or physical abuse. Or the absence of stress produced by the hostility of the two parents living together may reduce risk.

Like neglect, and unlike physical and sexual abuse, emotional abuse refers to integral aspects of the parent–child relationship rather than to an abusive experience or series of repeated events. Research has shown that the presence of an ongoing relationship with a non-emotionally abusive parent or close relative may afford some protection for the child from the worst effects of emotional abuse. Parental divorce or separation may remove this sustaining influence and benefit for the child.

A question, therefore, arises about what the likely effect will be of a permanent change in the family structure. In particular, it is important to ascertain what personal family and social resources will be available to the newly constituted family, both in residence and contact, and what new needs arise which, if not fulfilled, may once again place the children at risk.

Child indicators of concern

Reactive and adjustment disorders

Children are invariably affected by parental permanent separation and divorce. For a few children, the separation brings relief from intolerable tension and sometimes violence. For most children, there is at least some sadness, distress and anxiety. These feelings may be articulated explicitly. More often, they are expressed indirectly through physical symptoms such as bed-wetting or abdominal pain, manifested as behaviour problems, or there may be a deterioration in school attainments. These indicators of the fact that the children are being affected by the changes in their circumstances require attention. They can be lessened by honest, regular, explanations to the children, the affording of opportunities for the children to express their wishes and feelings, and by minimising their active involvement and recruitment into the parental differences.

These considerations notwithstanding, it cannot always be assumed that difficulties which a child shows in one or more domain of their functioning is related only to the fact and event of the divorce. It may well be that a child's difficulties are attributable to the effects of one or more of the parental factors described above, that the child continues to be adversely affected by the difficulties in the couple relationship, or that the effects of parenting difficulties and possible past abuse remain unresolved. It is therefore important to establish a profile of the child's functioning and the presence of difficulties in any of the five domains of:

    (1) emotional well-being (in particular, fears and anxieties, depression);
    (2) behaviour (in particular, attention-seeking, oppositional, withdrawn);
    (3) peer/social relationships (in particular, isolated, aggressive);
    (4) developmental/academic progress (in particular, under-achievement);
    (5) physical health (in particular, non-specific aches and pains, growth, wetting or soiling).

The presence of some of these difficulties can be reliably established by the use of the Strengths and Difficulties questionnaire. An indication of difficulties then calls for a determination of the duration of these difficulties and whether they are related to the current stressors or to previous parenting difficulties or adult issues.

There is, however, rarely an invariable or predictable relationship between causal events and experiences in a child's life on the one hand, and a particular resultant difficulty on the other. It is for that reason that a child's difficulties will be regarded as probably attributable to an experience rather than definitely caused by it.

Innate disorders

Some children have psychiatric disorders whose cause is not attributable to their environment such as learning disabilities, pervasive developmental disorders (autism and Asperger's Syndrome) or Attention Deficit Hyperactivity Disorder. These children are, nevertheless, particularly responsive to, and affected by, their care-giving environment. Such children may have particular difficulty in understanding the disruption to normal family life of separation and their own feelings and the feelings of those around them.

Particular difficulties are likely to be presented for a parent left alone to care for a child with a significant handicap with anger about their predicament and difficulties in coping. The role of the non-resident parent in such a situation needs careful consideration.

It is therefore particularly important that arrangements for changes in their care are managed in an optimal way. For these children, a consultation with their treating child psychiatrist or psychologist is indicated.

CONCLUSION

A change in the child's circumstances brought about by divorce both affords an opportunity for positive change in the child's life but may render the child more vulnerable to the effects of contact or care with a parent who continues to be troubled.

What remains unclear is who should be providing the court with the requisite information about the child's well-being. Section 37 reports (Children Act 1989) requested from social services may well be indicated for some of these children. The outcome of the present deliberations about the respective future roles of court welfare officers and guardians ad litem in family proceedings is keenly awaited.

REFERENCES

Amato P R and Keith B 'Parental divorce and the well-being of children: a meta-analysis' (1991) *Psychological Bulletin* 110, pp 26–46.

Block J H, Block J and Gjerde P F 'The personality of children prior to divorce: a prospective study' (1986) *Child Development* 57, pp 827–840.

Chase-Lansdale P L, Cherlin A J and Kiernan K E 'The long-term effects of parental divorce on the mental health of young adults: a developmental perspective' (1995) *Child Development* 66, pp 1614–1634.

Cummings E M 'Marital conflict and children's functioning' (1994) *Social Development* 3, pp 16–36.

Cummings E M and Davies P T *Children and Marital Conflict: The Impact of Family Dispute and Resolution* (Guilford Press, New York, 1994).

Cummings E M, Zahn-Waxler C and Radke-Yarrow M 'Young children's responses to expressions of anger and affection by others in the family' (1981) *Child Development* 52, pp 1274–1282.

Emery R E 'Family violence' (1989) *American Psychologist* 44, pp 312–328.

Fergusson D M, Horwood L J and Lynskey M T 'Family change, parental discord and early offending' (1992) *Journal of Child Psychology and Psychiatry* 33, pp 1059–1075.

Hetherington E M and Clingempeel W G 'Coping with marital transitions' (1992) *Monographs of the Society for Research in Child Development* 57, nos 2–3, serial no 227.

Jaffe P, Wolfe D, Wilson S and Zak L 'Similarities in behavioural and social maladjustment among child victims and witnesses to family violence' (1986) *American Journal of Orthopsychiatry* 56, pp 142–146.

FOURTH SESSION

Jenkins J M and Smith M A 'Marital disharmony and children's behaviour problems: aspects of a poor marriage that affect children adversely' (1991) *Journal of Child Psychology and Psychiatry* 32, pp 793–810.

McCloskey L A, Figueredo A J and Koss M P 'The effects of systemic family violence on children's mental health' (1995) *Child Development* 66, pp 1239–1261.

Shantz C U and Hartup W W (eds) *Conflict in Child and Adolescent Development* (Cambridge University Press, Cambridge, 1995).

Wallerstein J S, Corbin S B and Lewis J M 'Children of divorce: a 10-year study' in E M Hetherington and J D Arasteh (eds) *Impact of Divorce, Single Parenting and Step-parenting on Children* (Erlbaum, Hillsdale, 1988).

Zill N, Morrison D R and Coiro M J 'Long-term effects of parental divorce on parent–child relationships, adjustment and achievement in young adulthood' (1993) *Journal of Family Psychology* 7, pp 91–103.

Legal Services

FAMILY LAW PRACTICE IN ENGLAND AND WALES: THE FUTURE

Maggie Rae[1]

THE CURRENT POSITION

Solicitors and barristers undertake a form of training which is practically and academically based. Some of this training is common to both professions and some is separate, involving a mixture of examination work and on-the-job training. Once qualified, a lawyer (a term used here to encompass both solicitors and barristers), can practise in any area he/she chooses. So, by way of example, a law student who has chosen to specialise in shipping law and has during his/her training studied subjects applicable to that subject, could practise family law, a subject he/she has never studied, at least not in any depth.

After qualifying, solicitors must undertake a certain amount of post-qualification training each year. This system has now been extended to all solicitors, however long in the tooth they are! Solicitors can choose the courses they attend, and these do not have to be related to the subject in which they practise. For example, I, as a family lawyer, could choose to attend courses on French property ownership, a subject in which I am interested as I own a house in France.

Family lawyers have had and continue to have a poor public image. We are seen as confrontational, expensive and concerned to preserve a monopoly in relation to divorce work. There are also many complaints about our lack of competence. There are, undoubtedly, family lawyers about whom these complaints can justifiably be made. However, the profession is changing and has been in the process of doing so for some years now. The existence and continued success of the Solicitors Family Law Association (SFLA) is evidence of this. Recently, it has seemed that the Government has bought into the criticisms outlined above without recognising their limitations. For example, the way in which the Government introduced the Pilot Schemes for information sessions under the Family Law Act 1996, without any or only very scant involvement or consultation with family lawyers, appeared to indicate that it believed that family lawyers were likely to be opposed to clients or prospective clients receiving information from anyone but themselves. That is not true. Family lawyers know that a well-informed client is more likely to understand the process and we welcome that. I hope that most of us also recognise that we cannot do everything.

Family lawyers are also accused of stoking fires rather than of calming down them. Some undoubtedly do so but most do not and the accusation is not borne out by the evidence. A great many lawyers have now qualified as mediators, for example, and the Ancillary Relief Pilot Scheme was the brainchild of family lawyers. Both of these mechanisms have as their aim the reduction of conflict and its replacement with negotiated agreements.

Here, too, Government can help. It is dissapointing that the Government has delayed implementing Part II of the Family Law Act 1996 which would have introduced no fault divorce. Whilst the legislation was very complicated and may even have been unworkable, it introduced a much needed reform. The present system under which most divorce is brought on the 'fault' grounds is not fair and does nothing to reduce the level of acrimony between divorcing couples. There are too many examples of people being effectively coerced into divorce under the present system. It is to be hoped that the Government reintroduces this measure even though the Act may need to be amended to make it workable.

---

1   Maggie Rae, Solicitor, Clintons.

There is, however, one characteristic displayed by family lawyers which undoubtedly increases both the level of costs and the degree of animosity: the solicitors' letter. We do have to write letters. Too often though we litigate sensitive issues through correspondence and make matters a great deal worse as a result. Courts can and do give clear indications that such letters will not affect the outcome of cases and that they are to be deplored. It is a great pity that the practice continues to the extent that it does.

That said the system suffers I think from a number of defects which I set out below.

LACK OF SPECIALISATION

A great deal of family work is done by solicitors who are not specialists. The Law Society's Children Panel has done much to reduce the opportunities for non-specialist solicitors to practise in public law cases. If exclusive contracting comes in, it seems that the Legal Aid Board will require solicitors' firms applying for contracts to have at least one person in the firm who has a family law accreditation from The Law Society or SFLA schemes. The SFLA plans to publicise the names of those who are accredited, as will The Law Society, and solicitors will be able to publicise their acquisition of accreditation too. This is likely to encourage work away from general practitioners into the hands of family law specialists.

Exclusive contracting is also likely to lead to a reduction in the number of firms practising family law and to larger firms. This will almost certainly mean greater specialisation.

This will not mean, however, that solicitors without accreditation will be prevented from doing family work which is not subject to the requirements imposed by The Law Society or the Legal Aid Board.

Family law is a specialist subject and the profession as a whole needs to recognise this more widely and make that view clear to the public.

TRAINING

The training offered to those who study family law has changed greatly over the last decade. It is more practically based than hitherto, for example.

Despite these improvements, I would argue that it has a long way to go before it can be said to address the training needs of family lawyers. Like many solicitors, I have recently trained as a mediator and found the training of enormous help in daily practice. In particular, I received training in the mediation course in subjects which are simply not yet part of the normal training for solicitors. These included dealing with anger, investigating the research into family breakdown, negotiating and facilitating others to do so, an emphasis on face-to-face contact and against the habit of letter-writing to which solicitors often seem wedded and, most importantly, an emphasis on keeping the interests of children to the forefront. Additionally, many mediation courses stress the importance of ongoing support and supervision and the formation of buddy groups where participants can give help to each other. I think those in charge of our professional training could learn a great deal from this. These skills are extremely important to the good practice of family law.

ENCOURAGING NEGOTIATION

The Ancillary Relief Pilot Scheme (which will be implemented throughout England and Wales from June 2000) encourages negotiated settlements and provides a mechanism through which the court can actively assist in the process through the Financial Dispute Resolution appointment.

The Family Law Act 1996 has now been partly shelved by the Government and may never be brought into force. However, some parts of the Act have been brought into force and will continue. This includes an emphasis, where legal aid is sought, on encouraging the couple to attend mediation to sort out their problems.

Mediation is relatively new in the UK and is an option that most couples choose not to take up. There has been a significant increase in the numbers of solicitors qualifying as family mediators and specialist courses are run by the SFLA and Family Mediation.

Many family lawyers, though, are still resistant to the idea of mediation, seeing it as a threat to their livelihood. This is a mistake in my view since, in most cases, the couple will need both lawyers and mediators. It also seems that divorcing couples want the security of their own lawyer even if they choose to seek the assistance of mediation. There is also a reluctance by many clients to try mediation, often driven by a fear that the process will force them to agree to arrangements against their interests. It is therefore a process that has a long way to go before it becomes an integral part of our culture.

The mediation training I have outlined above also, I believe, gives solicitors more confidence in undertaking negotiation. It is still, however, hard to persuade many lawyers to try this approach. Better training and judicial encouragement could go a long way towards resolving this. Matters are not helped by the confusing application and interpretation of our discretionary system set out in s 25 of the Matrimonial Causes Act 1973. Experienced specialist practitioners can often find advising clients on quantum a difficult task. For those who are less experienced or specialist, the task can seem insuperable. It is even more difficult for lay clients.

The Government indicated a wish to reform the position. For the most part, the legal profession seems to want to continue with the present scheme. In my view, s 25 does lack the clarity that I believe people are entitled to expect and we as lawyers should think hard about reform.

THE ROLE OF OTHER PROFESSIONS

Many family lawyers acknowledge that others have a vital role to play in the resolution of family disputes. However, many do not. There are great disparities in the extent to which solicitors refer clients to counsellors, therapists and others who will often have a great deal to give. There is also still a tendency for solicitors to believe that they are the only people who matter in such situations. The training offered to mediators addresses this and needs to be more widely adopted.

There are also few opportunities for those engaged in work with families to understand and recognise the value of different professional roles and skills. This is something which can and should be addressed by all of us. It is heartening to see that the SFLA now offers training courses that frequently involve those from other disciplines. There is still a great deal to do here.

CONCLUSION

This is a time of transition. The changes we have seen and those proposed point to a move towards greater specialisation and concentration of family law work. As consumers of the service we provide become better informed, they will, I hope, be better able to make informed choices about the lawyers they choose. In turn, family lawyers will be expected to demonstrate higher levels of expertise than has hitherto been the case.

PART II OF THE FAMILY LAW ACT 1996 POSTPONEMENT – THE IMPETUS FOR CHANGE

Iain Hamilton[1]

Mr Hamilton *emphasised that there were considerable practice implications for family law solicitors, based on the knowledge and experience gained through the pilots and discussion, which could be discussed irrespective of whether Part II of the Family Law Act 1996 was implemented. Such changes (introduced by rule changes) could have a significant impact on this field. He posed four questions for consideration.*

(1) **Parenting Plans**
    Should they be implemented and their use made compulsory by those giving advice and information to those parents with children seeking divorce?

(2) **Should the use of Protocols be encouraged?**
    Mr Hamilton expressed the view that a protocol for divorce and children matters (including consideration of matters such as saving saveable marriages, providing information on mediation and marriage support services) would provide a vital focus on the relevant issues for those practising in this field.

(3) **Teaching of Family Law**
    Should this include some teaching on family dynamics and issues relating to child development on an inter-disciplinary basis?

(4) **Inter-disciplinary Training**
    The view was expressed that, if a decision to implement Part II is made, there was a need for a national programme of inter-disciplinary training similar to that introduced before implementation of the Children Act 1989.

INTRODUCTION

The decision of the Lord Chancellor to postpone implementation of Part II of the Family Law Act 1996 is one to be welcomed. It provides the opportunity for all those involved in the provision of services to families and children upon marriage breakdown to evaluate and reconsider their roles. It allows for reflection within the context of knowledge and experience gained through the implementation of the different pilot projects undertaken in relation to Part II.

One of the principal outcomes of the pilot projects, from a practitioner's perspective, is the fact that assisting families and children in relation to the resolution of issues which arise on marriage breakdown can no longer be seen as being the sole province of lawyers simply because it is litigation-based. The involvement of different professionals and organisations in the pilot projects relating to provision of divorce information and mediation has underlined that. The importance of the role of other professionals in the divorce process has been further highlighted by the discussion and debate generated in relation to the Family Law Act 1996.

There has been a significant shift in the perception of the range of services family lawyers should be able to provide and the way in which marital litigation should be conducted. An example of this is willingness of the legal profession to undertake training in mediation in response to the development of mediation services promoted by the provisions of Part II.

This paper does not seek to address whether or not Part II should be implemented nor to analyse what may be regarded as being the obvious benefits or deficits of the provisions of Part II. The paper is optimistically premised on the basis that, whatever decision may be made by the Lord Chancellor in relation to Part II and its implementation, the commitment to the introduction of 'no fault divorce' will be maintained. It advocates that the opportunity should be taken to build on lessons learnt during the past two years about the conduct of marital litigation, particularly where there are children involved,

---

1   Iain Hamilton, Solicitor, Jones Maidment Wilson, Manchester.

with a view to changing and improving the service which the legal profession offers to children and their families upon marriage breakdown. Suggestions for change are made relating to matters which, if there is the will to change, can be implemented now irrespective of the decision awaited in relation to Part II.

INTER-DISCIPLINARY TRAINING AND CO-OPERATION

The experience of the pilots has underlined the need for inter-disciplinary understanding and co-operation in providing appropriate support and services for families at the time of marriage breakdown. The perceived failure of the pilots may well be in part attributable to the failure of family law practitioners to recognise and promote the benefits of such services. While this may have been fuelled by the perceived threat to their role as gatekeepers of the divorce process, it is arguable that lack of knowledge and understanding about the process of divorce information giving and the mediation process contributed significantly to the failure.

The abandonment of fault-based grounds for divorce and its replacement by a framework for time-based no fault divorce requires practitioners to adopt an entirely new conceptual and philosophical base if they are to be effective in providing sound advice, assistance and representation to clients in the future divorce process. If they are to provide competent and well-informed advice, practitioners will be required to be able to embrace, accept and promote the philosophy of 'no fault'. The same is true of both the judiciary and the Bar. This will provide an enormous challenge to practitioners in relation to how they think about and practice marital litigation. Many family law practitioners remain sceptical about the advantages of 'no fault divorce', the provision of divorce information and mediated settlements or agreements in relation to children and money. New attitudes and understanding will not come overnight and arrive on the dawn of whatever day Part II or its successor is eventually to be implemented. If such scepticism and lack of knowledge is to be overcome, the profession needs to ensure that those who practice family law have proper opportunities for education and training about the essential processes which are central to the application of the provisions of Part II or its successor.

Solicitors are not well prepared for the practice of family law upon qualification. Teaching and training in family law does not currently embrace any requirement to have any knowledge or understanding of the complexities of family dynamics or the impact which the breakdown of emotional relationships might have on the psychological functioning of clients or the children caught up in the process. This is an area which has been neglected by The Law Society, family law practitioners and the academic institutions which provide qualifying courses for solicitors. No one who has significant experience of advising, counselling or representing persons involved in separation and marriage breakdown underestimates the importance of the complexity of the emotional states which those who are involved in the divorce process may undergo, or the extent to which their emotional state might affect their behaviour and their ability to make both choices and decisions. The inter-disciplinary debate and discussion in relation to the question of marital litigation has highlighted just how important it is that family law practitioners should have much wider training than at present is required.

QUALIFYING AND POST-QUALIFICATION TRAINING FOR FAMILY LAWYERS

Teaching and training in family law should address as core issues the opportunity to gain some understanding in relation to family dynamics and psychological functioning as well as child development and welfare issues. Teaching on these issues should be incorporated into the family law options studied as part of the process of qualifying as solicitors. Any curriculum should also provide knowledge and understanding of the research information available as to the effects of separation and loss on children and the impact of marriage breakdown.

It is suggested that the post-qualification training required by those who will deal with divorce and private law children's cases should replicate some of that which is compulsory for Children Panel Solicitors in relation to public law cases. This should be developed on an inter-disciplinary basis to provide a broader perspective beyond the narrow focus of the litigation process. This should be supplemented by a continuing education requirement for all practitioners. The mechanisms to ensure that such continuing training is undertaken exist for solicitors within the scope of the accreditation requirements for The Law Society's Family Law Panel and the Solicitors Family Law Association's (SFLA) more stringent Family Law Panel. It remains unfortunate that the Bar has not yet adopted any similar scheme of accreditation for family law practitioners.

The revision of training requirements in the qualifying courses offered to solicitors is something which is likely to take time to address. The impetus for change is present. The challenge is to take it up and develop increasing opportunities for inter-disciplinary training now.

INTER-DISCIPLINARY TRAINING PROGRAMME ON IMPLEMENTATION OF PART II

If a decision is made to implement Part II of the Family Law Act 1996, it is hoped that the Government will recognise the need to provide a programme of inter-disciplinary training prior to implementation. The Children Act 1989 was heralded by a massive commitment to training almost every conceivable professional participant in the forensic and other processes involved. The changes which would be brought about by the full implementation of Part II of the Family Law Act 1996 are no less significant or wide ranging and will have an impact on the huge numbers of children who are caught up in the divorce process each year. The significance and benefits of such a programme of training are self-evident and will do much to promote an acceptance and understanding of the essential concepts and philosophy of 'no fault' divorce amongst professionals.

PARENTING PLANS

The parenting plans developed by the National Council for Family Proceedings for use in connection with some of the divorce information pilot schemes are without doubt one of the most helpful and useful documents to have been produced to assist parents to consider and address questions arising as to what arrangements need to be made for the child(ren) upon marriage breakdown. The booklets are short, clearly written in easily understood language and sensibly address almost every question which needs to be raised to enable parents to agree appropriate arrangements for their children. It provides a document which, if completed by discussion between separating parents, can be regarded as an 'agreed plan' as to the arrangements for the children at the time of separation. The range of issues covered, about which parents are encouraged to think, discuss and agree upon, if possible, is extremely wide. Helpful essential basic information about what children who are involved in marriage breakdown need when planning for their future is given. Useful facts about contact visits are set out and there is helpful information about the importance of communicating with children and, indeed, each other. The questions raised in the plan itself are set within the context of this information. The questions address specific issues relating to the basics of living arrangements, holidays, school and school activities, health, religion and cultural issues as well as other arrangements and finance. Examples of some of the questions raised include:

- how will you discuss discipline of the children; what is allowed and what is not?
- what days are special for your family or community?
- which friends and members of the wider family do your children want to stay in contact with?
- how will the school be informed of the children's changed circumstances?
- how do out-of-school activities fit in with contact arrangements?
- if a child requires urgent medical attention, how will you let each other know what is happening?
- what will happen to family pets?

These are all the sort of questions which are not addressed at present by many couples at the time of separating and tend to be dealt with when an issue arises. They can then become a source of conflict. They are questions which practitioners frequently never seem to think of asking when advising generally on issues relating to residence and contact. They are examples of issues which at present often seem to be raised at the last minute and, as practitioners, judges and court welfare officers will be painfully aware, are the sort of 'fine details' upon which agreements and arrangements in relation to residence and contact founder. The consequences can be unnecessary, expensive and often painful litigation which could have been avoided if the questions had been raised and considered at an earlier stage.

More important, however, is that the questions address issues which can be of great importance or significance to children and yet are frequently overlooked by adults when considering the broader concepts of residence and contact.

Every family law practitioner should be familiar with the contents of the parenting plan booklets. It is suggested that their use should be mandatory in providing advice and assistance on issues of residence and contact. Considerable benefits might be gained if it were to be made a requirement that, on any application being filed in relation to contact and residence, etc in connection with divorce, the solicitor issuing should certify to the effect that he has specifically considered and discussed with his client all the issues and questions raised in the parenting plan booklet. Experienced practitioners would confidently predict that, if practitioners were subject to such a mandatory requirement to use the parenting plans when advising clients, even where mediation has failed, a large number of applications might never need to be brought to court or, if they are, it will mean that the 'fine details' or 'loose ends' will not prove to be the rock upon which arrangements will founder. The mandatory use of parenting plans can be introduced independently of any question relating to the implementation of Part II. It could be effected by changes to the Family Proceedings Rules 1991. It is suggested that it should not be delayed.

THE 'OVERRIDING GENERAL PRINCIPLES' – PROMOTING CHANGE

The well-being of children and provision for their welfare upon the breakdown of marriage is one of the core principles underpinning the exercise 'by the court *and any person* of functions in consequence of Parts II and III' of the Act. Marriages should be brought to an end with 'minimum distress to the parties and to the children affected' and in a manner 'designed to promote as good a continuing relationship between the parties and any children affected as is possible in the circumstances'. There is also the specific obligation expressed at s 1(d) to remove or diminish any risk arising from domestic violence to both children and the parties to the marriage.

These principles are to be welcomed. They should be seen as having significant practice implications. Family law practitioners, both solicitors and barristers, must recognise that the way in which they represent the interests of their clients will be subject to these 'overriding general principles'. No longer should they be able to claim that they are 'simply acting on instructions' when pursuing a course which may be to the detriment of the children. It is to be hoped that the court will play an active part in encouraging a proper and sensitive approach to the resolution of issues within the context of proceedings by visiting those who transgress with appropriate sanctions.

Some may argue that such an approach should not be necessary because family law practitioners have for many years adhered to those principles when acting for and advising clients. The SFLA has done much to promote a sensitive and conciliatory approach by its members to the advice and representation they provide for clients with an emphasis on consideration to the welfare of children of the family.

However, whilst the majority of SFLA members adhere to this Code of Practice, it is widely acknowledged that there are some who do not. It also has to be recognised that not all solicitors who practice family law are members of the SFLA (membership is approximately 4,500). A significant number of those who profess to practice family law do so without adhering to any credo or Code of Conduct other than that they are required to act in accordance with their client's instructions. Such practitioners create inordinate difficulties for families and their children, which include increasing acrimony, incurring unnecessary costs and creating delays in the issues being resolved. The existence of the 'overriding general principles' provides a real opportunity for the courts to exert some control over the conduct of marital litigation and the manner in which it will develop for the future. If sanctions are applied to those who fail to act in accordance with the principles, this will be a very positive step to be welcomed by all.

CHILDREN UNDER PART II – POTENTIAL FOR EXPLOITATION

Part II of the 1996 Act provides a framework for time-based no fault divorce which, where there are children of the family under the age of 16, means that, once a decision to divorce has been made by either or both of the parties to the marriage, they will have to wait a period of 80 weeks before a divorce order can be granted. The question arises as to what will happen during this period?

FOURTH SESSION

It is clearly intended that marriage counselling, other marriage support services, mediation and legal advice should come into play since no divorce order may be granted unless the parties comply with the requirements of s 9 of the 1996 Act which include being able to satisfy the requirements of s 11 in relation to the children and their welfare.

What if the parties or one of them is not prepared to wait? Are they likely to resort to seeking occupation or non-molestation orders to take advantage of the provision in s 7(12)(a) which removes the six-month extension of the period for consideration and reflection where there are children aged under 16 and such an order is in force? Section 7(12)(b) also enables the six-month extension to be avoided if the 'court is satisfied that delaying the making of the divorce order would be significantly detrimental to the welfare of any child of the family'. How are solicitors who are instructed to pursue such applications to respond?

Section 10 of the 1996 Act provides for an 'order preventing divorce' on the basis of hardship which can be 'financial or other hardship to the other party or to a child of the family.' It is open to speculation as to the extent that reliance might be placed on arguments relating to the interests of the children as a basis for preventing the divorce order being granted. The previous 'hardship' bar to divorce based on financial hardship has featured little in litigation under the Matrimonial Causes Act 1973. The test under s 10 is very much wider and clearly capable of being exploited as a litigation tool by those who are implacably opposed to divorce or who may wish to argue it for tactical purposes.

Section 11(2) gives the court the power to direct that a divorce order may not be made until the court orders otherwise where it is likely to exercise its powers under the Children Act 1989 relating to any child of the family but is not in a position to do so without giving further consideration to the case and there are exceptional circumstances making it desirable in the interests of the child to make such an order. The court is required to treat the welfare of the child as paramount in considering whether the circumstances of the case are likely to require it to exercise its Children Act powers. Is this likely to become a tactical tool which parties will wish to employ to seek to gain an advantage in the resolution of financial issues?

The provisions in ss 7(12), 10 and 11(2) clearly have the potential for creating a whole new area of jurisprudence relating to children and divorce. They have potential for being used as a genuine basis for either expediting or delaying the divorce process. Equally, however, each has the potential for being abused and being applied as a tactical device as a means of disrupting the divorce process or with a view to securing a strategic advantage in the resolution of other issues such as finances. Unhappily, the provisions of s 11(4)(b) relating to conduct of the parties will be brought into play in relation to these types of applications. This will provide the opportunity for those who wish to do so, to engage in hostile and vitriolic litigation, which is corrosive and undermines relationships with children and undoubtedly has an adverse impact upon them. These are areas of potential work which solicitors will undoubtedly be actively encouraged by their clients to explore and may replace some of the contact and residence cases which will be absorbed in and resolved by the mediation process.

Similarly, s 29 of the 1996 Act prevents a person being granted legal aid for 'proceedings relating to family matters' unless they have attended a meeting with a mediator to determine whether or not mediation is more appropriate. These provisions do not apply to applications under Part IV of the 1996 Act relating to domestic violence and occupation orders. There will be clients who will wish to take proceedings in order to obtain orders in respect of their children who will be unable or unwilling to participate in mediation if that can be avoided. The question arises as to whether this will result in an increase in applications under Part IV of the 1996 Act for which legal aid will not be restricted as a means of being able to invite the court to deal with issues relating to children sooner rather than later in the divorce process.

DIVORCE PROTOCOL – ENCOURAGING THE PACE OF CHANGE

The problems in relation to litigation involving children outlined above are just some of the potential difficulties which will have to be faced if Part II is implemented in its present form. Human nature will not change as a result of the implementation of Part II nor will the solicitor's duty to his client be affected until there are proceedings before the court when the implications of the 'overriding general principles' can be brought to bear. What can be done to avoid solicitors and their clients exploiting the above provisions and to ensure that the approach required by s 1 is encouraged and promoted?

It is suggested that the solution to some of the potential problems referred to could lie in the development of a divorce protocol along similar lines to the pre-action protocol for personal injury claims or the clinical negligence protocol which now apply as part of the Civil Procedure Rules 1998. There is already a proposal for an ancillary relief protocol to accompany the implementation of the new ancillary relief rules due to come into effect later this year.

A divorce protocol would be a means of promoting and encouraging the application of the 'overriding general principles' in s 1 in relation to advice and assistance given to clients by solicitors before proceedings are commenced. It would provide a means whereby solicitors could be required to provide and promote information about seeking help from appropriate agencies where there is some prospect of the marriage being sustained. There could be included a mandatory requirement for solicitors to provide clients with prescribed divorce information at first interview and, where there are children involved, a copy of the parenting plan booklet. Other issues, which could be covered, include provision of information in relation to mediation, screening for domestic violence, the conduct of the divorce and pre-action issues in relation to children.

If a divorce protocol can be developed and implemented, it should operate in the same way as the Civil Procedure Rules 1998 so that the standards set would be treated as the normal reasonable approach to the conduct of marital litigation. If proceedings are issued, the court should decide whether non-compliance with the protocol should merit adverse consequences.

It is suggested that a protocol, which has some 'teeth', may be an effective way of addressing what have been seen as some of the shortcomings of family law practitioners in the past. A protocol can be developed and implemented independently of any decision in relation to the implementation of Part II and yet can bring into play in a realistic and practicable way much of what Part II was intended to achieve.

CONCLUSION

Much has been learnt during the past two years about the services which families involved in marriage breakdown need. Lawyers have been under threat by being displaced from their traditional role of gatekeepers to the divorce process. The decision to postpone the implementation of Part II of the Family Law Act 1996 no doubt came as a great relief to many family law practitioners. Many may hope that Part II will simply disappear whilst others may hope that the Lord Chancellor will take the opportunity to amend some aspects of Part II which are identified as being unworkable.

There are few commentators who challenge the potential benefits of 'no fault' divorce or the change to the conceptual and philosophical framework for the practice of litigation on marriage breakdown which Part II provides. It is difficult to foresee within the current political climate whether or when Part II might be implemented or in what form. The suggestions for change addressed above can all be implemented independently of whatever fate might lie ahead for Part II. Postponement of the decision to implement has provided an impetus for change which it is hoped that those responsible for the development of family law policy, the training and recruitment of solicitors and the administration of family justice will be prepared to support and encourage in practicable and achievable ways.

FOURTH SESSION

THE IMPLICATIONS OF THE FAMILY LAW ACT 1996 FOR THE CHILDREN PRACTITIONER – WHOSE DIVORCE IS IT ANYWAY?

Peggy Ray[1]

*In considering the question of the child's voice in legal proceedings, **Peggy Ray** raised three points as central to the question:*

(1) **Information**

It was clear that children needed and wanted more information on divorce. She raised the possibility of children who have been through the process of a parental divorce talking about their experiences (eg in a leaflet) as a way of communicating to divorcing parents some of the concerns likely to be faced by their children;

(2) **How we view children in the divorce process**

The suggestion was made that one might consider every child involved in a divorce as a potential 'child in need' (as defined in s 17 of the Children Act 1989). Her proposal was that, on filing of a statement of marital breakdown, there would be a referral to the Unified Family Court Welfare Service and a case worker allocated to the child throughout the divorce process. There could be an initial appointment to see the child and then sporadic visits from time to time, as appropriate. She suggested that this might be seen as a supportive service, similar to the way in which parents viewed health visitors;

(3) **Getting the child's voice before the court**

Continuing the idea of allocating each child a caseworker, Ms Ray suggested that the caseworker could help the child go through the parenting plan and, perhaps, take back the child's views to the parents. Ultimately, she would like to see a situation where the caseworker would be asked to assist the child to endorse the parenting plan at the end of the s 11 process. There would then be a 'review' of the parenting plan by the caseworker six months after the plan had been endorsed (similar to the use made of six-monthly reviews in care proceedings, where the child's voice is heard far more). There could also be a referral mechanism back to the court if the plan had not worked out satisfactorily. Such an approach, in Ms Ray's view, would come much closer to meeting the needs of children to have their voice heard before the court.

INTRODUCTION

Despite the uncertainties in relation to the implementation of Part II of the Family Law Act 1996, it is still a useful exercise to consider whether the new legislation would materially affect the experience children have of divorce. It may be a requirement under the Act for solicitors to advise their clients to consider their children's welfare, *wishes and feelings*[2] (my italics).

At present, under the Matrimonial Causes Act 1973, there is no requirement that the court considers the wishes and feelings of any child involved, and the current prescribed statement of arrangements form makes no reference to a child's views of the proposals made by the parents. Under the Family Law Act 1996, the wishes and feelings of the children of the family are brought directly and immediately into the divorce process. This is reflected in Part I of the Family Law Act 1996 which establishes the principles underlying the Act[3] and by the introduction of the paramountcy principle into the court's considerations of the proposed or actual arrangements for the children prior to the making of a divorce order.[4]

However, what impact this will make in practice, if implemented, is uncertain. It is a time when children's needs and concerns can be easily overlooked. My concern is that the obligations which may be placed on legal advisers under s 12 of the Family Law Act 1996 will be treated by many in the same

---

1   Peggy Ray, Solicitor, Goodman Ray.

2   Family Law Act 1996, s 12(2)(iii).

3   Ibid, s 1(c)(i) and (iii).

4   Ibid, s 11(3).

way as the current requirement to certify whether or not the possibility of a reconciliation has been discussed.[1]

WHAT DO WE KNOW ABOUT CHILDREN'S EXPERIENCES OF DIVORCE NOW?

The research material set out in the accompanying papers confirms what many of us rely on as 'home truths' and which, in my personal experience, are often themes brought up by children I see who are in the current divorce process.

Children often feel responsible or guilty for the breakdown of their parents' relationship. We know that there is often a risk of the child being overburdened, becoming an inappropriate confidante to a distressed parent, or an unsuitable mediator between parents. The child as ally in court proceedings is known to all of us, and another difficult dynamic to untangle. These are examples of children being put under a great deal of pressure and anxiety, not by 'bad' parents, but by parents who, for a period, find it impossible to function well as parents and who can become overwhelmed by their own feelings of loss, failure and distress.

What are the implications for children caught in this process? A child may be living with tension and/or violence while (often on the advice of the lawyers) their parents remain together until financial arrangements are sorted out. It is the parents' imperative, which sustains this period often over many months. The emotional violence/abuse/harm to which these children may be exposed during the period of parental conflict is likely to be chronic and as damaging as physical violence.

In the short term, these children may lose developmental progress. They are likely to be exhausted by the uncertainty of their circumstances, the need for constant vigilance to confirm how Mum and Dad are in the absence of any concrete information, and subsequently caught or mesmerised by this preoccupation.

The other risk faced by many of these children is that of 'muddle'. Professor Christina Lyon, Edward Surrey and Judith Timms, in their research on support services for children when parental relationships break down[2] confirm children's overwhelming desire for information when parents divorce: 'All the evidence shows that children suffer from being protected by adults.'[3] Many parents state that they are delaying or avoiding talking to their children on the premise that it is better not to tell them anything until arrangements are definite. However, it is likely that children are well aware when hostility has broken out at home, however hard the parents may try to limit its expression in front of them.

The effect of this is that a child may see one thing while being told another or not being told anything at all. They may begin to doubt the validity of their own experience. This could lead to a loss of confidence in their own ability to make connections between what they experience and what they know. If this goes on for very long without accurate information, it can have an impact on the development of their own abilities to make secure relationships as they lose trust in their own sense of what they experience. It is important for professionals to be sensitive to the fact that children are vulnerable during this time in their lives.

THE NEW PROCESS: WILL IT SUIT CHILDREN BETTER?

The information meeting

Before a party can take any steps to dissolve the marriage legally, they must attend an information meeting.[4] I understand that some work has started on information being made available to the children of the family. One of the strongest messages which comes from the research is that children feel acutely the lack of information about their situation. The Lyons, Surrey and Timms research indicates that information may need to be gender sensitive as the female respondents to their study reported to have

---

1   Matrimonial Causes Act 1973, s 6.
2   Lyon, Surrey and Timms *Effective Support Services for Children and Young People when Parental Relationships Break Down – a child centred approach* (University of Liverpool, 1998).
3   Ibid, see p 171.
4   Family Law Act 1996, s 3(1)(b).

been more affected by contact problems than the males.[1] Ideally, material could be given to and discussed with children by both parents. I also suggest that some thought is given to the idea of a leaflet or other form of information being drafted by children for parents recounting the more common feelings children have during divorce. This could provide parents with direct information they may not be in a position to hear from their own children. This is an area where professionals can significantly help both children and their parents understand the process of separation and divorce.

The statement of marital breakdown

The 1996 Act provides that the divorce process will be commenced with the filing of the 'Statement of marital breakdown'. There is no fault-based ground on which the statement is to be based; an assertion that the party filing believes the marriage has broken down is sufficient. The fact that there will be a statement of 'bald' marital breakdown in the legal process is helpful to the courts and to the adults in terms of litigation but I wonder if it will affect the conversation and feelings swirling around the breakfast table?

The Act does provide for the *joint* filing of the statement of marital breakdown.[2] This is a significant change from the current position of having one parent petition the other parent even in those cases of a mutually agreed separation of two years. It affords much more scope for children to understand that both parents have agreed to part. One hopes that parents could also approach the proposed arrangements for the family on a more constructive basis. It is the one change which truly reflects, in my view, the 'no-fault' reality of the divorce order, *if* it is accompanied by an accurate explanation by the parent(s) to the child of why the divorce has happened. A risk of the 'no fault' divorce is that the child may believe that there could equally be a 'no fault' breakdown of the parent–child relationship which could jeopardise the child's security in the maintenance of those relationships. If Mummy can stop loving Daddy, she could stop loving me.

The period of reflection and consideration

The length of the period

Parties to a marriage are to reflect and consider for a period of nine months and 14 days, or if there are children aged under 16, for a period of 15 months and 14 days. It is likely that children will worry while their parents reflect. There is an interesting conflict between the Children Act 1989 which states as one of its underlying principles, that delay is prejudicial to the interest of the child,[3] and the Family Law Act 1996 which establishes as a presumption that those marriages in which there are children should be dissolved much more slowly than those without,[4] regardless of the particular facts of each case and whether satisfactory arrangements have already been made by the parents.

What will be going on for the children of a family during this period? Parents are likely to be negotiating or litigating over the financial arrangements, and applications under the Children Act 1989 may also be made. In addition, it will be open to a party to make an application for the extension of the period not to apply if the court is satisfied that 'delaying the making of a divorce order would be significantly detrimental to the welfare of any child of the family'.[5] The period can never be reduced to less than nine months. One can envisage the kind of litigation this provision may inspire. What is significantly detrimental? Is it that neither parent will leave the house voluntarily as they are respectively advised to stay put to protect financial interests, and the children are living in a continued and prolonged atmosphere of hostility? Is it the same as 'significant harm', a concept with which we are very familiar in the public law sphere and which is central to the operation of Part IV of the Act? Could the presumption not have been reversed to be consistent with the Children Act 1989? Why should the period of reflection and consideration be longer *unless* it is in the interests of the child? Any delay must be prejudicial as a general principle.

---

1   Lyon, Surrey and Timms, *Effective Support Services for Children and Young People when Parental Relationships Break Down – a child centre approach* University of Liverpool, 1998), pp 44–45.
2   Family Law Act 1996, s 6(3).
3   Children Act, s 1(2).
4   Family Law Act 1996, s 7(11) and (13).
5   Ibid, s 7(12)(b).

Mediation

During this period, the parties are encouraged to consider mediation. At present, it is rare for children to participate actively in the mediation process. Provision is made within the Act for there to be a code of practice which must include whether and to what extent children should be given an opportunity to express their wishes and feelings in the mediation. The mediator must be highly trained and be able to treat the child with respect as an individual who has as valid a contribution to make in the process in which he is involved as his parents. However, we are aware that the pilots report a very poor take up of mediation and this opportunity may not, in practice, be a real one. It remains unclear, therefore, whether, and if so, in what way, children may have more opportunities to have their views considered during the long months they wait before their parents are able to conclude the dissolution of the marriage.

It is not clear that there are sufficient safeguards to ensure an intolerable burden is not placed on the children of the family during this period.

The divorce order

No order for divorce will be made unless the court is satisfied that the arrangements for the children are such that they do not warrant the exercise by the court of its powers under the Children Act 1989.[1] The court will treat the child's welfare as paramount, and there is a form of welfare checklist,[2] which includes a consideration of the child's wishes and feelings. It is not clear how these will be ascertained, or whether the new prescribed form of statement of arrangements will provide a section for completion by a parent after a specific discussion with a child. 'Parenting plans' have been piloted with positive results.

The court also retains the power in exceptional circumstances to delay the making of a divorce order if 'it is in the interests of the child', or it is likely to be required to exercise its Children Act powers and is not in a position to do so immediately.[3] Again, it is of interest to note that the 'checklist' referred to above does not reflect the principle set out in s 1(2) of the Children Act 1989 that delay is prejudicial to the interests of the child. It does reflect a presumption in favour of continued contact with the absent parent but also includes reference to the risks which may face the child and which are attributable to the place the child is living (or proposes to live), any person with whom he is living (or it is proposed he will live) and 'any other arrangements' for his care. The conduct of the parties is a matter for specific consideration.

It is impossible to predict how s 11 of the Family Law Act 1996 will be interpreted in conjunction with s 1 of the Children Act 1989 when there are pending applications under the Children Act and the finalisation of the divorce may be inextricably linked, for example, in heavily contested contact proceedings. There is concern that applications under s 11 of the Family Law Act 1996 to bar the making of the divorce will or could be used for strategic purposes.

A PROPOSAL FOR THE SUPPORT OF CHILDREN

The State has accepted a mandate to become involved in the life of a family during divorce. Children are vulnerable during this process and may need a little or a significant degree of support from adults outside of their immediate family. Concepts from the public law sphere where the vulnerability of children, the identification of their needs, and the language of physical and emotional harm is in more common currency can be helpful in this context. Section 17(10) of the Children Act 1989 defines a 'child in need' as a child who is unlikely to maintain a reasonable standard of health or development without the provision of services, or his health or development is likely to be significantly impaired or further impaired without the provision of services, or he is disabled. The identification of a 'child in need' triggers a statutory duty to provide services by the local authority. A child undergoing divorce can be seen as a child in need, not in a 'child protection' sense, but rather as a child in need of support.

---

1 Family Law Act 1996, s 3(1)(c).
2 Ibid, s 11(4).
3 Ibid, s 11(2).

In this way, a service for children involved in divorce proceedings can be seen as a supportive service similar to the provision of a health visitor who visits every child born in this country. There are approximately 1 million births every year and each child is visited at least 2 or 3 times after birth. There are approximately 160,000 divorces annually of which 90,000 involve children under 16. The idea of a short-term focused engagement with a welfare professional was one of the innovative ideas under the Children Act 1989 in the form of a family assistance order. The proposal I put forward below is not without precedent. At this stage, these are preliminary ideas and I hope to be in a position to expand on them at a later date.

I suggest that on the filing of a statement of marital breakdown, a referral would be made to the new 'unified service' and a caseworker would be allocated. The caseworker would make arrangements to see the parents and children. That caseworker could remain allocated to the children throughout the divorce process. I depart from the view that access to the caseworker should be as requested by the parents. The research has highlighted that many parents do not recognise a child's need for information at this time. Once initial contact is made, I would suggest the caseworker is available if the child wishes to make contact but, in any event, makes sporadic visits throughout the 'period of reflection' to ensure that the child's interests are not lost. We who practise in the public law sphere have years of experience of those children who do not wish to see you – they communicate it very well – but the more common experience is as a welcome opportunity to seek information and to reflect on what is happening.

A VOICE IN COURT

I would also envisage a role for this caseworker to help the child participate in the formulation of the 'parenting plans' by the parents. Initially, my thoughts would be that the relationship between the child and caseworker would be a confidential one, with the caseworker acting as informal 'advocate'. The task would have to be well defined as it would not fall within the current tasks undertaken by court welfare officers or guardians ad litem, although well within the skills of both.

Again, to import a useful and well-known procedure from the public law sphere, something along the lines of 'child in care' review forms could be adapted to the current piloted 'parenting plan'. This would provide the child with an opportunity to record his views in writing, assisted by the unified service caseworker, on the arrangements proposed. I would not envisage a rigidly prescribed procedure. The information from the child/caseworker team could inform the parents' own negotiations in relation to plans for the future, usefully communicating the child's views to the parents through an independent professional.

Negotiated agreements could therefore include a section completed by the child, with the assistance of the caseworker. The parenting plan, so endorsed, would ensure that the child's voice is considered by the court as required by s 11 of the Family Law Act 1996, Article 12 of the United Nations Convention on the Rights of the Child and by Article 6 of the Convention for the Protection of Human Rights and Fundamental Freedoms.

Cases in which agreement over plans can not be reached would be litigated under the Children Act 1989 as they are now. I believe that, with the child's views having had a much more predominant role in the early stages, the litigation is likely to be more child focused than is often the case now. It is likely that it would be appropriate for a different caseworker to take on the 'court welfare officer' role in these circumstances, although a change of worker (from the child's point of view) would be undesirable. Issues of confidentiality would have to be worked through if the task for the caseworker were to change.

In exceptional cases, it is hoped that the implementation of s 64 will provide a child with the opportunity to be represented as a party in proceedings.

An allocated caseworker could also provide the court with an informed view of the child's best interests in those cases involving applications under s 7 (on an application for an order that the extension of the period of reflection and consideration do not apply) or s 11 (for an order that the divorce order be delayed).

Finally, I propose the caseworker from the unified service undertake a kind of 'check up' say 6 months after the divorce order, or any court order made in relation to the child. Arrangements could be 'tweaked' if necessary (outside the arena of the court) but there would be the power, if necessary, to refer the matter back to court. A relatively quick revisit of the arrangements made by a 'welfare professional' outside the court, could avoid problems becoming entrenched, while identifying at an early stage those cases in which the child's interests are not being met and a reconsideration is necessary before significant emotional damage is caused. It may just provide the flexibility which would avoid a return to the court in those cases where it is unnecessary and an early return to court where delay may make the problem a much more difficult one to resolve.

SUMMARY

I believe there are many positive features in the new legislation which could ensure a child's wishes and interests are not overlooked by both parents and professionals. There are also inherent difficulties. My concerns are primarily in relation to the period of reflection and consideration and the lack of any discretion to abridge that period. There is some scope within the Lord Chancellor's power to make regulations to improve on the current situation for children. The provision of information for children at the outset and ongoing through the divorce process is important. This was strongly promoted by the Children's Charities Consortium at the Bill stage.

Without information, it is difficult to see how the increased duties to ascertain and consider children's wishes and feelings will deliver a better experience of divorce for children. It is to be welcomed that the child's voice (in theory) is to be heard and it will be the responsibility of practitioners in all fields involved to ensure that this is facilitated. Listening to children in this way will make sense only if we understand more thoroughly what their experience of divorce is and recognise their part as members of the family in the divorce process. Providing children with a support service, including a mechanism to voice their wishes and feelings, to be heard by the court, and perhaps as importantly by their parents, would be a significant step in recognising that this is a process which involves them as much as their parents.

REFERENCES

Professor Christina Lyon, Edward Surrey, Judith Timms *Effective Support Services for Children and Young People when Parental Relationships Break Down – a child centered approach* (University of Liverpool, 1998).

Piper 'Barriers to Seeing and Hearing Children in Private Law Proceedings' [1999] Fam Law 394.

Sclater 'Divorce – Coping Strategies, Conflict and Dispute Resolution' [1998] Fam Law 150.

Cretney 'Lawyers under the Family Law Act' [1997] Fam Law 405.

FOURTH SESSION

THE JUDICIARY

THE NEW LAW OF DIVORCE: IMPLICATIONS FOR THE COURT

His Honour Judge Hamilton[1]

Judge Hamilton *explained how the courts on circuit are organised and noted that since the introduction of the Civil Procedure Rules 1998 each principal court had a designated civil circuit judge with a job description which requires him to compete with other judges, including designated family judges, for judicial resources. He lamented the fact that despite the introduction of the idea of the designated family judge in 1996, he was still without any definition of his role. The judge then went on to consider the impact on the family justice system if Part II of the Family Law Act 1996 were to be implemented. He posited the view that it was easy to think that 'no fault' divorce would automatically mean less litigation. However, the reality was that the divorce process envisaged by Part II would be likely to increase the amount of divorce litigation heard by circuit judges (eg on the question of the 'hardship defence'). The pressure on the family justice system's IT resources would also be greatly increased if one were to implement Part II and Judge Hamilton questioned the ability of the present IT arrangements to cope with the demands of implementation. In closing, the judge also noted that Part II would require a considerable degree of public education, which had not yet been properly done. The public at present were accustomed to the idea of a 'quick divorce' and it would not be easy to tell people that they would now have to wait for far longer periods to obtain their divorce. This would need to be addressed if Part II were to be implemented.*

EXPECTATIONS OF A DESIGNATED FAMILY JUDGE

Divorce under the Family Law Act 1996 is based on the same concept of irretrievable breakdown of marriage as divorce under the current law, dating back to the Divorce Reform Act 1969. The difference lies in the manner by which irretrievable breakdown may be proved. Under the current law, breakdown must be proved by one of five prescribed 'facts'; three of these connote fault: two of these fault-based facts (adultery and intolerable behaviour) provide the only means by which divorce can be sought at the point of breakdown, or perceived breakdown. The 1996 Act bases the finding of irretrievable breakdown on the passage of time alone and aspires to eliminate the element of fault.

One might expect the change to herald an easier life for both the administrative and the judicial functions of the court. First impressions may prove to be misleading.

Under the new law, the role of the court will commence when a statement of marital breakdown is lodged. Fourteen days after this, the period for reflection and consideration (which is at the heart of the system created by the 1996 Act) begins to run. The period is ordinarily nine months (s 7(3)) but:

(1) on joint notice from the parties it may be interrupted for an attempt at reconciliation requiring additional time (s 5(5) and (6)); and
(2) largely as a result of amendments made to the Bill in the House of Commons, s 7 contains a labyrinth of provisions which:
  (a) extend the period by operation of law in certain cases, but
  (b) exempt some of those cases from such extension, and
  (c) give the court discretionary powers in some cases to extend the period or, in others, to cancel an extension which would have taken place by operation of law.

Some of these extensions under s 7 come into force during the period of reflection and consideration: others take effect only on an application for a divorce order.

This is not the place to discuss the merits or even the substance of these provisions. I draw attention to them because, in effect, they require the court to generate and maintain in every case an accurate record

---

[1] HHJ Donald Hamilton, Birmingham County Court.

of the date upon which the period for reflection and consideration will expire. Without such a record, there is a real danger that divorce orders will be wrongly made or withheld.

It would not be appropriate to make junior clerical staff in the court office responsible for this record. The prescribed forms of statement of marital breakdown and application for a divorce order must be designed to draw attention to any factor which has the effect of extending the period for reflection and consideration but that alone will not deal with the other circumstances in which, by operation of law or judicial discretion, the period may be extended. The complexity of these provisions cries out for the use of a computerised case-record supported by a programme which, given the material information, will maintain an accurate record of the critical date as the case progresses.

Given such a record, the judicial workload in the divorce process itself seems likely to be reduced. No longer will it be necessary for the court to consider whether there is sufficient evidence of adultery or intolerable behaviour or whether the parties have really been living apart. There will still be a role for the judiciary, however, notably in dealing with attempts to prevent or delay divorce.

Section 7(4) confers on the court a discretionary power (exercisable on application by the recipient of a statement of marital breakdown) to extend the period for reflection and consideration where there has been 'inordinate delay' in service of the statement. It remains to be seen what delay will be considered to be inordinate but, in a few cases, the process to divorce may be significantly delayed: suppose, for example, that a statement is served only six months after it is lodged with the court. I would anticipate that applications under s 7(4) will be allocated to district judges.

Under s 7(10), where an application for a divorce order is made by one party, the other party may, without giving reasons, apply to the court within the prescribed period for time for further reflection and, provided that certain requirements are satisfied, the period for reflection and consideration will be extended by six months, regardless of the bona fides of the party seeking to delay the proceedings. This will not apply if an occupation order or a non-molestation order is in force in favour of the party applying for the divorce order or 'if the court is satisfied that delaying the making of a divorce order would be significantly detrimental to the welfare of any child of the family'. Again, in a few cases, this may give rise to contested hearings. In view of the role of child welfare, I anticipate that applications under this provision will be allocated to circuit judges and possibly also to district judges nominated to hear care cases who can already try contested applications under s 8 of the Children Act 1989.

A court cannot make a divorce order unless the requirements of s 9 (arrangements for the future) are satisfied. Deliberate delay in making such arrangements will not, ultimately, prevent a divorce but it could nevertheless be used to postpone it at least until the court can consider the matter. This may add to the number of applications for financial relief or for orders under s 8 of the Children Act 1989.

The provision which will generate most work for the judiciary, however, is s 10 which gives the court power to prevent a divorce if it is satisfied:

(1)   that dissolution of the marriage would result in substantial financial or other hardship to the respondent spouse or to a child of the family; and

(2)   that it would be wrong in all the circumstances (including the conduct of the parties and the interest of any child of the family) for the marriage to be dissolved.

This is not the place to consider this provision at length. No doubt, reference will be made to the similar provision of the current law, now contained in s 5 of the Matrimonial Causes Act 1973 (refusal of decree in five years' separation cases). There are three significant differences, however:

(1)   the hardship under s 10 of the 1996 Act need only be 'substantial' as opposed to 'grave' in the 1973 Act;

(2)   hardship to a child will suffice: the Government added this to the original Bill, apparently with the intention that the hardship should be objective hardship such as the need to sell a house adapted to meet the needs of a physically disabled child, rather than the child's distress;

(3)   Under s 5 of the 1973 Act, the court is required to dismiss the petition for divorce if it finds the conditions for this are satisfied: under s 10 of the 1996 Act, by contrast, the court is given a discretionary power in this circumstance to prevent a divorce: and this power will be exercisable in accordance with the general principles underlying Part II of the Act set out in s 1.

Section 5 of the 1973 Act is limited in its application (to five years' separation cases) and, even in the cases to which it applies, it has not proved to be a common means of preventing divorce. Section 10 of the 1996 Act, by contrast, is general in its application and less restrictive in its terms. It seems likely, therefore, that, in the small group of cases where one spouse feels that divorce is being imposed at the behest of the other, it will be more commonly effective. It is, therefore, likely to give the judges some work at least in the early years of the new law until it acquires a body of authoritative interpretation. Practice to date indicates that cases under s 10 are likely to be allocated to circuit judges, rather than district judges.

I close with a reflection on public attitudes to the new law when it comes into force. The public has become accustomed to think of divorce as a relatively speedy process. Commentators have suggested that there will be resentment at the new requirements to attend an information meeting and then to wait for a period of 12 or 18 months (the period for reflection and consideration preceded by a minimum of three months from the information meeting).

A court manager was being only slightly frivolous when she expressed to me her worry about the angry response which some spouses may display on being told of these requirements. I also have my own fear that a few spouses will be so affronted at the prospect of having to attend an information meeting that they will send 'deputies' in their stead. The court cannot make a divorce order unless it is satisfied that the requirements of s 8 about information meetings are satisfied. Rules made by the Lord Chancellor under s 12 of the Act will, I hope, contain a requirement for some sworn confirmation of the truth of the information given in a statement of marital breakdown. Other rules can impose a similar requirement on a spouse who is served with a statement of marital breakdown but has to show that he/she has attended an information meeting in order to make or contest an application with respect to a child of the family on relating to property or financial matters.

THE ROLE OF DISTRICT JUDGES UNDER PART II OF THE FAMILY LAW ACT 1996

The Senior District Judge, Gerald Angel

*The Senior District Judge, **Gerald Angel**, introduced his paper by reminding the conference that the present divorce procedure worked very well in practice: it was easily understood by litigants in person and was not really the subject of any major complaints. He noted that Part II of the Family Law Act 1996 was, in many ways, largely about procedure, and expressed the view that it had produced a very complicated procedural system for obtaining a divorce. He then took the conference through the step-by-step process which would be required to be undertaken by a district judge before a decree could be pronounced under Part II. In so doing, he admitted that he was attempting to demonstrate that the new procedure would be very difficult to administer and would take far longer for the district judge to complete. In answer to a question, the Senior District Judge estimated that, under Part II, he was clear that it would take a lot longer than at present and the whole process was likely to lead to many mistakes. His view was that the proposed procedure under Part II was so complicated that it might even be unworkable.*

Implementation of Part II of the Family Law Act 1996 is likely to lead to district judges playing no lesser role in marital proceedings than they do now in divorce and judicial separation cases. The prospect is that they will play a greater part.

At present, district judges deal with the interlocutory stages in all cases and in undefended cases they certify entitlement to the decree and pronounce it in open court. They consider the arrangements for children and approve consent 'ancillary relief' orders reflecting terms agreed between the parties for financial provision and property adjustment. The vast majority of contested applications for ancillary relief are determined by district judges. Under Part II of the Family Law Act 1996, perhaps even more of the process will be dealt with by district judges.

For the first time, there will be some general principles. These are stated in Part I of the Family Law Act 1996 and apply to Parts II and III. Thus, when dealing with cases, district judges will be required to have regard to these principles, namely that the institution of marriage is to be supported, parties are to be encouraged to take all practicable steps to save the marriage, marriages which have broken down should be brought to an end with the minimum distress to the parties and the children affected, at the same time promoting as good a continuing relationship between the parties and children as possible and without incurring unnecessary costs. The risk of violence is to be removed or diminished.

Marital proceedings, as they will be described, will be an entirely new type of matrimonial proceedings, not just in the way that has been publicised whereby 'quickie' divorce will disappear but in the whole concept of the proceedings. District judges will no longer be concerned to examine whether the particular state of affairs relied on to prove the irretrievable breakdown of marriage, for example whether adultery, 'unreasonable conduct' or separation for two or five years, is shown to exist at the date of the commencement of proceedings. What happened between the parties or the behaviour of one or other of them, however significant or important it may be to them, will not be directly relevant to the proceedings in the way it is now. For those of us who started when conduct conducing and condonation were an anxiety and when the suggestion of collusion was enough to threaten palpitations, these new proceedings are truly a different world.

The new regime, under which only during the course of the proceedings and then only by reason of meeting certain requirements as specified in the statute does entitlement to a divorce or separation order emerge, will present district judges with a fundamentally different type of case from existing matrimonial cases. Moreover, district judges will find marital proceedings much more complex than are matrimonial proceedings now. At the same time, marital proceedings will be set apart from the current trend to achieve swift conclusion of litigation. In this respect, they will be unlike applications, for example under the Children Act 1989 or 'fast track' proceedings under the civil procedure reforms where early conclusion of the case is the clear objective. In marital proceedings, a minimum period of not less than nine months (plus 14 days), will have to elapse in every case after the commencement of the proceedings as a prerequisite to entitlement to an order and no amount of case management by the court or anything else will effect a reduction of that period.

The Family Law Act 1996, s 3, expresses in simple terms the court's obligation to make a divorce or separation order if certain conditions are satisfied. Determining whether the conditions are met will fall to the district judge. Of the four conditions, only one of them is certain to be simple to decide; that is the formal one of there having to be an application for a divorce or separation order which has not been withdrawn. The second will be to decide whether the marriage has broken down irretrievably. For this, the district judge will have to ensure that the requirements of s 5 are met. Meeting the requirements of s 5 includes complying with s 6 (statement of marital breakdown) and completion of the period for reflection and consideration. This will require reference to s 7 (14 subsections) and to s 9 and to rules made under s 12. Thirdly, the district judge will have to be satisfied that the information meetings requirements are met (s 8). Fourthly, the requirements of s 9 about the parties' arrangements must be satisfied. Meeting the requirements of this section includes also those of s 11 (consideration of the welfare of children of the family), subject to the exemptions listed in Sch 1. For district judges and litigants alike, this journey is likely to be an intricate and sometimes frustrating journey. Apart, that is, from the complications which will arise if a spouse seeks and obtains an order preventing divorce under s 10.

In some cases, district judges may find themselves dealing with problems before proceedings are even commenced. Proceedings start with the filing of the statement of marital breakdown but, of course, it will have been necessary for the initiating party to attend an information meeting 'not less than 3 months' beforehand. That spouse having attended such a meeting, the other spouse may come to learn of it. That other spouse, faced with the prospect of marital proceedings, may decide to start disposing of assets or dealing with them so as to make them less readily available for distribution. Were that to happen now, as from time to time it does, application can be made to the court under s 37 of the Matrimonial Causes Act 1973 for an order to retrieve the position and for an injunction to prevent any further inappropriate dealings. In such cases, if there are no matrimonial proceedings in existence at the time of the application, commencement of proceedings forthwith or within a few days is invariably a condition imposed by the court. With Part II in force, the period which may have to elapse may be nearly three months. Hitherto, the passage of that sort of period before launching proceedings would have been regarded as quite unacceptable. Much may happen in those three months. An alternative possibility is that the spouse who has been to the information meeting is the one who decides to start disposing of the assets, putting the other spouse at a disadvantage. If the disadvantaged spouse then seeks an injunction urgently (no proceedings in existence), the court would have to be informed that he or she would not even be in a position to commence proceedings until attendance at an information meeting followed by a wait for three months.

The process after the filing of the statement of marital breakdown is not straightforward and will require considerable vigilance from district judges to ensure that the statutory provisions are complied with, and complied with within the period permitted. This latter period, the period beyond which the proceedings may not run, is in practice one year after the expiry of the nine months or (if there are children) the 15-month period for reflection and consideration. Contemporaneously, will be the settling of the parties' arrangements for the future.

The parties' arrangements for the future covers settling by agreement or otherwise financial arrangements and arrangements for the children. This latter aspect promises to be more significant than it has been. The court will be required to consider, as it does now, the arrangements for children of the family who are under 16 years of age and whether the circumstances of the case require it, or are likely to require it, to exercise any of its powers under the Children Act 1989. What will be new is the requirement for the court to have particular regard 'on the evidence before it' to the wishes and feelings of the child, the conduct of the parties in relation to the upbringing of the child, the principle that the welfare of the child is best served by regular contact with his parents and family and the maintenance of as good a continuing relationship with his parents as possible and then any risks to the child attributable to where or with whom he is living or will live or any other arrangements. The likelihood is that these provisions will increase considerably the investigation that has to be undertaken by the court, and hence by the district judge. Under this section, the court has the power in 'exceptional circumstances' to direct that the divorce or separation order is not to be made until the court directs otherwise. A spouse who is

THE
JUDICIARY

unhappy about the divorce may be tempted to use this as a way of delaying the making of a divorce order.

Then there is the resolution of the financial arrangements. When these are settled by agreement, that will be sufficient for the purpose of the proceedings. Where there is a dispute and mediation is unsuccessful in achieving a resolution, district judges will inevitably be involved in determining the dispute. The difference will be that, instead of these financial proceedings taking place and being resolved after decree, they will be taking place beforehand. In addition to the financial provision and property adjustment orders which can be made now, there will also be the power to make interim lump sum orders and pension-sharing orders. In addition to these contested cases, there will be those cases in which no settlement can be reached and application will be made to satisfy the court that one of the four exemptions in Sch 1 applies. Inevitably, district judges will be dealing with these applications, examining delay, obstruction, ill-health, injury, significant detriment to the welfare of a child or serious prejudice to the applicant, whether it has been impossible to contact the other party and, in cases where there is an occupation and non-molestation order, inability to reach agreement.

Then there are some other provisions with which district judges may have to concern themselves. Section 8(5)(b), which prevents a person who has not attended an information meeting from contesting an application made to the court with respect to a child of the family or some (yet to be prescribed) applications relating to property or financial matters, may give rise to some interesting cases.

Applications for orders 'preventing divorce' may come within the purview of district judges. They may also find themselves being required to deal with applications under s 9(3) for orders to facilitate the obtaining of a 'get'. The complicated provisions with regard to the length of the period for reflection and consideration include the power to prevent the six months' extension of the period where there is a child aged under 16, in cases where there is a non-molestation or occupation order and where 'delaying the making of the divorce order would be significantly detrimental to the welfare' of the child. District judges will hear these applications. Part II has much to keep district judges busy.

National Support Structures

Lord Justice Thorpe, His Honour Judge Hedley, District Judge Royall

*In opening the session, **Lord Justice Thorpe** noted that, although each of the three papers on national support structures had been written independently, there was very little difference between them: this perhaps indicated that the case for a national support structure within the family justice system was something on which all would agree. All three members of the judiciary who had written papers on this topic emphasised the importance of inter-disciplinary work in the family justice field. There was a collective role for the professionals involved in the family justice system to ensure that individuals involved in family proceedings received appropriate support for their particular needs. **District Judge Royall** expressed the view that it was important for any national structure to have a strong local base, allowing local professionals to have an imput on strategies for their particular area. This view was widely endorsed by the conference delegates and there was considerable support for the establishment of a national support structure with local committees. It was suggested that such a structure could build upon the excellent work done by the National Council for Family Proceedings, which as a small charitable organisation was inevitably limited in the scale of work it could undertake. There was unequivocal support for the suggestion that such a national structure should be established as soon as possible: it was not something that was dependent on implementation of Part II of the Family Law Act 1996.*

THE CASE FOR THE FAMILY JUSTICE CONSULTATIVE COUNCIL

Lord Justice Thorpe

INTRODUCTION

The purpose of this paper is to consider the need for a multi-disciplinary support network for the family justice system and how that need might be met. The title of the paper reflects the fact that the majority of those to whom I have spoken praise the work of the Criminal Justice Consultative Council (CJCC) and extol the benefits that it has brought to the criminal justice system. However, before considering the present needs of the family justice system, it would be useful to record in outline the relevant history.

THE PAST

Inter-disciplinarity on any significant scale arrived with the Children Act 1989. The steps taken by the government of the day to ensure the successful implementation of 'this wonderful legislative construct', to borrow the words of Stephen Cretney, included mixed training, the guarantee of a specialist judiciary at all levels and the creation of both business committees and service committees at each of the 50 care centres. With the advantage of hindsight, these essentially administrative arrangements can be judged an outstanding success. The business committees have proved a vital local facility for sharing problems and devising solutions in order to raise standards. The service committees failed to define their role and were in due course reinvented as forums. Part of the successful development of the business committees was their intercommunication and interdependence with the Children Act Advisory Committee so successfully launched under the chairmanships of Booth J and in due course Bracewell J. The Government's decision to terminate the advisory committee was widely regretted and criticised. Its dissemination of information and advice through its annual report and good practice guides had been widely appreciated. Similar intercommunication between the care centre forums and the annual inter-disciplinary circuit conference did not prove so fruitful. Over the past few years, a significant number of forums have either faltered or failed.

Partly to meet the criticism surrounding the termination of the Children Act Advisory Committee, in April 1997 the Lord Chancellor created the Advisory Board on Family Law which is now in its third year of successful operation and which has through its Children Act sub-committee published consultation papers on current policy issues in family justice.

At about the same time, the Lord Chancellor created the National Inter-disciplinary Forum as a representational and advisory body to promote inter-disciplinary co-operation in support of the information pilots at a national level, to consider reports from the local inter-disciplinary forums that supported the pilots, and to monitor the progress of the pilots. Within its membership, all the relevant professions and public services were represented. It met first in June 1997 and its latest meeting was in June 1999. Throughout that 24-month period, it has received reports from the research team led by Jan Walker and from the individual pilot projects that have been run in order to furnish the essential data for research.

Another recent arrival on the inter-disciplinary scene has been the National Convention of representatives from the business committees and forums. There have been two meetings to date and they have made a valuable contribution to developing a sense that we are all part of one uniform system rather than unconnected local cells.

THE PRESENT

Between the immediate past and the emerging present, I do not attempt to draw any clear boundary. Recent research conducted by the National Inter-disciplinary Forum establishes the vital effectiveness of the Children Act business committees. The state of the forums varies from dead and buried to alive and thriving. The causes of decline are as varied as human ailments. What is clear is that, where they have been the local focus of inter-disciplinarity, they have been hugely valuable and valued. I quote from a letter recently written by a consultant child psychiatrist to the Royal College of Psychiatrists:

> 'The family court forum ... has provided a very useful meeting place for social workers, mental health professionals, probation officers, magistrates, solicitors, guardians ad litem etc who work with young people who are in contact with the courts. We are still a long way from understanding each other's roles and function but meeting three times a year discussing matters of mutual interest in the welfare of children has contributed enormously to inter-agency joint working for the welfare of children.'

The principal task of the National Inter-disciplinary Forum has been successfully completed. The seven local pilots have concluded their trials. A report on the work of the National Inter-disciplinary Forum to date will shortly be published. In the meantime, the minutes of its meetings have been made available to the judiciary on FELIX. However, as local trials have reached completion the focus of debate has moved to the future. Further research demonstrates that all of the local inter-disciplinary groups remain in readiness and keen to participate in a multi-disciplinary launch of Part II of the Family Law Act 1996. The last meeting of the forum on 16 June confirmed this readiness in a lively debate of the issues which are at the heart of our conference theme. The Lord Chancellor's statement in Parliament on the following day came as a shock. His subsequent rationalisation focused on the same territory that we had surveyed, namely the pilots and Professor Walker's research. The interpretation of statistics from research may be necessarily subjective. I can only say that the Lord Chancellor's interpretation had not been perceived by our forum.

Obviously, the advisory board was equally unprepared for the Lord Chancellor's interpretation. At its meeting on 7 July, it, too, resolved that there were unanswered questions and issues unaddressed and that accordingly the chairman should seek clarification from the Lord Chancellor.

THE FUTURE

I turn from this uncertain present to consider our future goals and objectives. My own reaction to the Lord Chancellor's deferral is that our need for a fully identified and structured multi-disiplinary network to support the family justice system is immediate and in no way dependent upon the implementation of Part II of the 1996 Act. Of course, implementation without such a network would be foolhardy but it does not follow that the creation of the net can safely be deferred until the present political indecision is resolved. The promotion of good practice through inter-disciplinarity should no longer be dependent on a single charity, the National Council for Family Proceedings, and a number of unrelated and hesitant government trials. The family justice system deserves better, primarily because the quality of its function affects more and more people as relationships increasingly founder and as the need for child protection grows. The criminal justice system has its consultative council and I have taken my title from that obvious parallel. So what are the aims and objectives of the CJCC? The following statements are taken from its Summary of Activities 1997–1998:

'It aims to achieve the level of communication, co-operation and co-ordination amongst the component services necessary to advance a successful and respected criminal justice system. The council's role is to facilitate discussion and agree action across the criminal justice system.'

The work of its subordinate area committees is thus described:

'The area committees aim to promote better understanding, co-operation and coordination in the administration of the criminal justice system. Their terms of reference stress the importance of:
   –   the committees role as problem solving forums;
   –   exchanging information on local development;
   –   the locally co-ordinated introduction of national policies and initiatives;
   –   their close relationship with the council and other liaison groups; and
   –   the promotion of best practice.'

Are not those aims and objectives fit for our needs with little or no amendment? But it is easier to state the aim than to achieve it. The CJCC has developed a structure which has recently evolved into 42 regional councils following Criminal Prosecution Service (CPS) boundary lines. Those lines have little relevance for the family justice system nor do we start from scratch. Our natural evolution begins with the care centre business committees at the local level. These are solid foundations upon which to build. In my opinion, the obvious starting point is to designate the care centres, 'family justice centres'. The responsibility of the designated judge should cover the whole range of family justice. The existing inter-disciplinary committees should be expanded to include representatives of all the disciplines and services upon whose collaboration the family justice system depends. However, there is an obvious tension between judicial leadership and a perception of legal domination. I do not doubt that the designated circuit judge must be, and must be seen to be, the local leader. Most, if not all, designated judges have great experience in the chairman's seat and are respected within the local professional community for their capacity to focus discussion on the key issue and to ensure that decisions which are taken in committee are duly implemented. But it is important that discussion should not be dominated by the voice of the lawyer, particularly if disciplines and services not previously engaged are to be both attracted to and retained in the partnership.

But if that is to be the base of the pyramid what should lie between that and its apex? To illustrate the choices, I have obtained from Court Service a family justice jurisdictional map which illustrates the location of the care centres as well as the boundaries of the court groups and the circuits: see Figure 1. Just as the CJCC has its regional councils, so too should our ideal design. My reason for that conclusion is two-fold. First, intercommunication within the regional group enables the strong to support the weak as well as the dissemination of useful information, not only on practice issues but also on topical questions which all care centres within the region need to address. Secondly, it would permit regular meetings at a national level with each region sending its delegate. As our experience at the National Inter-disciplinary Forum has demonstrated, this is an effective way of finding a collective solution for problems whether they have been generally experienced or whether they have had an isolated incidence. If the channel of communication is extended so that it is impracticable to provide more than one annual meeting attended by representatives of each of the 50 care centres, the capacity to share problems and to achieve uniformity of practice and standards becomes inadequate. The drawing of the boundaries of the regional groups is perhaps a point of detail, albeit an important one. Obviously, consideration would be given to existing designations such as the court group or the circuit. My present view is that the former is too small and the latter too large. There must be an obvious possibility of including a number of smaller court groups within a single regional unit. Since this network has the object of promoting collaboration and good practice within the family justice system, boundaries which regulate the more general administration of that system seem most appropriate.

If a system were developed broadly in line with my proposals then it should replace the function of both the National Inter-disciplinary Forum and the National Convention. It would not in any way compete with or duplicate the responsibilities of the Advisory Board to guide the department on policy issues. Of course, any formulation of policy must be by a multi-disciplinary group but there is a clear distinction between policy makers and practitioners. All that I propose is an extension of existing institutions which contribute to inter-disciplinary exchange between practitioners so that their focus is not only, or

THE JUDICIARY

even principally, upon public law Children Act issues. We have an obvious responsibility to do for our divorce and ancillary relief law and practice what the Children Act 1989 did for our child law and practice: that is to say to make it relevant for contemporary social and economic conditions and to ensure that it delivers services and disciplines that are seen to be effective and fair, above all in determining disputed issues.

There are many proofs of the need for action and urgent action. I take one small instance. I heard recently from District Judge Payne of the spontaneous development of an inter-disciplinary support group in the Oxford care centre. This is his note describing the development:

'Oxford Interested Group Meetings

Conception
The Oxfordshire FCBC asked DJ Campbell to set up a small working party in advance of the implementation of the Family Law Act 1996. The aim was to establish a dialogue so that the various agencies involved in preparations for the Act did not find themselves vying with one another in the provision of relevant services and to identify areas of unmet need.

Participants
District Judges

Oxfordshire Family Mediation Service	RELATE
Solicitors Family Law Association	Court Welfare Service
Family Mediators Association	Legal Aid Board
Family Court Business Committee	Oxford Solicitor–Mediators

Meetings
A total of five, commencing in February 1997, held approximately every six months.

Achievements
1. *Sharing knowledge and information*
    (a) as to how the court, the profession, and others were geared up for the anticipated demands following the implementation of Part IV FLA 1996 in October 1997,
    (b) regarding information meetings. One member of the working party visited Australia and was able to report back on the various information sessions she had seen there.
2. *Liaison with the Legal Aid Board*
    The existence of the group undoubtedly helped to persuade the board that Oxford should be one on the areas included in the second phase of the implementation of s 29 FLA 1996. In connection with this the board held a 'roadshow' at the combined court centre a fortnight before s 29 was implemented. 98 people attended.
3. *Publicity*
    An information leaflet summarising the services offered by the various mediation and support groups such as RELATE is in the final stages of preparation.

Conclusion
The intangible but nonetheless valuable result is that the disparate organisations who will be in the front line when the Act has to be made to work now have a significantly improved understanding of the challenges each is facing. In addition there is now a forum at which problems can be informally discussed and differences resolved.'

Following the Lord Chancellor's announcement, the Oxford group has considered its future but unanimously decided not to disband. They are convinced that, whatever statute may be in force, there is the same priority for inter-disciplinary exchange.

I say that this is urgent business partly because I have learned from experience how hard it is to persuade government to accept a case for change and how slow is its subsequent realisation even when the case has been accepted. An even more important consideration is that the National Inter-disciplinary Forum has an army deployed widely in the field. To illustrate that point, I reproduce a map of the jurisdiction showing those parts of the jurisdiction in which a pilot scheme operated with local inter-disciplinary support: see Figure 2. Well over half the population of the jurisdiction lies within the areas which are coloured on the map. The local inter-disciplinary support groups are a precious band of committed volunteers. They are not disbanding but standing ready for the next call. The experience that they gained during the operation of the pilots is invaluable, but they cannot be expected to wait indefinitely and without any assurance as to their future role. It would be a serious misjudgement to allow their enthusiasm and their experience to go to waste.

Legend

Text	Combined Court Centre
Text	County Court
——	Circuit Boundary
——	Circuit Boundary
◆	Divorce Jurisdiction
◢	Family Hearing Centre
‡	Care Centre

As revised 16 July 1999

London County Court Group and Supreme Court Group

Uxbridge, Willesden, Edmonton, Ilford, Romford, Bow, PRFD, Brentford, Wandsworth, Bromley

North Eastern Circuit
1 - Newcastle Court Group
2 - Teesside Court Group
3 - Leeds Court Group
4 - Bradford Court Group
5 - Sheffield Court Group

Northern Circuit
1 - Central Manchester Court Group
2 - Outer Manchester Court Group
3 - Liverpool Court Group
4 - Preston Court Group

Midland & Oxford Circuit
1 - Birmingham Court Group
2 - Stafford Court Group
3 - Coventry Court Group
4 - Northampton Court Group
5 - Nottingham Court Group
6 - Lincoln Court Group

Wales & Chester Circuit
1 - Mold Court Group
2 - Swansea Court Group
3 - Cardiff Court Group

South Eastern Circuit
1 - Maidstone Court Group
2 - Lewes Court Group
3 - Kingston Court Group
4 - Luton Court Group
5 - Chelmsford Court Group

Western Circuit
1 - Exeter Court Group
2 - Bristol Court Group
3 - Winchester Court Group

THE JUDICIARY

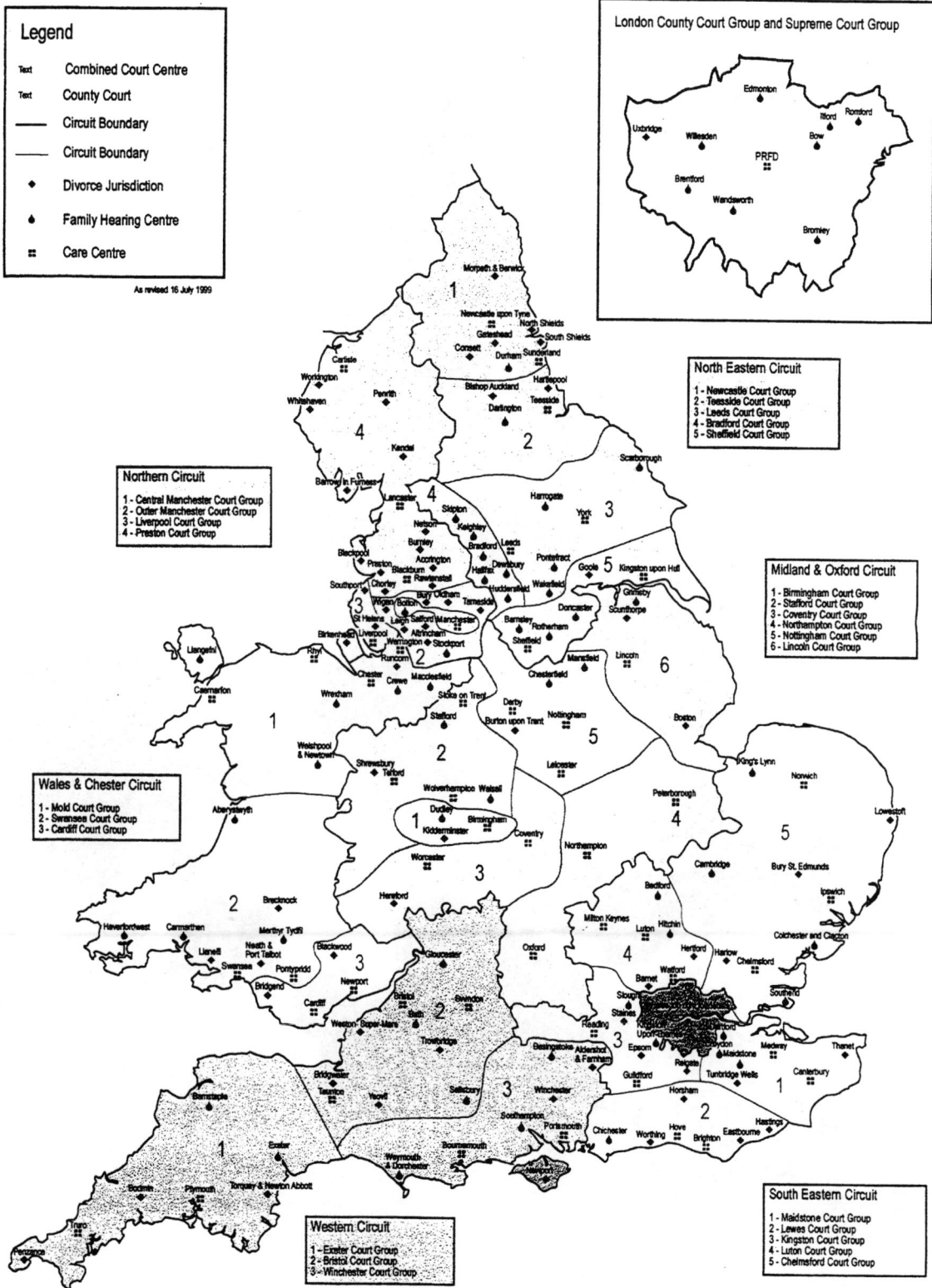

Figure 1. Courts with divorce, family or care jurisdiction in England and Wales

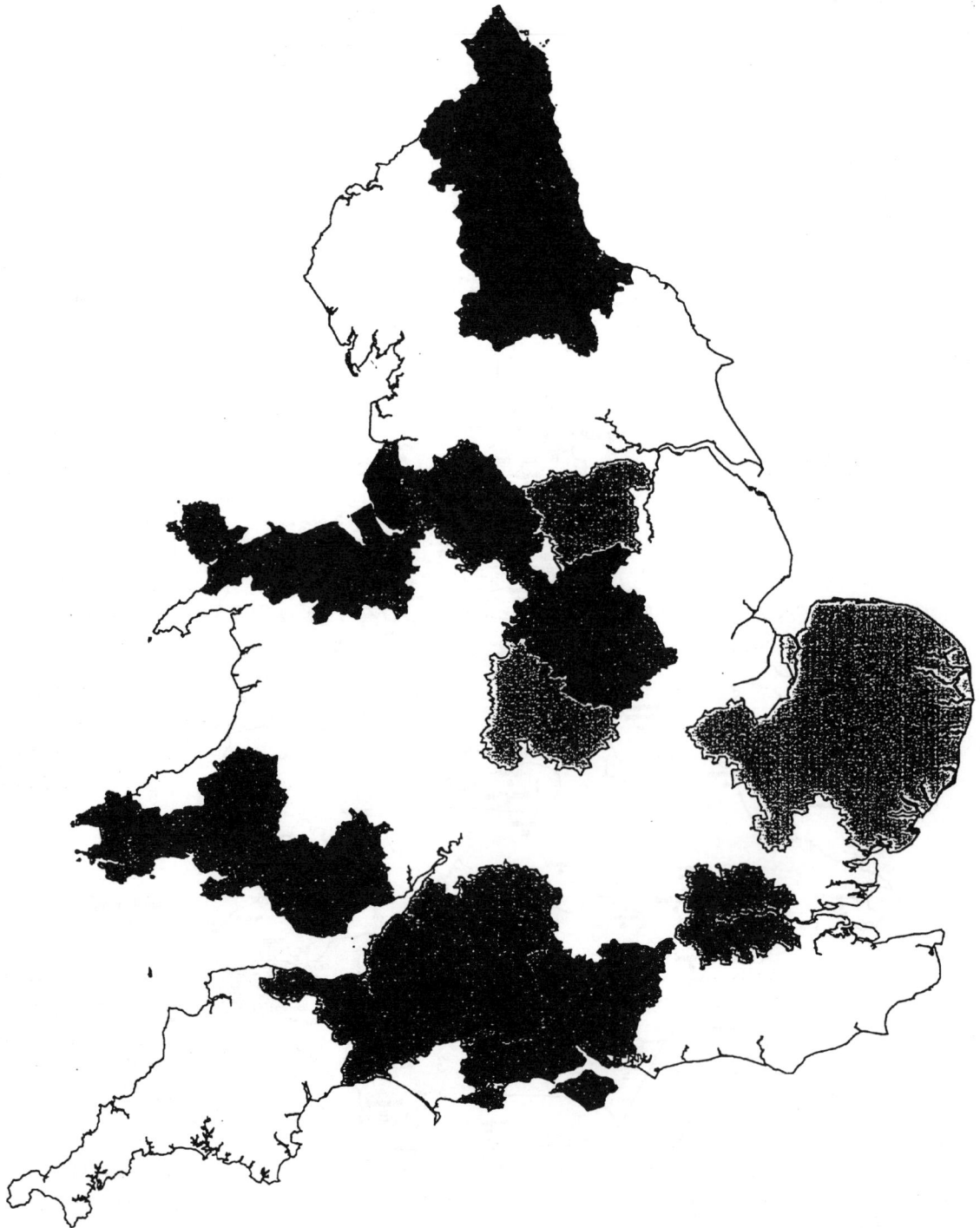

Figure 2. The pilot study areas

PART II OF THE FAMILY LAW ACT 1996: HOW DO WE MAKE IT WORK?

His Honour Judge Hedley[1]

When Part II is finally implemented then, if it is in a recognisably similar form to that at present, its success will be heavily dependent on effective co-operation across a range of disciplines. The courts are becoming increasingly aware of the need for such co-operation in a whole range of its work and there are interesting models not only in family law but in both the Criminal and the Technology and Construction Courts. The purpose of this paper is to address the issue of structures to ensure effective implementation and, in so doing, to see what can be learnt from other established structures.

The implementation of the Children Act 1989 was supported by the creation of Family Court Business Committees (FCBCs) in each of the established care centres linked to the central Children Act Advisory Committee (CAAC). Alongside this, the Family Forum (FF) was developed which was intended to facilitate rather more general interdisciplinary discussion than could be done at the FCBC. There is a general consensus that, whilst the effectiveness of the FF was patchy, there was general satisfaction with the rest of the structure and general regret when Government dissolved the CAAC even though some of its functions were taken over by the Advisory Board on Family Law (ABFL). Certainly this structure emphasised the value of meeting and co-operation between the various agencies and disciplines involved in family law.

Similar experience can be found in the criminal justice system. The Area Criminal Justice Committee, chaired by a senior Crown Court judge, draws together the different agencies involved in that system for the purposes of sharing information, concerns and insights with a view to a smooth and co-operative operation of the system. That is essentially based on police areas, although movements in police reorganisation may require some rethinking of that structure. These committees are coordinated by the Criminal Justice Consultative Council (chaired by the Vice-President of the Court of Appeal, Criminal Division) which again represents in its composition the varying agencies and disciplines involved in the system. There seems to be a general consensus that this structure makes a valuable contribution towards the operation of the system.

In the Technology and Construction Court the arrangement is less formal being effectively a court-user group convened by the relevant senior judge of the local court. Obviously the London court is more formally structured whilst outside London no court, I think, has more than one full-time judge of this court. In fact multi-agency working has been operating on a more or less formalised basis for probably longer here than in either the criminal or family justice systems.

Two obvious conclusions flow from this. First, multi-agency and multi-disciplinary meeting and co-operation offers potentially significant benefits for the proper running of a family justice system. Secondly, that the proper structure is that which is most natural and convenient to the particular group of agencies necessarily to be involved; however, the existence of both local bodies and a central body has been seen to be a source of strength. It may then be worth reflecting on how this could most usefully be applied to implementation of Part II of the 1996 Act.

In my view, the most significant factor is that there is already established an existing structure to support the family justice system. It is true that FCBCs are limited to a care centre. Nevertheless, each divorce county court has a care centre with which it can be easily associated. That structure is probably the least inconvenient, although other possible groupings might revolve around local authority boundaries or those of probation services or Petty Sessional Divisions or Court groups or Circuits. I do not see that any one of those has such advantages over the care centre grouping as to justify a new structure separate from the FCBCs.

---

1   HHJ Mark Hedley, Liverpool County Court.

It follows of course that the remit of the FCBCs will be significantly extended and their membership may need to be enlarged to include representatives of mediation schemes, other court staff and perhaps a greater District Judge representation. That said, the extra work will be of a similar kind to their present responsibilities and the total work involved should be less than would be caused by two separate structures. Where FFs were functional, they could be useful in dealing with some of the more general issues.

There is also a central body, ABFL. Its present remit is policy but once again it would seem sensible to build on the established rather than create something new. An effective chain of communication was established between FCBCs and the CAAC: is there any reason why that should not be replicated with the ABFL? Certainly a means by which shared concerns and effective solutions could be widely shared would be a key contribution to effective implementation.

That leaves the issue as to whether there should be any intermediate structure. Most circuits have an annual interdisciplinary conference; perhaps there is a case for a business equivalent covering the whole of the family justice system. I am not sure myself of the present need for a formal intermediate structure. Others no doubt will disagree. We all need to start with an open mind and hear the perceptions and ideas of others.

THE FAMILY AND CHILDREN BUSINESS COMMITTEE

District Judge Martyn Royall[1]

PREAMBLE

Shortly after my appointment in April 1992, I was invited to attend a three-day residential seminar for nominated care judges from both the Circuit and District benches. Dame Margaret Booth chaired the seminar. She was then the first chairman of the Children Act Advisory Committee. She enthused that the Children Act 1989 was a revolutionary piece of legislation. Not only did it set new rules, and a new philosophy in relation to parents and children, but also enabled judges to adopt an investigative and interventionalist approach; a role almost unheard of for English judges.

It turned out to be a steep learning curve for practitioners, the judiciary and, more importantly, for those children and families involved. The process was considerably assisted by the Children Act Advisory Committee and, as importantly, the Family Court Business Committees chaired by the designated family judge and based upon care centres which thus took on a central role.

I have been fortunate to serve on both the Family Court Business Committee and the Family Court Services Committee (renamed subsequently the Family Court Forum) for the Norwich Care Centre since 1992. I understand that Family Court Business Committees throughout the country have been extremely successful in local implementation and in dealing with issues of both local and national importance. The Family Court Forum was initially useful but has lost some impetus and, in many parts of the country, has become defunct.

Over a period of five years, with the leadership from the Advisory Committee and substantial input from the local committees, there grew a united strength culminating in guidance as to best practice across the whole spectrum of the Children Act 1989.

THE 1996 ACT

I do not apologise for the preamble, for it is against this background that the implementations of the Family Law Act 1996 should be considered. It follows the Children Act 1989 well, supporting both an investigative and interventionist approach. One only has to consider Part I of the 1996 Act:

'1. The court and any person, in exercising functions under or in consequence of Parts II and III, shall have regard to the following general principles–
    (a)   that the institution of marriage is to be supported;
    (b)   that the parties to a marriage which may have broken down are to be encouraged to take all practicable steps, whether by marriage counselling or otherwise, to save the marriage;
    (c)   that a marriage which has irretrievably broken down and is being brought to an end should be brought to an end–
        (i)   with minimum distress to the parties and to the children affected;
        (ii)   with questions dealt with in a manner designed to promote as good a continuing relationship between the parties and any children affected as is possible in the circumstances; and
        (iii)   without costs being unreasonably incurred in connection with the procedures to be followed in bringing the marriage to an end; and
    (d)   that any risk to one of the parties to a marriage, and to any children, of violence from the other party should, so far as reasonably practicable, be removed or diminished.'

Part I itself could be described as an exultation to all those practising in family law and the provision of services to help assist and befriend the family. The implementation of this exultation will involve substantial co-operation between all agencies involved in family provision, from the public, private and voluntary sectors. To ensure, in the first place, that those involved understand the greater responsibility

---

1   District Judge Royall, Norwich County Court and District Registry.

placed upon couples to make their marriage or relationship work, but if this is unsuccessful to deal with all aspects of family breakdown in accordance with these overriding objectives. Each area must have in place the necessary machinery and infrastructure.

Without a cohesive approach and inter-disciplinary planning, both nationally and locally, there is in my view a real risk that the overriding Part I principles will be lost. The Act requires and embodies more than a court process, and inter-disciplinary planning is essential. The machinery and infrastructure for this must be in place before implementation and thereafter to provide a smooth transition and to deal with any deficiencies enabling divorce or separation to take place within the spirit of the Act.

A BEGINNING

A start has already been made. Local Inter-disciplinary Forums were set up in the Summer of 1997 to assist in the advancement of the information meeting pilots, to develop inter-disciplinary co-operation in the promotion of the information meeting pilots, and to consider any resultant implications upon needs and resources. All pilots, having now been completed, have shared a common view that inter-disciplinary awareness has increased. This remit related only to a very small part of the Family Law Act 1996. Mediation is also being piloted, but unfortunately in isolation to the information meeting pilots. In some areas, both were piloted at the same time.

I quote from some of the comments made at the end of the East Anglian Second Pilot in May of this year.

From a magistrate:

> 'I feel that I have little direct input in the local group as our work on the family panel does not really touch the mediation side, and where it does the Court Welfare Officer has a key role. I therefore write to you more in the position of observer and I have found this interesting, mainly learning and/or reading about the work of the other agencies involved from whom I have learned a good deal.'

From a senior family court welfare officer:

> 'On a wider aspect there are so many changes taking place in the way that family law, in its widest sense, operates; and if we are to offer the very best service to both adults and most importantly the children, who are the innocent victims, we must ensure that all service providers, from marriage counselling through to Family Court Welfare are communicating with each other.'

From a solicitor:

> 'There is an important part to be played, in my view, in continuing to pool information regarding change and how change is perceived by us all in our individual ways to affect the public at large. Any process by which such information can continue to be collated and used to achieve a better way of guiding people through their difficulties has to be worthwhile.'

It is clear, both from my local knowledge of the East Anglian Pilot, and as a member of the National Inter-disciplinary Forum that considerable benefits have already inured from the inter-disciplinary approach undertaken within the pilot project, with national representation of organisations not simply involved in the court process, but involved in mediation, marriage guidance and marriage care in its various forms. This has produced better understanding of each organisation's perceptions, strengths and, indeed, weaknesses as we all embark on a new beginning.

As an example, during the East Anglian pilot, it became clear that there was a lack of mediation services in Suffolk. With the assistance of the Forum, and of its members, arrangements were able to be made to service that need in the short term whilst other arrangements were made.

THE PRESENT

I am sure that we are all concerned not to proliferate committees or forums. There is already in place the Family Court Business Committee based upon each care centre. As the title of these committees implied, they are primarily business orientated, their function being to examine the process of litigation involved under the Children Act 1989, and to ensure that cases pass through the process efficiently and effectively. Their concern is the management of the case-loads in terms of the availability of resources, priorities in relation to other litigation, and sound practice. The membership includes the designated

Family Judge, Court Administrator, District Judge, representatives of Justices' Clerks, representatives from Local Authorities from the Guardian Panel, the Legal Aid Board, and in the case of Norwich, a practising Barrister and a Solicitor. The membership of the Family Court Business Committee, however, is not written in tablets of stone. It has formal terms of reference but it might be explained as a strategic working group dealing with matters of Family Court policy on both a national and local basis.

The terms of reference of the Family Court Forums are wider but do afford to be considered in relation to this new chapter. They were established to promote discussion and encourage co-operation between all the professionals, agencies and organisations involved or concerned with the family, to consider issues which arise locally in the conduct of proceedings and the practice of the court, to recommend action which can be taken locally to improve the service provided to the family, and to consider whether special events seminars, study days or conferences are required locally to disseminate good practice, new arrangements and ideals, or to examine problems. The membership of the Family Court Forum is far wider than that of the Family Court Business Committee and includes representation from a wide range of organisations involved directly in families and children.

THE FUTURE

In my view, in the light of the success of Family Court Business Committees, their role should be extended to include, in equal part, the implementation, and in due course, the best practice, with regard to the Family Law Act 1996; and, more importantly, of its overriding principles.

I thought initially that this was original thought on my part but, in referring to the Lord Chancellor's Department's paper in regard to Family Court Business Committees, I read:

> 'In the longer term it is hoped that these Committees will play a role in the organisation of all Family Business, not just Children Act proceedings.'

Their formal terms of reference need to be substantially increased. The current terms of reference for the Family Court Business Committee are:

(a) to make sure that arrangements are working properly at local level, in particular allocation and transfer arrangements, meeting agreed targets where appropriate;

(b) to seek to achieve administrative consistency between the two tiers of the courts;

(c) to ensure that the Guardian ad Litem and Probation Services are aware of the needs of the court, but avoid making unreasonable demands on their services; and

(d) to liaise with Family Court Service Committees, now known as Family Court Forums.

In my view, reference (d) should be replaced, and additional terms of reference be added:

New   (d) consider the arrangements for, and the provision of, appropriate advice for families whose relationship is in difficulty or who are contemplating proceedings;

(e) to consider and seek provision for facilities available locally for assisting divorced and separated parents with their children;

(f) to consider public awareness by way of education, training and development of a multi-disciplinary approach to provide greater awareness;

(g) to ensure consistency of facilities within the area of the Committee.

This will, by its very nature, involve an increase in the size of the present Committee to involve senior representatives of the service providers, more particularly with regard to the provision of information and of mediation; but it should remain, as it always has been, a Committee with an emphasis on strategy, policy, and local provision to be known as the Family and Children Business Committee.

I would propose that this Committee should meet quarterly.

I am concerned with the effectiveness of a Family Court Forum, but recognise the importance of the wider views of those people involved 'on the ground', and more particularly the local input that can be obtained from representation from Social Workers, Health Visitors, General Practitioners, Voluntary Groups including Relate, Citizens Advice Bureaux and, indeed, family academics, and I would propose that two of the four meetings of the Family and Children's Business Committee should include an Open Forum and representatives of these organisations be invited to attend. Here there can be a wider and broader discussion by practitioners from the different disciplines and agencies of matters regarding the family in its widest context.

REGIONALISATION

I have throughout referred to the new committees being based upon care centres, obviously with representation from other Family Court Centres. I do not make this suggestion lightly, but I do so for one reason, and one reason only, that the strength of the current Family Court Business Committees has been based on 'ownership': all those involved have been concerned with the provision of services locally. I am aware that there has been an increasing move towards regionalisation, but I am convinced that if these new committees are seen to be too remote, local interest and input will be lost.

I accept that in other parts of the country, and indeed on other circuits, the difficulties which are evident within the South Eastern Circuit, because of its huge geographical size, may not exist or may exist to a lesser extent.

My experience is of the East Anglian pilot area, which included Norfolk, Suffolk and the major part of Cambridgeshire. Each of these counties has its own mediation groups, its own marriage counselling groups, separate Court Welfare Services (although I accept this is probably to change) and in my view there were real problems in conferring, in each of the counties, the sense of ownership.

I am equally aware of the inconsistencies of approach which have occurred under the current system, and it may be that it would be helpful to have a regional body with responsibility for overseeing the local committees based on the care centre areas.

NATIONALLY

There should, of course, be a central committee to facilitate a dialogue between local Family and Children Business Committees and the central body so as to develop, within the Family Law Act 1996, best practice.

A start has been made. The Information Meeting pilot established a national forum, its membership being drawn from organisations involved in family matters together with representatives of the Lord Chancellor's Department and judiciary. This could be considered as a framework for a national advisory committee, subject to suitable additions to its membership.

It may be that a member of the Central Committee should take regional responsibility rather than set up a further tier of bureaucracy which, without strong leadership may create a mere 'talking shop'.

WHAT NEXT?

I wrote this paper prior to the Lord Chancellor's announcement on 17 June.

It is my understanding that the only decision which has been made is that the decision as to implementation has been postponed until next year.

It is not too early, in my view, now to establish a local and national organisation, to be ready for the implementation of the Family Law Act 1996. Anything that can be done to improve inter-disciplinary knowledge and co-operation must be of benefit to the family. There is much work that can be done at this stage to address issues, with regard to the current legislation, that would benefit the family and to lay a strong basis for the implementation of the Act, or its successor, at a future date.

CONCLUSIONS

THE WAY FORWARD

Lady Justice Hale DBE[1]

In many ways, the conference was much more exciting and constructive following the announcement that Part II of the Family Law Act 1996 was not to be brought into force next year than it would have been as a simple preparation for implementation. For such a diverse group, delegates were remarkably united in their support for the fundamental principles behind the 1996 Act:

(1) the introduction of genuinely no-fault divorce;
(2) the principle that, so far as practicable, arrangements for the future should be made before rather than after the divorce was granted;
(3) the provision of reliable but neutral information to both parties to the divorce and to their children; and
(4) the availability of good quality mediation services as and when the parties wanted them.

Participants also had some constructive suggestions for what could be done whether or not Part II was implemented soon. We were all looking for ways in which the system as a whole could offer a better *service* for separating and divorcing couples whether married or unmarried and above all for their children. What follows is a synthesis of the resolutions passed in the various groups and some concluding comments which are all my own.

NO FAULT DIVORCE NOW

The conference was unanimously in favour of the *speedy introduction of no fault divorce* in line with the philosophy of the Family Law Act 1996:

'"No change" is not an option, given the widespread acceptance that the present law is unsustainable.'

Some were concerned that, even without the difficulties presented by the need for information meetings, the present hurdles in Part II were unduly complex and would require some ingenuity from practitioners and the courts to make them workable. Many would favour *amending legislation* to produce a scheme much closer to the original recommendations of the Law Commission but the difficulties of securing Parliamentary time and support for this course were also recognised. The general feeling was that delegates would rather have the present legislation and make it work than have no change at all.

INFORMATION

Everyone supported the provision of good quality information. There was a need for this information *well before* any proceedings were brought by anyone. Leaflets, videos and CD-ROMs could be made available through community sources, including DSS offices, CABx, public libraries, post offices, GP surgeries and supermarkets.

There was a strong feeling that *unmarried couples* needed this information just as much did married. One opportunity of reaching them which has not yet been exploited is at *birth registration*, particularly as both unmarried parents must normally be involved if the father's name is to be registered. A simple booklet explaining the legal position and containing a parental responsibility agreement which could be

---

1   Lady Justice Hale, a Lord Justice of Appeal; formerly a Judge of the High Court; before that, as Professor Brenda Hoggett, the Law Commissioner in charge of the Commission's programme of family law reform.

sent off for registration there and then would be an obvious solution without the need to amend the Children Act 1989.

There was an even stronger feeling that *children* needed access to good quality and age appropriate information from a neutral source. Some parents may be able to help their children through the troubles of their separation but many may not. Children should be able to go elsewhere for information and, if they needed it, for help. We were impressed with some of the materials currently being developed by the research team for children to use.

All of this applied irrespective of whether there were any proceedings. The Government should continue to *offer information meetings* on a voluntary basis and to *sponsor research* into the best ways of providing the information which all family members need.

There was support for the principle of compulsory information-giving in the 1996 Act, especially for couples with children. Those with no children under 16 (or 18 if in full-time education) might be exempted. Imaginative use might be made of the exemption provisions in order to make the formal scheme in the 1996 Act workable.

However, any opportunity to amend the Act so as to provide for *greater flexibility* and choice in the ways in which information might be provided should be grasped. While some people might prefer an individual meeting, it was difficult in practice to provide a useful one to one encounter when questions about their particular circumstances could not be answered for fear of trespassing into advice.

Others might prefer group meetings, interactive CD-ROMs or video presentations. The conference was impressed with the accounts of group meetings in Canada and Australia. There is also a need to engage ethnic minorities who are unlikely to be reached through conventional means.

It was felt that any information provided, especially on a formal basis, should be neutral and not with a view to securing some stated aim.

In any event, the opportunity should be taken now of providing appropriate information leaflets which should be *sent out with the court documents* when proceedings were begun: this would enable information to be given to *both parties*.

MEDIATION

Everyone affirmed their support for *widely available* and *well-publicised* mediation services. These services should be properly funded, organised and regulated and have a uniform set of standards and code of practice.

Mediation should be available at all stages. It might be particularly helpful *before* any proceedings were launched. It could also be helpful at a *later* stage when protracted litigation was proving counter-productive.

The present 'either/or' approach under Part III of the 1996 Act might not be the best. Greater flexibility between legal and mediation services might be better. There were points in the process where legal services might be the more appropriate and points where mediation might be better. *Limited legal aid certificates* should be made available to enable people to receive legal advice before being required to attend a meeting with a mediator or engaging in mediation.

Participation in mediation itself should remain voluntary but the receipt of information about it should be compulsory.

The essence of *s 12(2)* (duty of legal representatives to give information about mediation) and *s 13* (the court's power to direct parties to attend a meeting for the purpose of having mediation explained to them) should be implemented immediately by rules. The same could apply to *s 14* (power to adjourn proceedings for a limited period for this purpose or in order to enable disputes to be resolved amicably) which is already widely done in practice but without the safeguards contained in s 14.

LEGAL SERVICES

The lawyers at the conference proved themselves stalwart defenders of the value of specialist legal services to separating and divorcing couples. However, they also emphasised the need for *accreditation schemes* for family law practitioners, and there was support for making such accreditation a requirement of practice in this field.

Accreditation should include a compulsory continuing education element. Legal training for family practitioners should include issues of *interpersonal and family dynamics*. Lawyers had much to learn from other disciplines.

The provision of legal aid and the basis of remuneration for lawyers should be *front loaded* so as to encourage the early resolution of disputes.

Pre-action protocols should be devised for divorce proceedings, along similar lines to those now being devised for some civil proceedings under the Woolf reforms.

CHILDREN

Everyone was impressed with the value of *parenting plans* as a useful tool for parents to think through and agree the agreements they wished to make for their children.

The conference was also impressed with the need for *the children themselves* to have access to good quality age appropriate *information* and somewhere they could turn for independent *support and advice* should they want it. Secondary school aged children might have information through schools, youth clubs, and other youth organisations, but we were reminded of how important the *Internet* is in enabling them to find out what they want to know privately and in their own time. Younger children may need someone to talk to if they want. Children aged from 6 to 9 are particularly vulnerable. Community-based services, including primary care services, should try to develop ways of achieving this.

One group suggested that all children whose parents initiated divorce or separation proceedings should have a face-to-face interview with a case worker and a follow up to discuss any parenting plan or other arrangements. While not going as far as this, others could see a role for *the new unified welfare service* in supplying a contact point for children who wanted information or support.

The conference was less impressed with the *role of the court* as laid down in s 41 of the Matrimonial Causes Act 1973, or its replacement in s 11 of the 1996 Act. Some would simply repeal it. Others would try to improve it.

The present forms were poorly designed to enable the court to identify those cases where it should execise its powers under the Children Act 1989. Immediate consideration could be given to improvements which would more effectively identify children who may need further consideration by the court or the provision of further services. Some thought that it would be appropriate to seek the views of an independent professional involved with the family, such as a teacher or health visitor, others that to provide an independent and objective view in every case would be 'unjustifiably intrusive into the very large majority of families as well as prohibitively demanding of resources'.

Judicial experience of these provisions suggests that, unless there is a dispute between the parents, the court is not well equipped or well suited to identify the problem cases. Section 11 will be no improvement upon s 41 in this respect. It is very difficult for the court to get an accurate picture without arranging for a court welfare officer's investigation. This is not practicable in all cases. It is also difficult to know what the court would do with the information collected other than to pass it on to social services if appropriate.

Where there is a dispute, the main conduit for the child's views to be made known should continue to be court welfare officers, social workers, guardians and advocates. Nevertheless, the courts could relax their present very restrictive approach to meeting children face to face. Teenage children should be able to attend court at 'some appropriate juncture' if they want.

THE COURTS

Judges and magistrates should receive training designed to give them a full understanding of the mediation process. This would also enable them more effectively to engage with litigants in court, and to conduct the mediation required in financial dispute resolution appointments. (I would also add the need for judicial training in interpersonal and family dynamics.)

Immediate consideration should be given to reforming the Family Proceedings Rules 1991 so as to modernise and humanise the procedures and the language.

SOME CONCLUDING COMMENTS

The 1996 Act was emphatically not concerned with making divorce either easier or harder for the families involved. One wise observer of the Parliamentary debates commented how cleverly the opponents of no fault divorce had combined to produce a scheme which might be seen as well nigh unworkable. They cannot all have been unaware that the present law permits one party to obtain a very speedy divorce whether or not the other party wants it and then to delay the working out of the practical and financial consequences almost indefinitely. Participants in this conference were only too well aware that in doing so it is letting down everyone involved, not only the parties, but also their children and the wider community.

Even within the present law, there is much we could do to offer them a better service. The idea of offering the public a service is commonplace in many other areas of activity but something of a novelty in this context. It is nevertheless the clearest message to come out of this conference.

The conference was full of thoughts about information and mediation services, all of which could be improved within the present legislative framework. The main messages here are that we need to help rather than to preach at the adults and that we need to consider the children as real people and active participants rather than passive recipients of the adults' decisions.

The conference was less full of thoughts about how we could better adapt the present court processes to the needs of the people rather than the professionals involved. Many of us can remember the 1970s' debates about the failings of the court structure: an incoherent patchwork of substantive law in which the principles and the remedies applicable to exactly the same set of facts depended upon the court in which the proceedings were brought. By and large that is all behind us now. The same principles apply at all levels in the court system and there is ready transferability between them.

But we have still not got to grips with the idea that most people who are undergoing family transitions have a range of decisions to take, many of them inter-dependent. They do not parcel these up into discrete issues to be resolved separately from one another, according to different processes with different timetables. Somehow the law has managed to produce a situation in which one divorcing couple can go through five separate sets of proceedings, in five different venues, and according to five different timetables. Thus:

(1) Applications for protection against molestation or to secure the short-term occupation of the family home are brought under Part IV of the Family Law Act 1996, either in a family proceedings court or in any county court where they are first heard by a district judge.

(2) Petitions for divorce or judicial separation are brought under the Matrimonial Causes Act 1973 in a divorce county court. Unless they are defended, which is extremely rare, they are determined on paper by a district judge after the court staff have checked the forms. This will include consideration of the arrangements for the children under s 41 of the 1973 Act.

(3) Applications for contact, residence or other orders about the children's upbringing are made to a family proceedings court or a county court with private law jurisdiction under the 1989 Act. Most contested proceedings are heard by a specially qualified circuit judge. The procedures under the Children Act 1989 entail active court management and timetabling.

(4) Applications for financial provision or property adjustment (apart from periodical payments for children) arising out of a divorce or judicial separation are made to the divorce court, most being heard by a district judge. Procedures which entail active court management and timetabling are only to be introduced nationwide next June.

(5) Applications for child support are made to the Child Support Agency where they are determined administratively with appeals on some matters to the DSS independent appeals service.

The confusion which this must cause to the participants, the anxiety and distress provoked by a multitude of court hearings before different judges and sometimes in different buildings, and the sheer expense entailed in all those hearings and in all the different documentation involved, are little short of scandalous. Of course, there are families who agree about some things but not about others. Of course, there are families where the process of fact finding on some issues is more complex than on others.

But in ordinary civil proceedings the decision to separate the various issues arising out of a particular incident or transaction is taken deliberately and for good reason. In family proceedings, on the other hand, we start from the proposition that each issue must be determined separately. It is sometimes possible to bring them together, but only with some ingenuity, and usually *after* the separate processes have begun. There is plenty of scope for the powerful and resourceful to gain tactical advantage. The lawyers have real difficulty in seeing that things might be done any differently, whereas the mediators have known for a long time that their clients do not put their problems into these neat little boxes.

It cannot and should not be beyond the wit of those responsible to devise a comprehensive procedure which could be employed by all families to resolve all the problems which they need the court to resolve in a way which suits the needs of that particular family. This is what the Law Commission had in mind when it recommended the concept of divorce as a 'process over time'. Even if the breakdown of the marriage has still to be proved in the old ways, there is nothing to prevent us from trying to devise such a process within the existing law.

We must address this problem urgently. The present system allows and even encourages the parties to spend a quite disproportionate amount of their resources (or the resources of the legal aid fund which will usually be recouped from them) upon legal proceedings. Small wonder that many of those who have been through it once are reluctant to risk it again by remarrying. More and more young people are choosing to postpone or even reject marriage altogether. It may already be too late to halt that trend, but they are deluding themselves if they think that living together without marriage carries any less risk of legal proceedings. If anything, their problems are even more complex. The price of keeping the individualised discretionary approach to resolving family problems is that we must make the process as genuinely user friendly and as cost effective as we possibly can. Proportionality should be our watchword here as everywhere else in the civil justice system.

CLOSING REMARKS

Lord Justice Thorpe

Lord Justice Thorpe expressed his thanks to the planning group who had been responsible for organising the conference over the preceding 15 months, with particular thanks to Peter Harris for collecting in all the papers and to the Family Policy Division of the Lord Chancellor's Department for their distribution. Thanks were also expressed to the Judicial Studies Board for their organisation of the conference and, of course, to all the authors who had given their time so generously in their written and oral presentations.

Lord Justice Thorpe went on to remind delegates of the important role the conference and the President's Inter-disciplinary Committee play in the development of the family justice system and its procedures, with the potential for even greater influence. He emphasised the need for a united inter-disciplinary voice to be heeded and thus, hopefully, to have a greater influence over the development of law and practice in the family justice system. Finally, he expressed the thanks of all the delegates to the retiring President for his considerable support of the committee and its work; he would be greatly missed.

APPENDIX

LIST OF SPEAKERS AND PARTICIPANTS

Names   *Organisation*

SPEAKERS

The Senior DJ Gerald Angel   Principal Registry Family Division
William Arnold   Head of Family Policy, Lord Chancellor's Department
Sir Stephen Brown   The President, Family Division
Dr Christopher Clulow   Tavistock Marital Studies Institute
Mary Corbett   Marriage Care
Professor Gwyn Davis   Bristol University Faculty of Law
Thelma Fisher   National Family Mediation
Pat Fitzsimons   Relate
Dr Judith Freedman   Portman Clinic
HHJ Donald Hamilton   Birmingham County Court
Iain Hamilton   Jones, Maidment Wilson, Solicitors
Peter Harris   Ex. Official Solicitor
HHJ Mark Hedley   Liverpool County Court
David Hodson   Family Law Consortium
Robert Hutchinson   Director of Social Services (Portsmouth)
Professor Christina Lyon   University of Liverpool, Faculty of Law
Penny Mansfield   One Plus One
Professor Mervyn Murch   Cardiff Law School
Maggie Rae   Clintons, Solicitors
Peggy Ray   Goodman Ray, Solicitors
Professor Martyn Richards   Centre for Family Research
DJ Martyn Royall   Norwich County Court and District Registry
Lord Justice Mathew Thorpe   Royal Courts of Justice
Dr Judith Trowell   Tavistock Clinic
Professor Janet Walker   Newcastle Centre for Family Studies
Mr Justice Wall   Royal Courts of Justice
Elizabeth Walsh   Chief Executive, UK College of Mediation
Dr Anne Zachary   Portman Clinic

PARTICIPANTS

Florence Baron QC   Barrister
Susan Bindman   NAGALARO
DJ Roger Bird   Bristol County Court
Eddie Bloomfield   Family Policy Division, Lord Chancellor's Department
Dame Margaret Booth   Chair, UK College of Family Mediators
Sir Thomas Boyd-Carpenter   Family Law Advisory Board
Jacqueline Brown   Family Policy Division, Lord Chancellor's Department
Elizabeth Clarke   Barrister
Jonathan Creer   Family Policy Division, Lord Chancellor's Department
Dr Stephen Cretney   All Souls College, Oxford
Nicholas Crichton   Inner London Family Proceedings Court
HHJ Susan Darwall-Smith   Bristol County Court
HHJ David Davies   Rhyll
Tess Duncan   GALRO Panel, Surrey
Amanda Finlay   Director of Public and Private Rights, Lord Chancellor's Department
Dr Danya Glaser   Great Ormond Street Hospital, London
Anna Gledhill   Relate
Mrs Justice Hale   Royal Courts of Justice
Julia Hennessy   Essex County Council
Mr Justice Holman   Royal Courts of Justice
Professor Joseph Hornick   Canadian Research Institute
John Hughes   Cambridgeshire Probation Service
Kathryn Hughes   Farleys, Solicitors

Diane Hulin	Private Office, Lord Chancellor's Department
Dr Brian Jacobs	Maudsley Hospital, London
Peter Jeffries	ILPS
Mr Justice Johnson	Royal Courts of Justice
Jenny Kenrick	Tavistock Clinic
Mr Justice Kirkwood	Royal Courts of Justice
Vicky Leach	NCH Action for Children
David Lock MP	Parliamentary Secretary, Lord Chancellor's Department
Laurence Oates	The Official Solicitor
Stephen Orchard	Legal Aid Board
Arran Poyser	Department of Health
Patt Monro	Lawyers for Children
Nigel Shepherd	Addleshaw Booth and Co Solicitors
Jenny Stevenson	Psychologist
DJ Dinah Stocken	Doncaster County Court
Dr Claire Sturge	Northwick Park Hospital
Mr Justice Sumner	Royal Courts of Justice
Valerie Vaughan	Family Mediation Service
Robert Verity	Kent Probation Service
Peter Watson-Lee	Williams Thompson Solicitors
Tony Wells	Family Law Advisory Board
Judy Wenban-Smith	Psychologist
Sarah White	Legal Aid Board
Susan Winfield	Information Meetings

JSB STAFF

John Jacomb